POIGNANT, HILARIOUS, FRESH, MOVING!

The thirty-three essays appearing in this volume appeared (sometimes in slightly different form) in such publications as the old *Saturday Evening Post, Esquire, Atlantic Monthly* and *New York*. Taken together, they represent the best of one of the most remarkable sensibilities in America today.

Dunne finds his subjects in a tiny desert community on the edge of Death Valley, in a missile silo in Montana, in a town on San Francisco Bay.

He inhales the aroma of a small-time fight club.

He experiences the doldrums of a road trip with a big-league baseball team.

He visits a private detective who specializes in lost cats and spends the day with a stunt man who falls on his head for a living.

Books by John Gregory Dunne

Quintana & Friends
True Confessions

Published by POCKET BOOKS

QUINTANA & FRIENDS

BY

JOHN GREGORY DUNNE

WASHINGTON SQUARE PRESS
PUBLISHED BY POCKET BOOKS NEW YORK

WSP

A Washington Square Press/Pocket Books Publication
POCKET BOOKS, a Simon & Schuster division of
GULF & WESTERN CORPORATION
1230 Avenue of the Americas, New York, N.Y. 10020

Published by arrangement with E.P. Dutton
Library of Congress Catalog Card Number: 78-18209

ISBN: 0-671-83241-7

First printing September, 1980

10 9 8 7 6 5 4 3 2 1

WASHINGTON SQUARE PRESS and colophon are trademarks
of Simon & Schuster.

Printed in the U.S.A.

For Alice
and Calvin Trillin

"When I am in California,
I am not in the West.
I am west of the West."

—THEODORE ROOSEVELT

and nibbling cold cuts, watching the reporters wag

CONTENTS

3. TINSEL

4. CONTINENTAL DRIFT

Acknowledgments

The author is grateful to *Esquire*, the *Saturday Evening Post*, *Holiday*, the *Atlantic Monthly*, the *Los Angeles Times Book Review*, *New York* and *National Review* for permission to print in this collection pieces that appeared in their pages under his by-line, although sometimes in slightly different form and with different titles.

"Tinsel" and "Memento Delano" first appeared in the *Atlantic Monthly*, and "Pauline," "Ex Post Facto" and "Apostasy" in the *Los Angeles Times Book Review*. "Golden Boys," "Realtor to the Stars," "Mad Milo," "Quintana," "Memories of a Left Fielder," "Fractures," "Friends," "Gone Hollywood," "Bottled Poetry" and "Stunts" all appeared in *Esquire*.

"Sanctuary," "Winter Cruise," "Buck," "Texas Poor," "Apollo 204," "The Nightingale of Jackrabbit Flats," "Induction Day," "Building 590," "Maye & Leroy," "Marvin in Manialand," "Quebec Zero," "Port Chicago," "King Tiger," "Nevermore, Quoth the Eagle," "Case No. 68-401-356" all appeared first in the *Saturday Evening Post*.

"Letter from Portuguese Bend" appeared in *New York* and "Sneak" appeared first in *The Studio*, published by Farrar, Straus & Giroux, copyright 1969, John Gregory Dunne.

Introduction

I think I became a writer because I stuttered. I still stutter, although I can disguise it so well that unless I am tired or drunk the stammer is almost imperceptible. Like all stutterers, I have my own Distant Early Warning system. I have become adept at recognizing two or three sentences ahead of time those hard consonants that will trip me up and I have a warehouse of soft and sibilant synonyms to transport me across the shoals of speech. The effect of this personal DEW line is to give my diction an odd, herky-jerky cadence, making me sound like nothing so much as a simultaneous translation into English from another language. But when I was a boy in school, and had neither the wit nor the vocabulary to summon synonyms, I sat mute in class, terrified that the nuns would call on me to recite. In compensation, I had to learn to express myself on paper. I listened to the way people talked, becoming in the process a rather good mimic, and grew so precociously observant that my mother once complained that I never missed a twitch or a droopy eyelid or the crooked seam on a stocking. When I was a young writer, I thought this facility a virtue, but with age, or perhaps tolerance, I am less sure. This kind of observation should be seasoning rather than the meal itself; put a writer with a tendency for misanthropy in front of a typewriter and the possibility exists that someone, usually someone unsuspecting, is going to get mugged. I recognize an occasional absence of charity in myself, and it was for this reason that I began to put myself in my work; if I exposed my own mosaic of petty treasons, perhaps the people I was writing about would have less reason to complain.

The legacy of my stammer makes me a terrible reporter in one sense: I hate to ask questions. In any event I am not interested in the answers. There is a kind of reporter who thinks that the answers to the questions he asks matter. I don't. If I talk to someone who is practiced in giving answers, I will get his standard programmed answers; if I talk to someone who is not practiced in giving answers, I will not find out what is on his mind by asking him, either because he does not know or because he has not given it much thought: the answers are irrelevant and so are the questions. As usual, it was Murray Kempton who put the whole matter of Q-A in proper perspective. Reviewing a journalist's memoirs in the *New York Review of Books,* Kempton said that the journalist had not been told anything on or off the record in thirty years that could not be printed on the pedestal of a monument.

Hating to ask questions and never trusting the answers has defined the type of reporting I do. What I do is hang around. Become part of the furniture. An end table in someone's life. It is the art of the scavenger: set a scene, establish a mood, get the speech patterns right. What matters is that the subject bites his nails, what matters is that he wears brown shoes with a blue suit, what matters is the egg stain on his tie, the Reader's Digest Condensed Books on the shelves, the copy of *Playboy* with the centerfold torn out.

In general, I stay away from the "big story," the front-page murder or the important social action event. Too many reporters mean too many fingerprints smudging up the story. I like to find something that no one else has done, then go out on the outskirts of the story and look back in on it. Out there at the city limits of a piece, at the county line, I find people who truly interest me. All they want is a piece of the action, or if they already have a piece, they probably got it through the back door; maybe they even jimmied the lock on that back door. There is probably no place in America that so epitomizes this moral county line where I am professionally comfortable as Las Vegas, Clark County, Nevada. I have a weakness for Vegas, for the people I find there, for the stories I hear there. Let me tell you one story: it will suggest the kind of thing you will find in this book. I was, for reasons that escape me, at a luncheon for the Italian wine industry. All the freeloaders in town were there. A couple of movie stars. A delegation of Italian bureaucrats representing the wine industry. And a Vegas comic in an orange cardigan. At the end of the lunch, the head of the Italian delegation got up and in painfully broken English thanked us for drinking his booze. Up jumped the comic. "Let me translate Dr. DeLuco's remarks," he said. Then he scrunched his neck down between his shoulders. "You know why Italians got no necks?" he said. Down went his neck even further between his shoulders, and he threw out his arms. "It comes from saying, 'What gun?' " The rest of the guests were appalled. I laughed so hard I made a rude noise and had to excuse myself from the table.

The introduction to a collection of pieces seldom acknowledges that much of what a writer does was written to pay a bill or to meet a deadline, that phrases, sentences, even whole pieces have been polished to remove the tarnish, that the garbage has been culled and burned, as if its absence from the collection is proof that it never existed, was never written. The pieces in this book were selected from almost seventy-five written over a period of fifteen years. I have arbitrarily divided the book into four categories: "Software," personal pieces; "Hardware," about the social stresses of the 1960s; "Tinsel," about Hollywood; and "Continental Drift," a geologist's phrase defined in the *Random House Dictionary of the English Language* as "the hypothetical tendency or ability of continents to drift on the earth's surface because of the weakness of the suboceanic crust." I come from generations in the East, I have settled in the West, and if there is a single thread in this book it is the confrontation of the transplanted Easterner with the culture of the contemporary West. Or perhaps, with the writer's ego, I only think that the continent has drifted West with me.

Finally, these pieces would not have been written, this book even contemplated, had it not been for two people. The first I shall not name. Because of the cargo of time, the shifting freight of personal relationships, we no longer speak, but he was as close to a mentor as anyone I have ever known. When I arrived in New York in 1956, a retired PFC in the Army of the United States, I was the quintessential Ivy League graduate, a receptacle of received wisdom, a memory drum of fashionable and right-minded and untested opinion. I met him at a party, he insulted the hostess and most of the guests, and left. It still takes my breath away when I think of that evening. In the polite middle-class Irish Catholic circles in which I grew up, a guest did not call his hostess "trash." Neither did a guest, when introduced to a Middle-European count, say pleasantly, "Scratch a Hungarian and you'll find a Jew," even though he correctly intuited that the count was a poseur and remittance man. The count, as I remember, threw a drink at him; it was the first of many drinks I was to see thrown at him over the next eight years. I was both aghast and exhilarated, and was only to learn later that he believed in the social benefit of making a scene, that he was discomfited only when people did not react to his outrageousness.

He was like a stick of unstable dynamite, socially irresponsible, a respecter of no race or tradition or station. He was also smart as hell. He called himself a writer, but as he seldom wrote, for all the typewriters he borrowed and never returned, it would be more accurate to call him an oral historian. I was soft and he became the DI of my intellectual boot camp, a professor of life itself. I ranged over New York with him, picking up his lessons by osmosis, Sancho Panza to his demented knight. I met the Gallos and the widow of the celery king of the Harlem Market. I went to VID meetings in the Village with him, and Lexington Avenue Democratic Club parties; he would insult the VID and the Lexington Avenue Democrats, disrupt their events and push off into the night. At an Athletes for Nixon fete in 1960, he asked Frank Gifford (this was before Gifford was absorbed by the Kennedys) why he pronounced "athlete" as a three-syllable word. I attended right-wing galas and met the Buckleys; he insulted both the Buckleys and their followers. His idea of high good humor was to send a right-wing dialectician, who had abandoned both Judaism and the Communist Party for the Right and Anglo-Catholicism, an Episcopalian hymnal. He introduced me to Norman Mailer; then he called Norman, in print, "a pain in the ass." He liked Carmine DeSapio and did not insult him. He also liked Adam Powell; in fact, he thought an indictment an indication of character. His style, when he did write, was that of an axe-murderer, albeit a funny one. As an *obiter dictum* in a review of Gore Vidal's play, *Romulus,* he characterized an early Vidal novel, which looked askance at the United Fruit Company, as "Positively the only anti-fruit thing" Vidal ever wrote; in *Esquire,* he hacked gleefully at the Goldwater Revival (a cause he supported), dismissing the Revival's more perfervid supporters (at many of whose tables he had dined) as "the acne and the ecstacy." The worst word in his lexicon was "ingrate," and when I sometimes hinted that he too fell from grace, he would jab a finger into my shoulder: "Don't do as I do, do as I say." Another jab into the shoulder: "Get the picture?"

He taught me to accept nothing at face value, to question everything, above all to be wary. From him I developed an eye for social nuance, learned to look with a spark of compassion upon the socially unacceptable, to search for the taint of metastasis in the socially acceptable. He was truly my Bessemer converter. "I must love him," Norman Mailer once told me, "otherwise I'd kill him." I feel much the same way.

The other person responsible for this volume is my wife, Joan Didion. We have been married for fifteen years. I do not guarantee that we will be married sixteen, yet we did not guarantee to each other at the end of the first week that we would still be married at the end of the second, at the end of the fifth year that we would make it through the sixth, at the end of the ninth through the tenth. I think it is sufficient to say that she is the center from which the rest of my life proceeds.

1.

SOFTWARE

QUINTANA

Quintana will be eleven this week. She approaches adolescence with what I can only describe as panache, but then watching her journey from infancy has always been like watching Sandy Koufax pitch or Bill Russell play basketball. There is the same casual arrogance, the implicit sense that no one has ever done it any better. And yet it is difficult for a father to watch a daughter grow up. With each birthday she becomes more like us, an adult, and what we cling to is the memory of the child. I remember the first time I saw her in the nursery at Saint John's Hospital. It was after visiting hours and my wife and I stood staring through the soundproof glass partition at the infants in their cribs, wondering which was ours. Then a nurse in a surgical mask appeared from a back room carrying a fierce, black-haired baby with a bow in her hair. She was just seventeen hours old and her face was still wrinkled and red and the identification beads on her wrist had not our name but only the letters "NI." "NI" stood for "No Information," the hospital's code for an infant to be placed for adoption. Quintana is adopted.

It has never been an effort to say those three words, even when they occasion the well-meaning but insensitive compliment, "You couldn't love her more if she were your own." At moments like that, my wife and I say nothing and smile through gritted teeth. And yet we are not unaware that sometime in the not too distant future we face a moment that only those of us who are adoptive parents will ever have to face—our daughter's decision to search or not to search for her natural parents.

I remember that when I was growing up a staple of radio drama was the show built around adoption. Usually the dilemma involved a child who had just learned by accident that it was adopted. This information could only come accidentally, because in those days it was considered a radical departure from the norm to inform your son or daughter that he or she was not your own flesh and blood. If such information had to be revealed, it was often followed by the specious addendum that the natural parents had died when the child was an infant. An automobile accident was viewed as the most expeditious and efficient way to get rid of both parents at once. One of my contemporaries, then a young actress, was not told that she was adopted until she was twenty-two and the beneficiary of a small inheritance from her natural father's will. Her adoptive mother could not bring herself to tell her daughter the reason behind the bequest and entrusted the task to an agent from the William Morris office.

Today we are more enlightened, aware of the psychological evidence that such barbaric secrecy can only inflict hurt. When Quintana was born, she was offered to us privately by the gynecologist who delivered her. In California, such private adoptions are not only legal but in the mid-sixties, before legalized abortion and before the sexual revolution made it acceptable for an unwed mother to keep her child, were quite common. The night we went to see Quintana for the first time at Saint John's, there was a tacit agreement between us that "No Information" was only a bracelet. It was quite easy to congratulate ourselves for agreeing to be so open when the only information we had about her mother was her age, where she was from and a certified record of her good health. What we did not realize was that through one bureaucratic slipup we would learn her mother's name and that through another she would learn ours, and Quintana's.

From the day we brought Quintana home from the hospital, we tried never to equivocate. When she was little, we always had Spanish-speaking help and one of the first words she learned, long before she understood its import, was *adoptada*. As she grew older, she never tired of asking us how we happened to adopt her. We told her that we went to the hospital and were given our choice of any baby in the nursery. "No, not that baby," we had said, "not that baby, not that baby . . ." All this with full gestures of inspection, until finally: "That baby!" Her face would always light up and she would say: "Quintana." When she asked a question about her adoption, we answered, never volunteering more than she requested, convinced that as she grew her questions would become more searching and complicated. In terms I hoped she would understand, I tried to explain that adoption offered to a parent the possibility of escaping the prison of genes, that no matter how perfect the natural child, the parent could not help acknowledging in black moments that some of his or her bad blood was bubbling around in the offspring; with an *adoptada*, we were innocent of any knowledge of bad blood.

In time Quintana began to intuit that our simple parable of free choice in the hospital nursery was somewhat more complex than we had indicated. She now knew that being adopted meant being born of another mother, and that person she began referring to as "my other mommy." How old, she asked, was my other mommy when I was born? Eighteen, we answered, and on her stubby little fingers she added on her own age, and with each birthday her other mommy became twenty-three, then twenty-five and twenty-eight. There was no obsessive interest, just occasional queries, some more difficult to answer than others. Why had her other mother given her up? We said that we did not know—which was true—and could only assume that it was because she was little more than a child herself, alone and without the resources to bring up a baby. The answer seemed to satisfy, at least until we became close friends with a young woman, unmarried, with a small child of her own. The contradiction was, of course, apparent to Quintana, and yet she seemed to understand, in the way that children do, that there had been a millennium's worth of social change in the years since her birth, that the pressures on a young unmarried mother were far more in 1966 than they were in 1973. (She did, after all, invariably refer to the man in the White House as President Nixon Vietnam Watergate, almost as if he had a three-tiered name like John Quincy Adams.) We were sure that she viewed her status with equanimity, but how much so we did not realize until her eighth birthday party. There were twenty little girls at the party, and as little girls do, they were discussing things gynecological, specifically the orifice in their mothers' bodies from which they had emerged at birth. "I didn't," Quintana said matter-of-factly. She was sitting in a large wicker fan chair and her pronouncement impelled the other children to silence. "I was adopted." We had often wondered how she would handle this moment with her peers, and we froze, but she pulled it off with such élan and aplomb that in moments the other children were bemoaning their own misfortune in not being adopted, one even claiming, "Well, I was almost adopted."

Because my wife and I both work at home, Quintana has never had any confusion about how we make our living. Our mindless staring at our respective typewriters means food on the table in a way the mysterious phrase "going to the office" never can. From the time she could walk, we have taken her to meetings whenever we were without help, and she has been a quick study on the nuances of our life. "She's remarkably well adjusted," my brother once said about her. "Considering that every time I see her she's in a different city." I think she could pick an agent out of a police lineup, and out of the blue one night at dinner she offered that all young movie directors were short and had frizzy hair and wore Ditto pants and wire glasses and shirts with three buttons opened. (As far as I know, she had never laid eyes on Bogdanovich, Spielberg or Scorsese.) Not long ago an actress received an award for a picture we had written for her. The actress's acceptance speech at the televised award ceremony drove Quintana into an absolute fury. "She never," Quintana reported, "thanked *us*." Since she not only identifies with our work but at times even considers herself an equal partner, I of course discussed this piece with her before I began working on it. I told her what it was about and said I would drop it if she would be embarrassed or if she thought the subject was too private. She gave it some thought and finally said she wanted me to write it.

I must, however, try to explain and perhaps even try to justify my own motives. The week after *Roots* was televised, each child in Quintana's fifth-grade class was asked to trace a family tree. On my side Quintana went back to her great-grandfather Burns, who arrived from Ireland shortly after the Civil War, a ten-year-old refugee from the potato famine, and on her mother's side to her great-great-great-great-grandmother Cornwall, who came west in a wagon train in 1846. As it happens, I have little interest in family beyond my immediate living relatives. (I can never remember the given names of my paternal grandparents and have never known my paternal grandmother's maiden name. This lack of interest mystifies my wife.) Yet I wanted Quintana to understand that if she wished, there were blood choices other than Dominick Burns and Nancy Hardin Cornwall. Over the past few years, there has been a growing body of literature about adoptees seeking their own roots. I am in general sympathetic to this quest, although not always to the dogged absolutism of the more militant seekers. But I would be remiss if I did not say that I am more than a little sensitive to the way the literature

7

presents adoptive parents. We are usually shown as frozen in the postures of radio drama, untouched by the changes in attitudes of the last several generations. In point of fact we accept that our children might seek out their roots, even encourage it; we accept it as an adventure like life itself—perhaps painful, one hopes enriching. I know not one adoptive parent who does not feel this way. Yet in the literature there is the implicit assumption that we are threatened by the possibility of search, that we would consider it an act of disloyalty on the part of our children. The patronizing nature of this assumption is never noted in the literature. It is as if we were Hudson and Mrs. Bridges, below-stairs surrogates taking care of the wee one, and I don't like it one damn bit.

Often these days I find myself thinking of Quintana's natural mother. Both my wife and I admit more than a passing interest in the woman who produced this extraordinary child. (As far as we know, she never named the father, and even more interesting, Quintana has never asked about him.) When Quintana was small, and before the legalities of adoption were complete, we imagined her mother everywhere, a wraith-like presence staring through the chain-link fence at the blond infant sunbathing in the crib. Occasionally today we see a photograph of a young woman in a magazine—the mother as we imagine her to look—and we pass it to each other without comment. Once we even checked the name of a model in *Vogue* through her modeling agency; she turned out to be a Finn. I often wonder if she thinks of Quintana, or of us. (Remember, we know each other's names.) There is the possibility that having endured the twin traumas of birth and the giving up of a child, she blocked out the names the caseworker gave her, but I don't really believe it. I consider it more likely that she has followed the fairly well-documented passage of Quintana through childhood into adolescence. Writers are at least semipublic figures, and in the interest of commerce or selling a book or a movie, or even out of simple vanity, we allow interviews and photo layouts and look into television cameras; we even write about ourselves, and our children. I recall wondering how this sentient young woman of our imagination had reacted to four pages in *People*. It is possible, even likely, that she will read this piece. I know that it is an almost intolerable invasion of her privacy. I think it probable, however, that in the dark reaches of night she has considered the possibility of a further incursion, of opening a door one day and seeing a young woman who says, "Hello, Mother, I am your daughter."

Perhaps this is romantic fantasy. We know none of the circumstances of the woman's life, or even if she is still alive. We once suggested to our lawyer that we make a discreet inquiry and he quite firmly said that this was a quest that belonged only to Quintana, if she wished to make it, and not to us. What is not fantasy is that for the past year, Quintana has known the name of her natural mother. It was at dinner and she said that she would like to meet her one day, but that it would be hard, not knowing her name. There finally was the moment: we had never equivocated; did we begin now? We took a deep breath and told Quintana, then age ten, her mother's name. We also said that if she decided to search her out, we would help her in any way we could. (I must allow, however, that we would prefer she wait to make this decision until the Sturm and Drang of adolescence is past.) We then considered the possibility that her mother, for whatever good or circumstantial reasons of her own, might prefer not to see her. I am personally troubled by the militant contention that the natural mother has no right of choice in this matter. "I did not ask to be born," an adoptee once was quoted in a news story I read. "She has to see me." If only life were so simple, if only pain did not hurt. Yet we would never try to

9

influence Quintana on this point. How important it is to know her parentage is a question only she can answer; it is her decision to make.

All parents realize, or should realize, that children are not possessions, but are only lent to us, angel boarders, as it were. Adoptive parents realize this earlier and perhaps more poignantly than others. I do not know the end of this story. It is possible that Quintana will find more reality in family commitment and cousins across the continent and heirloom orange spoons and pictures in an album and faded letters from Dominick Burns and diary entries from Nancy Hardin Cornwall than in the uncertainties of blood. It is equally possible that she will venture into the unknown. I once asked her what she would do if she met her natural mother. "I'd put one arm around Mom," she said, "and one arm around my other mommy, and I'd say, 'Hello, Mommies.' "

If that's the way it turns out, that is what she will do.

1977

EX POST FACTO

The drama of a terminal illness is not proud. One gradually accepts the imminence of death, and even when the patient rallies in a kind of desperate, gasping euphoria, continues to make arrangements for the future, looking as it were at the annuities, the life insurance policies, the promises once idly made that now can be, *must be,* cashed in. These small treasons obscure not only the agony of the dying, but one's own real feelings about the victim as well.

So it was with the *Saturday Evening Post*. In the last four years of its existence, my wife and I wrote fifty-three pieces for the magazine. It made us financially independent at the same time its own fortunes were sliding irretrievably toward ruin. Only when its death rattle was too loud not to be heard did we realize that what we were losing was not a source of sustenance but nothing less than a surrogate family.

The surrogate father for those of us who wrote for the *Post* during its final throes was Otto Friedrich, the magazine's last managing editor. Working for the *Post* during the seven years that Friedrich was there must have had the same eerie fascination as being permanently attached to the Vietnam war. Indeed the Curtis Publishing Company bore a startling resemblance to MACV, bloated with age, fat, fear, fatigue, incompetence and just plain laziness. Advertising was ambushed, losses mounted, the body count of writers, editors and executives mounted alarmingly. The *Post*'s format seemed to change with the regularity of search-and-destroy missions, and with about as much success. Commander succeeded commander, each claiming to see that light at the end of the tunnel. With a persistence that ultimately became beguiling, each new Curtis administration launched another Operation Total Victory into the Fishhook and Parrot's Beak of Madison Avenue. It was an absurd campaign, begging for a superior diarist to set down each surreal twist and turn. In Friedrich the *Post* found its Pepys.

The *Post* heaved into the sixties already at the point of metastasis. Its board was dominated by octogenarians (presumably, to paraphrase Clemenceau, because there were no nonogenarians around) who had an editor of *Holiday* fired because he ran filler advertisements that said, "Support the United Nations"; its editorial policies were still dictated by the shade of the late George Horace Lorimer, a great editor who had made the *Post* a great magazine by scoring the

11

lyric of Middle America. But Lorimer died in 1937, and on the eve of rock and rebellion, of Castro and Cleaver, the *Post* was still paying $50,000 each for the novels of the eighty-year-old Clarence Buddington Kelland, novels with first sentences like: "Garland Lee owed much of her glamorous success to the fact that she looked like the wholesome girl next door."

The dilemma of the *Post* was simple: Middle America read the magazine, but wasn't buying the products advertised therein; the people whom the advertising was designed to reach didn't read the magazine; change the magazine and you lost the readers. The situation was complicated by the fact that the business acumen of Curtis's management was the sort that once led it to decline an offer to buy the entire CBS network for $3 million. It was a time for plots and plotters.

As managing editor, Friedrich was perfectly situated to "set down every sign of lesions or bleeding, every symptom of the inevitable death." His eye is unsparing, his ear acute. Though generally compassionate, he is occasionally an exquisite executioner. What he has written in *Decline and Fall* is not only a brilliant memoir of the decline of an American institution, but also a painful metaphor for the way we live now. There are no real villains in Friedrich's cast, only men with larger flaws and meaner spirits than their colleagues. Always a sense of madness seems to have prevailed. At the Downtown Club in Philadelphia, the president of Curtis forces an elderly Irish waitress to tell the board of directors a dirty joke; at a dinner for South Vietnam's Madame Nhu, the editorial director for all the Curtis magazines refers to her country throughout his speech as South Korea.

The closest the *Post* had to a hero was its last editor, William A. Emerson, a large Rabelaisian Southerner who in the darkest days claimed that his middle initial stood not for Austin but for Appomattox. Emerson liked to manipulate words to make them sound more impressive, as in "preposterosity" or "fornification." Morale at the *Post* when Emerson took over was, to use his word, "horribilous." At times it was counted an achievement to get through the day without a knife in the back. Gamely Emerson tried to put out a magazine, railing at the "ninnyhammers" and the "piffleniffers," the "cretins and miscreants" who ran Curtis, cutting his staff, his budget and even the size of his pages. "It is," he said, "like getting nibbled to death by ducks."

With each act the comedy grew blacker. At the end, left little more than a husk by a generation of mismanagement, Curtis attracted a fledgling *conglomerateur* named Martin Ackerman. "I am thirty-six years old and I am very rich," he told the staff when he took over. He also had an enormous oil portrait of himself carrying a copy of the *Wall Street Journal*. And so a magazine that began with Benjamin Franklin fell into the hands of Sammy Glick. Disarming and disorganized, Ackerman tried to forestall doom by discarding half of the *Post*'s subscribers, only to find that he had accidentally canceled his own subscription. Eventually he killed the *Post*.

In retrospect, it seems a miracle that the *Post* was able to publish more than two hundred issues during the years of turmoil. And yet, since the *Post*'s demise, I have wondered if, without the conspiracies and the revolutions, it would have been as good a magazine as it was during those dark years. A successful magazine is essentially a product, directed by a strong editor and/or publisher toward a well-defined reader market. Lorimer's *Post* was such a product. Today *Cosmopolitan* exists for what its editor Helen Gurley Brown has called "the girl with not an awful lot going for her," *Playboy* for the urban consumer-masturbator, *Newsweek* for the PTA liberal, *Time* for the locker-room progressive. Writing for these magazines is as invigorating as writing a segment for Bonanza; the formula is set, don't mess with it.

It was precisely because the *Post* wasn't a product that it was such a splendid magazine in those last years and so much fun to write for. They were willing to try anything—a Saran minister in San Bernardino, the diary of a Broadway flop, a Maoist splinter group in Watts with six members. Respect was grudgingly given, but once granted, the editors would follow you out onto the longest limb. In 1965, I peddled a story idea about a small California labor strike all over New York, and was turned down everywhere. "Who the hell has ever heard of Cesar Chavez?" asked one editor who has since nominated him for sainthood. The editor I finally approached at the *Post* asked only one question: "Is what's going on in Delano a good story?" I said yes. "Then do it."

I think now that had the *Post* turned the corner and become a successful product a lot of the spontaneity would have gone. It was that sense of impending doom that had drawn us all together. In closing I would like to tell you what it was like. A year ago, just a few months after the *Post* folded, I published a book (a book, in fact, that had been underwritten by the *Post*) and my publisher gave me an enormous party at the Huntington Hartford Museum in New York. I had asked a number of *Post* editors, all of them now scattered to the four winds, and to my surprise they all came, inconvenient though it must have been. We fell upon each other, sharers of a unique experience, a family. I was absurdly touched and finally saddened. The last lines of Friedrich's book explain the sadness: "Nobody had added a postscript on what eventually happens to families. We grow older and we grow apart, and our own children return to us only on Christmas visits, as strangers."

1970

BUCK

In late May of 1951, when Willie Mays and I both were young, I drove to the Polo Grounds one evening to see the Giants play the Boston Braves. The reason for my outing was less to take in the ball game than to avoid a sociology exam. I was flunking sociology that spring—*Middletown in Transition* conflicted with what I then perceived as the pursuit of the good life— and at Princeton, where I was, in the words of my faculty advisor, "wintering," one could escape the tarnish of a failing grade simply by reporting sick, not taking the exam, and making up the credit in a later semester. And so as I took my seat in the upper deck behind first base, a doctor's certificate stating that I was being tested for incipient mononucleosis in my pocket, I felt only a sense of relief at having deflected the inevitable. I had no way of knowing that I was about to witness what was to be, in the circumscribed world of baseball, a historic event, the first major league home run of Willie Mays.

I had never seen Willie Mays until that night. He had reported to the Giants just three days before in Philadelphia after opening the season at Minneapolis, in the American Association, where in thirty-five games he had amassed seventy-one hits, knocked in thirty runs, was batting .477, and had hit one ball so hard in Milwaukee, it was said, that it had actually driven a hole through the outfield fence. The Giants were going nowhere. They had lost eleven of their first twelve games and were anchored in the second division. So vigorously did the Minneapolis citizenry protest at Mays's recall that the Giants placed advertisements in the local papers apologizing for the act. Willie Mays was twenty years old.

He had gone 0-for-12 in a series in Philadelphia and for this game, his first in New York, the Boston pitcher was Warren Spahn. "If you're going to guess when you come up to bat," Willie Mays said later, "might as well guess on the first pitch. And might as well guess fast ball is what he's going to throw." Mays guessed right. The first pitch Spahn threw was a fast ball that Mays hit into the darkness beyond the left-field roof.

That was 1951. The Giants lost the game that night 4-to-1 and in the newspapers the next morning there were stories of other home runs (Luke Easter hit one, as did Bobby Doerr and Ralph Kiner) and of more cosmic events: Mohammed Mossadegh was defying Sir Winston Churchill over the nationalization of the Anglo-Iranian Oil Company, Senator Robert Taft complained about the conduct of the MacArthur hearing before the Senate Foreign Relations and Armed Services committees, and Sergeant Claiborne W. Hodges captured 112 Reds as the 28th Division pushed into North Korea. There is something sad and dated about those headlines today as there was something precocious and unexceptional about a first major league home run in 1951. As I looked back at that first home run at the start of this season, fifteen years later, Willie Mays seemed to me a figure from some other time, more a memory of my own youth than the only man with a shot—a long shot to be sure—at the all-time record of 714 home runs set by Babe Ruth.

I had not seen him play in those fifteen years, seen none of the intervening five hundred-odd home runs. Between him and Ruth stood only three men—Mel Ott with the National League record of 511 and Ted Williams and Jimmy Foxx with 521 and 534 respectively—all three of whom he seemed certain to pass this year. And so in much the same spirit as I had gone that night to the Polo Grounds (which sadly is no more), I flew to Houston to see Willie Mays in quest of a record, to see what that record meant to the man of thirty-five still living the dream of the boy of twenty.

The Giants were staying at the Shamrock Hotel, itself a faded vestige of the $20-million folly that Glenn McCarthy had opened in the mudflats of southwest Houston on St. Patrick's Day in 1949, an opening which had drawn three thousand guests whose din drowned out the special radio broadcast of the event and who created a telephone emergency which was equaled in the records of Southwestern Bell only by the Galveston Flood of 1909. The hotel now seemed almost shabby and was taken over that afternoon in late April by the convention of the Texas Butane Dealers' Association. In the lobby, a tired girl in black tights, mesh stockings and a white ribbon which identified her as "Miss Friendly Flame" was passing out blue lollipops. "Blue for *bu*tane," she kept repeating wearily.

Shortly after four o'clock, Mays emerged from the elevator into the milling throng of butane dealers and their wives. As he picked his way across the lobby, a conventioneer in boots and Stetson who had passed most of the afternoon in the hospitality suite said loudly to his companion, "Who's the nigra?"

"That ain't no nigra," his friend said. "That's Willie Mays."

"Well, what do you know," the butane dealer said. "I gotta get his autograph." He tried to place his drink on the edge of a table, but it fell to the floor, splashing bourbon on the ankles of Miss Friendly Flame. Without looking back, He pushed after Mays, calling "Hey, boy . . ."

If Mays heard, he gave no notice.

He had come into Houston with 509 home runs, only two behind Ott's National League record and, with a good chance at least to tie it in the four-game

17

series against the Astros, he was besieged by local sportswriters in the Giant dugout before the first game. With reporters he does not know, Mays is wary and slightly antagonistic. He never looked at his questioners, but kept his eyes fixed on the batting cage, where Houston was taking pregame hitting practice.

"Look," he said finally, "you writers are keeping closer tab on that record than I am. Me, I'm not antagonizing any pitchers by talking about it. If I get conscious of it, I'm afraid it'll jinx me. So ask me something else."

It was that strange diction of the professional athlete, in equal parts self-conscious, defensive and patronizing.

"What about the book, Willie?"

"What about it?" Mays said. His autobiography, ghosted by San Francisco novelist and sportswriter Charles Einstein, had just been published and in it Mays had discussed his disenchantment with former Giant manager Alvin Dark over Dark's allegation that Negro ballplayers were not as mentally alert as whites.

"Have you talked to Alvin about it?"

"There's nothin' to say," Mays said. "I said that in the book. Ain't you read the book?"

The sportswriter was apologetic. "Actually, no. But I've read a lot about it."

"I think you're just trying to see if I read my own book," Mays said. "Haven't read it and asking me all those questions about it."

"I thought I'd wait until it came out in paperback," the Houston writer laughed nervously.

"Don't do me no favors," Mays said.

The reporter quickly changed the subject. "Have you thought who'd play you if there's a movie sale?"

"Sidney," Mays said. "He's the only one got the right build."

"Sidney who?"

Mays stared at the questioner and after a moment said quietly, "*Poitier*, man."

The Giants were now taking hitting practice and

Mays took a bat from the rack and stepped into the batting cage. He hit the first three balls thrown to him deep into the left-field seats. "Shoot," he said to no one in particular, "trying to find out if I read my own book."

As he left the cage, I introduced myself and said that I had seen his first home run in the Polo Grounds fifteen years before. He looked at me impassively and said nothing. Beside him, Giant coach Larry Jansen began to laugh.

"Buck," Jansen said (all the Giants call Mays "Buck"), "if everyone who's told you this past week they were in the Polo Grounds that night was actually there, that game must have drawn a hundred thirty-eight thousand people."

"I was thinking a hundred and fifty," Mays said.

I tried to strike up rapport in another direction. Knowing that Mays and his wife, from whom he is now divorced, had adopted a three-day-old baby in 1959, I told him that my wife and I had recently done the same.

"How 'bout that," Mays said wearily. Nothing further was volunteered.

The Giants were shut out that night and again the next afternoon in the first game of a day-night double-header. The only home runs were hit by Houston players and when they were struck, the message board which circles the outfield lit up in a tooting, blazing Western cartoon with fireworks, rockets, bomb bursts, snorting cattle, galloping horses, pistol-packing cowboys and ricocheting bullets. (A home run by a visiting player is greeted only by a ticking time bomb flashing "Tilt.") It occurred to me that the Astrodome was to the old Polo Grounds as Andy Warhol is to James McNeill Whistler, and as one with a strong sense of nostalgia, I found the display disconcerting.

Before the night game, the crowd was serenaded by the Kilgore Junior College Rangerettes. Dressed in red, white and blue cowgirl outfits, the Rangerettes resembled the chorus line in a Busby Berkeley musical. Waving flags and kicking their booted legs in a parody of the Rockettes, the girls swung into their finale, a neo-rock-'n-roll version of "God Bless America." In the Giant dugout, the players perused them like practiced flesh peddlers.

"Third from the end," one of the Giants said. "She's got that anxious look."

"Naw," said another. "Her legs don't quit."

"There's one there got her eyes on you, Buck."

Mays laughed and lifted his arms helplessly over his head.

"Buck thinks that's trouble he don't need."

The Houston pitcher that night was Robin Roberts. Now thirty-nine and in the last flickering twilight of his career, Roberts had won 281 games since he broke in with the Phillies in 1948 and was trying desperately to hang on until he won three hundred, a mark reached by only fourteen pitchers in major league history. His fast ball but a memory and armed only with guile and faultless control, Roberts held the Giants to one run in six innings and that run scored when the Houston shortstop dropped a pop fly. But with two outs in the seventh, and the score tied 1-to-1, Mays lashed a home run five rows deep behind the 406-foot sign in left field. When the ball was hit, Roberts's shoulders sagged and he did not bother to turn around to watch it go out.

"It wouldn't have brought it back," he said later in the Houston clubhouse after the Astros lost the game 2-to-1. He has a handsome, gentle face and lines of fatigue were etched around his eyes. "You been around as long as I have, you know when it's gone."

"How do you pitch to him, Robin?" a reporter asked.

Roberts took a long drink from a carton of milk before answering, as if wondering how many times he had been asked that question in the last eighteen years. "You move the ball in and out. If he guesses wrong, you got a chance. If he guesses right . . ." He shrugged.

20

'How many has he hit off you, all told?''

Look, why don't you ask him?'' Roberts said with
ash of impatience. "I just lost the game. He won
it.''

In the Giants' locker room, Mays could not remember exactly how many home runs he had hit off Roberts. "Four or five," he said. "He's been over in the
American League a long time.''

"That's the 241st game he's lost," a Houston writer
said.

"He's won a couple, too," Mays said succinctly.

"I guess he didn't do too bad for a guy thirty-nine
years old," the reporter persisted.

"Man, you got something against a guy getting
old?" Mays said.

The next day—Sunday—Mays did not take batting
practice, as he seldom does, now that he is older,
when a day game follows a night game. Nor does he
ever take fielding practice, again in an effort to con-
serve his energy. In the Giant dugout, the players,
many of whom hate to fly, were talking about the National League's contingency plans to restock a ball
club with players from other teams in the event of an
air disaster.

"Hey, Buck," one of the Giants said, "I knew a
guy hated to fly and would only take trains. Then he
got killed in a train crash.''

"What happened?" Mays said.

"A plane hit the train.''

Mays shook his head and the dugout broke up in
macabre laughter. Walking back into the Giant clubhouse, Mays had the trainer put an ice pack on his left
hand, which was bruised and sore, causing him to lose
control of the bat. As he soaked his hand, he listened
expressionlessly while equipment manager Eddie Logan, who has been with the Giants since the days of
Mel Ott, reminisced about Ott and the record.

"Ottie would have been glad it's staying with the
Giants," Logan said.

"Haven't broken it yet," Mays said.

"It's only a matter of time, Buck," Logan

"You ever seen him play?"

"Only in the newsreels," Mays said. "He was on a little guy. Don't know how he ever hit kicking out his foot like that." He took the ice pack off his hand and clenched his fist several times. "I guess that'll have to do it," he said.

It was another tough game. The Houston pitcher was Larry Dierker, a slender nineteen-year-old who was only four years old when Mays broke in with the Giants. Into the seventh inning, Dierker shut the Giants out, but tiring, he allowed a run and was relieved by right-hander Jim Owens. With two outs in the eighth inning and the Giants down a run, Mays came up with no one on. On the third pitch, he sent a drive crashing toward the left-field stands. He took two steps toward first base, then stopped and watched the ball as it disappeared into the crowd.

In the press box, a member of the Giants' party asked Judge Roy Hofheinz, owner of the Astros, to let loose the pyrotechnics on the message board, which had never before been lit up for a visiting player's home run.

"That one only tied the record," Judge Hofheinz said. "If he breaks it, we'll see."

Mays did not come to bat again.

The Giant clubhouse after the 4-2 victory was crowded with press and photographers. The celebration had all the spontaneity of an elaborately choreographed Japanese *No* drama. The festive postgame clubhouse seemed to exist only in the minds of reporters with deadlines to meet and headlines to match. Only when a camera was pointed at one of the players did he rouse himself from his torpor, smile animatedly, and say, as if by rote, that he would tell his grandchildren that he had seen Willie Mays tie the National League home-run record. Those players not being interviewed sat quietly before their lockers drinking beer and nibbling cold cuts, watching the reporters clusered around Mays's cubbyhole, as if wanting to point out to the press that this was only the twelfth game of the season, that there were 150 left, and that baseball was, after all, a business.

Mays sat in front of his locker, naked except for the uniform shirt he had put back on for the benefit of the photographers. Patiently he observed the ritual he had gone through so many times before.

"Were you thinking of Ott when you circled the bases, Willie?"

"No."

"What were you thinking?"

"Tie score."

A park policeman broke through the crowd to tell Giant manager Herman Franks, a portly, balding man who affects an air of permanent anger, that the fan who had caught the record-tying ball in the stands was at the clubhouse door. Franks eyed the fan suspiciously.

"A lot of foul balls went into the stands today," he said. "How do I know this is the one?"

"You don't," said the fan, a husky, barrel-chested brakeman from the Missouri-Pacific Railroad, who had driven 152 miles to the game from his home in east Texas. "You just gotta take my word for it."

"I'll give you fifty for it," Franks said.

The brakeman took the fifty dollars from Franks and carefully counted it to see if it was all there.

"Christ," Franks said, "he doesn't trust me."

An iced bottle of champagne had been sent down to the clubhouse and Franks popped the cork. Mays sipped a glass for the photographers and then passed it to one of the other players. A photographer asked Franks to pour some over Mays's head.

"Shit, not that picture again," Franks said disgustedly. "Don't you guys ever get any new ideas?"

With a pained look on his face, he asked Mays if he minded. Mays shook his head and dutifully submitted to the dunking.

It was a half-hour before Mays could finally get to

the shower. When he emerged, the clubhouse was all but deserted. Someone asked him if he wanted the record-tying ball.

"Naw," Mays said. "It's Herman's fifty. Let him keep it. All it means to me is something else to dust."

It seemed certain that Willie Mays would hit his National League record-breaking 512th home run on San Francisco's ten-game home stand, and the Giants made plans for the event as if it were a diamond jubilee. A multitiered cake was baked with the number 512 embedded in the frosting with tiny silver sugar beads. One hundred dollars was earmarked for the fan who caught the record ball. In the photographers' booth at Candlestick Park, fifteen camera crews from local and network television moved in to record every move Mays made. From the Giant front office came an endless stream of arcane statistics: the first major league home run was hit by Ross Barnes of the Cincinnati Red Stockings off "Cherokee" Fisher of the Chicago Cubs on May 2, 1876; in running out his 511 home runs, Mays had trotted 183,960 feet around the bases, or 34.6 miles. A list was compiled of the thirty-one pitchers off whom Mays had hit five or more home runs (leading the parade, with eighteen, was Warren Spahn), and the homers themselves were broken down by day and night games, left-handed versus right-handed pitchers, by club, by date, by park. In the San Francisco papers, sports pundits, who reflect their city's almost maniacal resentment of all things New York, set out to prove that Mays's 511 home runs had actually traveled farther than Ott's, bulwarking their arguments not only with comparative fence distances but also with the variation between East and West Coast wind currents.

But then Mays and the Giants stopped hitting and the victory cake began to get stale.

Nine days passed. Atlanta, Cincinnati and St. Louis came and went without number 512 being struck. There was standing room only in the press box, and as the games went by, the headlines got bigger and the stories thinner. A rumor was investigated that the Braves had formed a pool on which one of their pitchers would serve up the record breaker. Outfielders were questioned as to how close to the fence they were when they caught long fly balls hit by Mays. Former National League batting champion Ernie Lombardi, who is now press box custodian at Candlestick Park, was interviewed about the number of home runs he had hit. "I seen on one of them bubblegum cards it was a hundred ninety-seven, a hundred ninety-eight," Lombardi said. "Anyway less than two hundred." The theft of Giant president Horace Stoneham's Cadillac by a North Beach beatnik was duly recorded as was the death of a seventy-year-old retired Navy lieutenant commander who became Candlestick Park's first heart attack victim of the season on Senior Citizens' Day.

At the plate, Mays began to press and tumbled into a slump that saw him get only three hits in twenty-five at bats. Dogged at every step by photographers, it was an effort for him not to lose his patience.

"How can I not think of the record?" he snapped after a loss to the Braves. "You guys remind me of it every time I turn around."

Nor did four losses in five games improve Herman Franks's disposition. "Go ahead, just don't stand there," he growled at a reporter after a loss to Cincinnati. "Ask me something silly."

As if his slump were not enough, Mays was also hurting. With the Giants down 11-to-0 against the Braves, he was rested midway through the game more for artistic reasons than anything else. "It just wouldn't be right if Willie hit it in a game like this," said Giant public relations director Garry Schumacher. But the next day, with the Reds battering the Giants, he was removed from the game in the fifth inning with a cold and upset stomach. Though ordered to stay in bed, he showed up at the park the following afternoon shortly before game time and began getting dressed, only to have Franks send him back home again to rest.

"Dick as he was, he thought he could do something to help," Franks said.

"When will he be back in the lineup, Herman?"

"How the hell should I know?" Franks rasped. "Now I suppose tomorrow you'll say that Franks answered that in his usual grouchy style."

Mays was back in the lineup against the Cardinals on Friday night, with the cameras once again recording his every sneeze. But on Sunday, running out an infield roller, he stumbled over first base, wrenching his knee. As he limped from the field, someone in the photographers' booth yelled, "Strike the set." Before Mays was in the dugout, the camera crews were packing their equipment. An inning later, it was pointed out in the press box that last year, when Mays hit his personal high of fifty-two home runs, he had once gone twenty-two days without a homer. It was a statistic that cheered only the freelance television cameramen. "I hope he never hits the sonofabitch," said one. "I get $82.50 every game I'm out here."

On Wednesday, May 4, ten days after Mays hit his record-tying home run and after tailing him around for two weeks, I found myself succumbing to the old sports page adage that no story is complete without either a child or a priest. I struck out with the child, but from a Jesuit friend I learned the name of the Reverend Peter Keegan, a curate at St. Cecilia's Roman Catholic Church in San Francisco and one of Mays's closest friends. I called on Father Keegan at St. Cecilia's rectory and was in luck. He had just come from lunch at Mays's home and told me that he had given him a pair of rosary beads and a St. Christopher's medal.

"For good luck," I said. Even as I said it I realized that I too had become a student of the memorabilia of a nonevent.

"Well," Father Keegan said, "actually it's his birthday Friday. But it won't do any harm and if it works I suppose you could call it a good-luck charm."

"Did you talk about the record?"

"I said he's been pressing and told him he was going to hit it tonight."

"What did he say?"

"He said 'I hope so, Father.' "

That night, shortly before the game with the Los Angeles Dodgers, I asked Mays if he was wearing his talisman. He stared at me suspiciously.

"The medal," I said.

"How did you know about that?" Mays said.

I told him I had seen Father Keegan that afternoon.

"Man," Mays said, "you guys are really following me around."

The Dodger pitcher that evening was Claude Osteen, who had not thrown a home run ball in 96 2/3 innings. Twice Osteen struck out Mays, each time making him look bad. But in the fifth inning, with two outs, Osteen threw Mays a high change-up. With seemingly only a flick of his bat, Mays sent a drive arcing in a high parabola over the right-field fence. As he circled the bases, Candlestick Park erupted. Whistling, cheering and stamping their feet, the crowd interrupted the game for five minutes and twice brought Mays from the dugout to doff his cap with the chant, "We want Willie."

The rest of the game was an anticlimax. In the Giant clubhouse, television cables were strewn all over the floor and floodlights burned down on Mays's locker. Someone kicked over a carton of fan mail, littering Mays's cubbyhole with letters. Interviewed on two postgame shows (throughout one of which he called the sportscaster by the wrong name), Mays did not arrive in the locker room for twenty minutes after the game ended. As he entered, Franks whispered to him that the boy who had caught the record-breaking ball was asking $1,000 for it.

"He wants a thousand, he can keep that mother," Mays said.

For nearly half an hour, flashbulbs popped and microphones were pushed into Mays's face, as reporters

and newscasters elbowed each other out of the way.
Occasionally tempers flared. "Just wait a goddamn
minute," a reporter shouted at one broadcaster. "I
was asking him a question."

"What did you feel, Willie?"

"Relief," Mays said.

"What do you want to do now?"

"I just want to get the hell out of here and go home,
that's what I want to do."

"Give us a smile, Willie."

"I don't have no more smiles, fellows," Mays said.
"I am just smiled out."

Only once did Mays seem genuinely amused. That
was when a newscaster from ABC's *Wide World of
Sports* pumped his hand and said, "Willie, you are a
great credit to the game of baseball."

"Why, thanks, man," Mays said.

Almost as an afterthought, the cake with the 512
lettered on it was wheeled in front of Mays's locker.
Mays cut into it for the photographers, but the cake
was by now so stale that it crumbled like a tenement
under the wrecker's ball. He held a piece in front of
his mouth, then threw it back on the plate when the
photographers left. No one else touched it.

When the crowd finally thinned, Herman Franks,
wearing nothing but a shirt, shower clogs and his
Giant cap, pulled up a stool in front of Mays's locker.
Puffing on a cigar, Franks said, "Now you can relax
until you get seven hundred and something."

"Shoot," Mays said. "There's Williams and there's
Foxx and then it's going to start all over again. Ain't
that right?"

"No," Franks said. "You've got a breeze now for
five years."

"I hope you're right," Mays said tiredly.

No one knew better than Mays the odds against his
catching Ruth. "I'm thirty-five now," he said. "I'd
have to average forty a year to catch up with that guy.
I don't think I can do it."

He wrapped a towel around his middle and plodded

slowly into the shower. The cameras were gone and the flashbulbs were no longer popping. The newsreel cables had been removed and the clubhouse was almost empty. On the bulletin board was chalked a message: "Plane leaving for St. Louis Friday morning, 8:15, TWA flt. 162. Please be at airport 7:45. Arrive St. Louis 1:40."

1965

MEMORIES OF A LEFT FIELDER

This is my last season. This is the year I hang up my spikes and give my glove to a children's hospital and take off the white uniform with the blue number 90 on the back—there's a story on how I was assigned a number that high, but I'll get to it later—and shake hands with Nobe Kawano, the clubhouse boy (it's funny calling Nobe a boy; he's older than I am), and probably with Tommy LaSorda, although as far as I'm concerned, Walter Alston will always be *the* manager of the Dodgers (I remember last year when Allen Malamud of the *Herald-Examiner* said Walt was out of touch with us players and should quit, and Walt called Malamud "fat," which under the circumstances probably was not the smartest thing for the Skip to have said, but as facts go, it was more accurate than anything you're likely to see in the *Examiner* on any given day) and walk out of the Dodger clubhouse for the last time. That's right, I am packing it in. I suppose there'll be a "day" for me—the last home stand against Houston—and I suppose if we make it into the playoffs and the series my retirement will be postponed, but what happens in October happens. All I know is that in 1978, I will no longer be in left field for the Los Angeles Dodgers. I am sick of the travel and I am sick of the aggravation, and now LaSorda sits me down against certain right-handers. Bleep that, say I. There's never been a pitcher born I couldn't hit; you can look it up—I'm .303 lifetime against Seaver, and him and Marichal and Gibson are the three best I ever hit against, not a petunia in the bunch, and in case you're interested, I'm .297 lifetime against Marichal and .316 against Gibson. So that's it, goodbye, Charlie, sayonara, Old John is calling it quits. . . .

It may come as a surprise to some readers to learn that I have been the regular left fielder for the Dodgers, in both Brooklyn and Los Angeles, for the last thirty-five years. At any given time, my actual tenure in left field has only been for some fifteen or twenty of those thirty-five years, for as I grew older in my nonuniformed life, I kept pushing up the date of my rookie year from 1942 to 1947 to 1953 and finally to 1958. In my frivolous life, I write the odd book or the odd film for the likes of Pacino or Streisand, but that is strictly a Clark Kent or Bruce Wayne cover. No literary friend has ever penetrated my double life (it would, after all, be rather difficult for Joan Didion to accept the fact that for the last fifteen years she's been sleeping with a five-time National League batting champion), although twice on the field I nearly blew my cover with an unthinking reference to belles lettres. The first was in the old Forbes Field in Pittsburgh, when I told Jim Gilliam one day that what I liked about Red Smith's sportswriting was the particular undulating rhythm of his sentence structure. Jim just looked at me for a while and finally he said, "I got to take infield." From that day to this we've never had much to say to each other beyond "His fast ball tails away" or "His curve ball breaks straight down" or "Attaboy" or "How to go." The second time was in Oakland during the '74 series. I saw Roger Angell before the third game and told him that reading him on baseball was like reading Trollope on mid-Victoriana—you both, I said, understand the social architecture. I never saw anyone look so surprised. I suppose it had never occurred to him that a left fielder with a pulled hamstring (I still hit .337 that year, even with no leg hits because of the hamstring) might have read the Palliser novels.

There will be some who will suggest that I suffer from a serious schizophrenia, that fandom has skidded across the county line into a dangerous and perhaps committable fantasy. So be it. I just happen to love the Dodgers in more ways than Elizabeth Barrett loved Robert Browning. When I was a very young boy I believed that I personally controlled the destiny of the Dodgers, that the team's won-lost record was determined by my manual transgressions of the sixth commandment. In 1944, when the team finished in seventh place and lost ninety-one games, I was convinced that my palm would become hirsute and that I would grow no taller than a jockey. Nearing six feet and rampantly, even ostentatiously, carnal, I stopped equating the supine with sin; the 1963 season was bliss itself—ninety-nine wins and a four-game sweep of the Yankees in the series.

Oddly enough, I find my occasional forays into the Dodger clubhouse infinitely sad. I have now reached the age where I see these young athletes in various stages of undress not as boys of summer but as the car dealers of the not too distant future, the insurance salesmen, pitching coaches, beer distributors—men of autumn, in other words—the more fortunate among them pauchy panelists on *Hollywood Squares*. The diamond is fantasia, the locker room a real world where a pitcher discusses how to apply K-Y jelly to the private parts of a Philadelphia groupie, and the manager in the middle of a losing streak tells a sportswriter that there are two things everybody has one of—an opinion and an asshole. There is an autographed picture of Frank Sinatra in the manager's office and three photos of Don Rickles; the message board blinks A DODGER STADIUM WELCOME TO JILLY RIZZO. In fantasy, however, the mystery remains. In the major league of the mind, Pete Rose does not pose for Jockey shorts, two weighted bats over his shoulder, his basket encased in a pair of camouflage green Metre Brief International Skants. Can Chrissie Evert for Feminique be far behind, or Johnny Bench for Detane, the Climax Control for Men? Who will step up for Prelude 3, the new dual-intensity vibrator, or Texture Plus with Pleasure Dots?

Nor, as it happens, am I much of a student of the sports pages. A quick look at the box score, a computation of batting averages on my pocket calculator, and that is it. Although from April to October I regard my time in front of a typewriter as much a front as Clark Kent's chores on the *Daily Planet,* a certain residual professionalism makes me look with distaste upon the Quintus Slides of the local sporting press. A year or so ago, I was at Dodger Stadium one Sunday when a man and his son leaped from the stands and the father tried to burn an American flag in center field. Rick Monday, then of the Chicago Cubs, now the Dodgers' center fielder, raced from his position, grabbed the flag from the arsonist and was saluted on the message board: RICK MONDAY YOU MADE A GREAT PLAY. The firebug, one William Errol Thomas, Jr., thirty-seven, unemployed, was arrested, given the choice of a $60 fine or three days in the slammer, served the time and disappeared. I personally find flag burning stupid and always, as it most certainly was in this case, counter-productive: Monday was named grand marshal of Chicago's "Salute to the American Flag" parade and was honored for his deed at baseball banquets throughout the winter; the photograph of him rescuing the flag was a poster given to fans at Dodger Stadium on Flag Day this year. "If he's going to burn a flag, he better not do it in front of somebody who doesn't appreciate it," Monday told writers. "I've visited enough veterans' hospitals and seen enough guys with their legs blown off defending that flag."

The Dickensian irony of Monday's statement was unremarked upon by the sporting press. It is seldom if ever mentioned in the sports pages that while the magnates of baseball have an almost mystical devotion to the flag, this devotion, during the Vietnam war, did not extend to volunteering their athletes to get shot in defense of it. The military history of the major leagues during Vietnam was essentially a history of National Guard weekends and evening reserve meetings, a kind of legal draft dodging that carried with it credentials of patriotism denied those who bugged out to Canada. Robert James "Rick" Monday, Santa Monica High School, '63, Arizona State, '67, six feet three, 195 pounds, was not paid a bonus of $104,000 to get his ass shot off in Nam; a tour or two or VA hospitals passed for service in the boondocks. I do not mean to be harsh on Monday, only on that Captain America persona concocted in the press box; he was only another of his generation, too aware to enlist in a war where niggers got killed and greasers and rednecks, not graduate students or bonus babies. What grievance sparked William Errol Thomas, Jr., was impossible to discover in the sports pages, let alone what bargain he had struck with his draft board. Not long ago, more than a year after the fact, I tried in vain to find him. I went to the criminal courts building and pulled the record on Case No. 31-543367. Thomas, William Errol, Jr., Viol. Sec. 602 (J) P.C., one year probation, not to enter Dodger Stadium during probationary period. No personal information. His attorney in the public-defender's office said that Thomas was an American Indian, a transient living out of the back of his car. The Department of Motor Vehicles yielded no information as to his whereabouts, nor did the registrar of voters, nor the Veterans Administration. The Bureau of Indian Affairs in Phoenix could not help, nor could the Navajo Area Office in Window Rock; the sixth office I tried at the Pentagon said it would take a month to discover whether Thomas, William Errol, Jr., had ever done a hitch in the military. The absence of Thomas's name from the bureaucracy's computer printouts seemed to speak more volumes than the tedious saga of Captain America, but these volumes will never be read in the sporting green.

It is because of such temporal matters that I rarely sit in the press box at Dodger Stadium. Better to wander alone through the grounds at 1000 Elysian Park. One Thousand Elysian Park Avenue—has any ball yard ever had a more evocative address? Even the best way to get there is through a time warp, down Sunset Boulevard, through Silver Lake and Echo Park. This is Philip Marlowe country, where the detritus of the 1940's radiates from every crumbling bungalow; peeled gold lettering on a second-floor window summons pedestrians to LEARN THE RHUMBA. Then left up that Angeleno Champs-Elysées at the top of which stands Walter O'Malley's Arc de Triomphe. I make the trip fifteen or twenty times a year, always by myself; alone in Elysium I am not burdened by nonbelievers who would question my lifetime batting average of .34973, which rounded to the nearest decimal gives me a b.a. over the last twenty years of .350. On the bulletin board in my office, there is pinned a ragged piece of paper on which are printed my stats since 1958. (When I first joined the Dodgers in 1942, I always intended to retire in twenty years; an eraser changes the twenty-year span every spring.) During the off-season, I ravage *The Baseball Encyclopedia* for pertinent figures. I am first in lifetime doubles with 800, seven ahead of Speaker, and second in triples with 301, after Wahoo Sam Crawford. I've never been much of a home-run hitter (nineteen is my high in the bigs; I average fourteen or fifteen a season), but ten times I accounted for at least 200 runs a season—that's RBI's plus runs scored, minus home runs (because homers are included in both RBI's and runs). Gehrig did that thirteen times; Ruth, eleven; Jimmy Foxx, nine; Charlie Gehringer, eight; Willie Mays only did it twice. Speed was always my game. The doubles and triples tell you that, and the 724 lifetime stolen bases (eight years, more than fifty); you walked me and I was as good as on third. Of course, what everyone talks about are the ten years with over 200 hits (once more than Cobb, twice more than Rose) and the two years in a row I hit over .400 (me, Cobb and Hornsby are the only ones ever to do it twice in a row, and no one has even hit .400 since Teddy Ballgame in 1941; my license plates are 403 JGD and 405 JGD in case you're wondering what my b.a. was those two years), but you know what I'm proudest of? The year I hit in 135 out of the 156 games I played, and for consistency, I'd put that against Joe D. and his fifty-six-game streak.

But those are only numbers, and numbers don't tell you about the good times, or the bad. I suppose you could call my contract battles with Walter O'Malley epic. They were never over money, but over the First Amendment: Walter did not like the idea of my writing books in the off-season and I was such a militant supporter of Marvin Miller and the Players' Association that he thought I was a Red. I always was one to speak my mind and the only two words Walter liked to hear a ballplayer say were "Yes, sir." It was my big mouth that got me my number 90. I was eighteen when I joined the Dodgers, a bonus baby, and I couldn't be farmed out, and Jackie Robinson didn't think much of bonus babies and insisted I be given a bat boy's number, and I said to him, "Listen, fella, the day you can hit as good as number ninety is the day you start pissing holy water." I shouldn't have said it, but of course I was right, and the number 90 has become as much of a trademark as Red Grange's 77.

It hasn't been a bad life, but the pulled hamstring has become chronic and I've got a novel coming out in October, and while I might come back next spring, it's time to start the rest of my life. I've given my farewell address a lot of thought, and this is what I'm going to say on my day, that last home stand against Houston:

". . . And now it is time to say goodbye. . . ."

(The 56,000 people in Dodger Stadium will cry as one, "NO!")

". . . It is not an edifying spectacle to see a grown man cry, but bear with me . . ."

("NOOO, NOOO . . .")

". . . I have worn this uniform for twenty years. I am a Dodger; I always will be a Dodger. . . ."

(Sandy Koufax and all my teammates of the last thirty-five years will be weeping along the third-base foul line.)

". . . Thank you for these twenty years, thank each and every one of you . . . . thank you . . . thank you . . . and goodbye."

1977

LETTER FROM
PORTUGUESE BEND

One morning recently, I awoke with an indefinable sense of anticipation and suddenly realized that it was Friday, Friday being *New Yorker* day in Portuguese Bend, on the Palos Verdes Peninsula in the southern section of Los Angeles (county, not city), and a day on which *New Yorker* devotees, to insure that they might obtain one of the few available copies of this weekly magazine, which arrives on the newsstands two and sometimes three weeks after distribution in the East, must plan their day to include a trip to Palos Verdes Estates, eight miles distant, where the magazines are sold. Accordingly, as I arose slowly, as is my wont, and circled past my sleeping wife in her blue Dacron crepe nightgown and entered the bathroom, my thoughts turned naturally to the *New Yorker* and how to obtain it. Standing under the shower (not one of the new American Standard models, but an old Crane with a stainless steel handle, a dormitory model similar to those found in the shower stalls in the basement of Joline Hall at Princeton University, where coincidentally I spent my undergraduate years), I reflected upon the magazine and upon the pleasures my wife and I have derived from its pages, over the admittedly short course of our marriage. A favored parlor game in our house in Portuguese Bend involves the naming of towns and cities not yet visited by Philip Hamburger, the gazetteer. Often, while driving on the Los Angeles freeway system (a typical trip into Beverly Hills for us necessitates use of both the Harbor and the San Diego freeways, while a trip to Chavez Ravine involves brief passage on the Pasadena Freeway, though this is a trip usually taken only between April and October), we are reminded of Janet Flanner, and the lucid communiqués in which she describes the various traffic problems encountered around the Étoile and the Bibliothèque Nationale during the course of her week in Paris.

Accordingly, over breakfast, my wife and I discussed the best routes into Palos Verdes Estates, eight miles distant. As I buttered a piece of raisin toast, I looked at Joan, my wife, who was sipping her second cup of black coffee, and spoke. "The north road," I said. Joan laughed, I agreed. While Joan dressed, I checked the Chevy II Nova station wagon which we have leased until our new poppy-red six-cylinder Mustang convertible arrives from the Ford factory at River Rouge, near Detroit, forty miles distant. Ten minutes later, Joan appeared in a black-and-white sleeveless print dress. "Are you ready?" I asked. "Yes," she laughed.

On the north road, Palos Verdes Estates is eight miles from Portuguese Bend. The Peninsula, as the natives laughingly call the peninsula, is roughly lump-shaped, and covers some 16,000 acres. It was once owned by the Palos Verdes Corporation, a five-man syndicate headed by Frank A. Vanderlip, former president of the National City Bank of New York, which coincidentally is the same city where the *New Yorker* is published. After the end of World War II, this syndicate began s......ng off the land to real-estate developers, and today it is one of the two or three most choice residential areas of Los Angeles, the others being the Wilshire district, Pasadena and Beverly Hills. Although tract houses tend to obscure the view of the ocean, the Peninsula is not without its scenic attractions. Seven-tenths of a mile north of our house on the north road is the celebrated Swedenborgian Wayfarers' Chapel, designed by the son of Frank Lloyd Wright. (In a witty moment, Eliel Saarinen, father of Eero and himself an architect, called Wright Senior "Frank Lloyd Wrong.") As we drove past the chapel, my wife reminded me that Jayne Mansfield had been married there to Mickey Hargitay, the former Mr. Universe. "Yes," I reminded her, "and Virginia Warren to John Daly, the broadcaster." I should have realized that this reference to the oldest of Earl Warren's three daughters would upset my wife, for she is an arch-conservative and has strong feelings about what she laughingly refers to as "the Warren Court." To change the subject, I reminded her that Henry, William and Alice James's father (some people, perhaps, would remember him better as the uncle of Minnie Temple, the model for Millie Theale in his son Henry's book *The Wings of the Dove*) had been a Swedenborgian, and an ardent one. We discussed for a moment whether Minnie Temple had ever visited Portuguese Bend (the Wayfarers' Chapel was built after her death) and decided that, to the best of our knowledge, she had not. Neither, in fact, has Philip Hamburger, the gazetteer. Half a mile farther along the north road, to our left, which is the west, we glimpsed Marineland of the Pacific. "That's Lloyd Bridges's house," Joan laughed, referring to the popular television program, *Sea Hunt*, which was filmed there, and which starred the actor, Lloyd Bridges. I agreed. The road into Marineland is lined with bougainvillea and shaded by an avenue of pepper trees. In the center of the road, a split rail cross is embedded into the asphalt. The arm pointing north reads "Entrance," while the arm pointing south reads "Exit."

The village of Palos Verdes Estates resembles a cloister, except that the fourth, or ocean, side is open. The architecture is of the Spanish Mission style, of the type introduced by the late Father Junípero Serra in the eighteenth-century missions of San Juan Capistrano, San Diego, San Miguel, San Carlos, San Carlos Borromeo, San Luis Obispo, San Jose, Santa Barbara, Santa Dolores and San Juan Bautista, where coincidentally my wife and I were married. A tiled, covered arcade shelters the shops along the three enclosed sides of the rectangle. Though it was midday when we finally pulled into the village, there were few people about. "It's lunchtime," Joan explained. I agreed. We repaired to the drugstore in the southwest corner of the arcade where magazines, including the *New Yorker*, are sold. "Do you think there will be any copies left?" Joan asked. I laughed. She agreed.

This is the first of two parts on buying the New Yorker *in Portuguese Bend.*

1966

NEVERMORE,
QUOTH THE EAGLE

I remember in my formative years being given wise counsel by a friend who had emerged emotionally scarred and tangibly poorer from an encounter with the Internal Revenue Service. "Don't ever," my friend warned, "mess with the eagle."

Over the years I have assiduously followed that advice. Each April my tax return is prepared by an accountant so fiscally conservative that he makes Calvin Coolidge look like John Maynard Keynes. I never carry money on my person. Instead I carry twenty-two credit cards, permitting me to charge (and deduct) everything from movie-theater popcorn (business entertainment, Section 162, Internal Revenue Code) to a sauna bath (emotional wear and tear: medical expenses, Section 213, Internal Revenue Code). It is a system which has always given me a secure feeling. And then, last summer, I messed with the eagle. Over, of all things, my laundry.

It all began one afternoon when I drove into San Pedro, California, to pick up my shirts and sheets. The scene outside the New Deal Laundry had all he elements of Black Tuesday, 1929. A crowd of angry housewives was peering into the window and pounding on the padlocked door. In the window was a sign: CLOSED FOR NONPAYMENT OF INCOME TAX. INTERNAL REVENUE AGENT WILL BE ON PREMISES AT 2 P.M.

It was then a quarter to four and the sullen crowd

began to close around me. "Are you this agent?" a woman asked truculently.

"No," I said, and fled to my car.

When I arrived the next day, I squinted through the window, and all I saw was a pile of empty polyethylene bags. The proprietor of the store next door told me the IRS man had come, distributed all the laundry and left. Someone, I thought, was twelve shirts and sixteen sheets to the good.

From a pay phone on the corner I called the Internal Revenue Service and asked the name of the agent in charge of the New Deal Laundry caper. His name, I was told, was Mr. Hakimura. "May I speak to Mr. Hakimura?" I asked. The voice parried. What did I want to speak to Mr. Hakimura about? "The whereabouts of certain property," I said, slipping easily into what I imagined was IRS diction, namely, my laundry." There was a pause. "Mr. Hakimura will get back to you," the voice said.

Three days passed. By this time I was a little gamey, twelve shirts being three less than I own. I kept badgering the IRS until finally, after I made a veiled threat of an appeal to higher authority, I was told that Mr. Hakimura might be found at the main branch of the New Deal in Long Beach. By now I felt distinctly committed. I drove to the branch, where I encountered a tall, slender Japanese.

"Mr. Hakimura, I presume," I said.

Mr. Hakimura perused me inscrutably. I produced my ticket and said that I would like my laundry back. He replied equably that he had given back all the laundry. I asked him where he thought mine might be.

"That," Mr. Hakimura said, "is a good question."

Pressed, he suggested that the laundry might be in the truck owned by Mr. Whiffle, the tax-delinquent laundryman. Mr. Whiffle's phone had been disconnected, and it took me two days to track the truck to a San Pedro garage. When I got there, I found the truck padlocked. Maneuvering around me on a skateboard, a mechanic told me that the IRS had sealed it.

My temper was beginning to fray, and during the ensuing days I prowled the corridors of the IRS offices in downtown Los Angeles, belligerently asking strangers, "Where's Hakimura?" But Mr. Hakimura had dropped from sight. Eventually one of his associates suggested that I call the cleaning plant where the New Deal sent its laundry. "I don't have access to the name," he said, "but it's in the book."

There are five telephone books in Los Angeles, but by deducing that the plant would be within a twenty-five-mile radius of the New Deal, I located it on the thirty-seventh call. I explained who I was and asked if they had my shirts.

"We might," a voice answered. "Or we might not."

"What's that supposed to mean?"

"We're under orders not to give out any laundry information."

"I'm not asking about the Polaris missile system."

"It's a federal affair, Mac."

I called the IRS and told an agent that the cleaning plant had taken the Fifth. He assured me that no injunction had been issued against the dissemination of laundry information. I again called the plant. Just before they hung up, I could hear a voice saying, "It's that nut who wants his shirts back."

Very coolly I dialed the IRS, and this time got Mr. Hakimura. "Where are my shirts?" I asked evenly.

"Have you investigated the possibility that they might be on Mr. Whiffle's person?"

I hung up. That night I dreamed of a very fat man roaming the streets wearing twelve shirts and sixteen sheets.

In the morning I drafted a combative letter to the Commissioner of Internal Revenue. But before sending it, I called Mr. Hakimura and offered to read it.

"Just make sure you spell my name right," he said. "H-a-k-a . . ."

"No!" he shouted. "H-a-k-i . . ."

"All I want is my shirts."

"Tough luck, buddy."

I was stamping the envelope when the phone rang. It was Mr. Hakimura. I refused to take the call: the federal government and I were through, finis, kaput. Mysteriously, Mr. Hakimura asked my wife to appear that afternoon at the IRS. At four o'clock she drove there and was handed a large bundle of dirty laundry. The shirts, Mr. Hakimura said, had been found in a rag bin at the cleaning plant. On hands and knees, my wife counted the laundry before an office full of IRS agents. She discovered that we had been given two extra shirts and three extra sheets. Mr. Hakimura refused to take them back. "We're not in the laundry business," he said grandly. "And one more thing. Your husband's a grouch."

Actually there was one more thing. This year, on my return, a deduction for the cleaning and pressing of office curtains (business maintenance, Section 162, Internal Revenue Code) is being questioned by the eagle.

1965

CASE 68–401–356

The weekend my house was robbed began inauspiciously. I was supposed to fly to Montana, but shortly before departure time, fog descended on the Los Angeles International Airport, causing a three-hour delay in all flights and making it impossible for me to make my connection in Spokane. It was New Year's weekend and there were no other planes available. My wife had already left with our daughter to spend the holiday with her parents in Sacramento. I was finally able to book a flight to Sacramento two days later, but when I came downstairs at 6:30 that morning, I found the dining room filling with water. A pipe had burst and the soggy plaster in the ceiling was sagging ominously. I canceled my ticket and called the plumber, who informed me ("so you won't be surprised by my bill, friend") that he got double time over a weekend, $24 an hour. Fifty-four dollars and a gaping hole in the ceiling later, the leak was fixed. I booked still another flight to Sacramento, but once more, this time while I was sitting in the plane, my seat belt securely fastened, observing the NO SMOKING sign, fog settled over the airport. I trudged off the plane. I knew I was fated not to leave Los Angeles. I felt like Job, wondering what would happen next, knowing something would.

The next day my wife called and asked if I would do some marketing before she returned home. I was gone for less than an hour, stocking up with $18.13 worth of items like grapefruit juice and applesauce and rib-eye lamb chops for my daughter. I had left the door unlocked. When I returned, it took a few moments to realize that something was wrong. I am naturally messy when left alone, and the broken Christmas-tree ornament I had neglected to sweep up and the coat that had fallen on the floor were still in the hallway. But now there was something different. The door on the Victorian commode had been wrenched off its hinges, and the desk drawers in the living room were thrown open and the contents strewn over the floor.

An almost surreal calm took over me, a calm as unnatural in its way as the irrationality that was to seize me later in the day. I felt as if my body were packed in ice, the adrenaline frozen, my blood pressure dropped to almost nothing. I went into the kitchen and put away the groceries, stacking each can neatly in the cupboard, taking each egg out of the box and placing it in its nest in the refrigerator. Then I washed my hands and walked back into the front hall. "Is there anyone in this house?" I called absurdly up the stairs. If I am not a coward, neither am I a brave man, and I don't know what I would have done had anyone answered. The adrenaline was beginning to thaw and I went upstairs. Every room had been ransacked. I knew I was not supposed to touch anything, and left the debris where it lay. Nothing appeared to have been taken, save a $2 bill I had been given four years ago by a miner in a little bar east of Death Valley. He worked in a mine called the Queen of Sheba, which always paid off in $2 bills. His name was Jim, he had been married seven times, and he was on his way across the desert that night for a liaison in Barstow with a girl named Suanne. I called my wife, and then I called the police.

I must tell you here how I felt, why I remembered so much about the miner named Jim. Robbery is so commonplace that one forgets that it is also frighteningly personal. What terrifies the victim is not so much the threat of physical danger as the vivid evidence that someone unknown and perhaps only obscurely rational has singled him out. The mind crawls at the thought of this unknown presence pawing through one's life, exposing his delusions and vanities. There is no reasonable, cerebral reaction. I felt defiled, my privacy invaded. In every room, all over the floor, were the artifacts of another time, another place—an old New York apartment lease, expired charge cards, out-of-date passports, old bankbooks, the keys to a second-hand red Fiat (the first car I ever owned), carbon copies of letters I wished I had never written. To anyone else they meant nothing, but to me it was as if a cobwebbed file had been opened, spilling out its secrets of past affairs and promises unkept, of small defeats and minor triumphs. I wished the thief had taken the tape recorder and the television set and the two portable typewriters, and left the drawers to my past closed. Insurance, at least, could replace a stolen television set.

I waited for the police. And waited. One hour, two, three. I suppose I should have been annoyed, but in a way I was glad to be alone. I sat in the dusk and tried to put a face on the anonymous intruder who had ransacked my house. One can attach purpose, however wrong, to a face. I stared out the window at the people passing by. I had never noticed so many strangers on the block. A duffel coat, a mustache, a way of walking, they all seemed an index to the criminal personality. Why had nothing been taken but that $2 bill? I wondered if it were all happening in my imagination and toyed with the idea of making the house look worse than it actually did, of emptying a few more drawers, overturning a table, breaking a lamp.

A detective finally came six hours after my first call. I must admit that while I am not a cop hater, policemen scare me. As the detective asked his questions, I found it difficult to look him in the eye. I wondered if I were talking too much, wondered if he thought I had done it (but done *what?*) for the insurance. My palms began to sweat. I kept smoking and mixing myself another drink.

The detective went through the rooms, dusting for fingerprints. The house seemed a debit against me, deliberately decorated to remain immaculate of evidence. The wood on the Victorian commode was too grainy, the leather case on the triptych too porous. He finally found a set of fresh prints on a can of mothballs that had been thrown out of a bedroom closet, but I had to admit that the can was the only thing in the house I had picked up after the robbery. Without comment he fingerprinted me. I realized that he had to distinguish my prints from the intruder's, if there were any, but I could not help an almost paranoid resentment at having my prints down in the files of the police department. It was still another incursion into my privacy.

When the detective left, he gave me a card that stated that my case number, for insurance purposes or to report to the police anything else that might have been stolen, was 68–401–356. He said that the intruder was probably a youth looking only for cash and that there had been a similar housebreaking in the same neighborhood earlier that afternoon. I began putting back the drawers. The depression that had seized me earlier that afternoon returned, and when I finally went to bed that night I wondered whatever had happened to the miner named Jim.

1967

FRACTURES

I had intended, when I began this piece, to write about *The Mary Tyler Moore Show*. I spent an afternoon in Studio City watching the run-through of the 147th segment to be filmed since the show first went on the air seven years ago. I made the requisite notes about the fastidious professionalism of my friends Jim Brooks and Allan Burns, who created the series in 1970 and have become very rich writing and producing it ever since. I noted the terminal ennui that sets in after seven years, an ennui that has led Mary Tyler Moore and her organization to make the unprecedented decision to take the show off the air voluntarily at the end of this season. I read all the clips about Mary Tyler Moore and grew irritated at the lust of interviewers to ferret out flaws we would accept without question in children or lovers. "Chain-smokes."

47

"Reserved in front of strangers." "Private."
"Disciplined." "Whim like steel." (She sounded like
a winner to me, and in the parlance of my father-in-
law, who spends a lot of time around crap tables,
"only the winner goes to dinner.") I meant to talk
about the social and professional chasm that exists in
Hollywood between movie and television people, with
television on the ghetto side of the tracks. And I intended to write about my mother, who was in many
ways the quintessential *Mary Tyler Moore* viewer, a
strong, tough, funny woman with an eminently rational view of the human condition. In 1972 she
changed her mind in the polling booth and voted for
George McGovern, whom she detested, because she
did not think anyone deserved to get beaten as badly
as he was going to be, especially by Richard Nixon.
Even in the intimidating presence of death, she never
lost her sense of humor. "One good thing you can say
about dying," she told me shortly before she did, "I
won't have to read about Patty Hearst anymore."

In other words, I didn't have much. It was an hon-
orable idea for a column. Serious. Not very interesting. Which was why breaking my elbow seemed a god-
send.

A natural disaster, a domestic crisis—such are the
secret yearnings of a writer with an idea he doubts will
work. My house was burgled twice and the two re-
sulting pieces netted me a lot more than the burglars
got. I can recall one columnist who eked three col-
umns out of his house burning down, one on the fire,
a second on the unsung dignity of fire fighting, and a
third on his insurance adjuster and a long view on the
charred artifacts of a lifetime. So avid for material is
your average columnist that once, when my daughter
caught my wife and me in flagrante delicto, I seriously
wondered if there was a column in it. (As it turned
out, only a column mention.) And so, as I lay in my
driveway, pain radiating up and down from the bulge
on my elbow that was obviously a broken bone, my

immediate thought was that I was saved from bidding adieu to Mary Tyler Moore.

It was my third break. I worked my first, a collarbone, into a backgrounder for the *Kingswood News;* I was eleven and the *News* was my school newspaper. I never used my second, a broken toe; how does a grown man confess, without sounding deranged, that he kicked his bathtub in a rage after reading the sports pages about a dispute between Alvin Dark and Charlie Finley? As material went, this third break would have been better had I done it in the classic Hollywood manner, punching out a producer or director (and I had several candidates in mind, including at least one woman), or à la Walter Wanger plugging Jennings Lang in his south forty after a parking-lot dispute over Joan Bennett. (Actually I was in a parking-lot dispute a couple of years ago. It was the day before Christmas at a liquor store in Malibu and I honestly don't know how it started. As I picked myself up off the asphalt, my opponent was getting into a dusty pickup with Oklahoma plates along with a girl who called him "Lew Bob.") Alas, this break seemed to offer little opportunity to exhibit grace under pressure. Indeed the only note of fashion I could introduce was that I was wearing Gucci loafers, which may or may not have been the reason why I slipped and fell in my driveway while bringing up the garbage.

I was trundled to a hospital that looked like a rainy-day set for a beach movie. The people in the emergency room reminded me of a remark by the late Johanna Mankiewicz Davis, who once said not only were there no blacks in Malibu, there were no brunettes either. Everyone there seemed to be blond and wearing a wet suit and there was sand all over the floor. Surrounded by these clones, it occurred to me that I was acting out an episode of *The Mary Tyler Moore Show*. All around were scalps wounded by flying surfboards and there I was, less the sardonic Lou Grant than the self-absorbed Ted Baxter, trying to imply that the garbage pail I had been heading for was in the vicinity of the Banzai Pipeline.

Instead of saying farewell to Mary Tyler Moore, I found myself trapped in what seemed an endless segment, playing all the parts, my dignity constantly assaulted by a phantom laugh track. I had not anticipated, even as my arm was wrenched to a right angle and encased in a cast from shoulder to fingertips, the constant pain. The X-rays showed the ulna fractured (already I was putting on airs: other people's bones were "broken"; mine was "fractured") in three places and it felt as if someone were playing snooker with the three errant bone chips; at times I was sure that I could feel the muscles atrophying. Unable to shave, I vowed to grow a beard; my wife gave her permission only if it made me look like the survivor of a plane crash in the Andes and not like someone who drove a Mercedes. A friend suggested I run up and down the sidelines at the Dallas Cowboys training camp in Thousand Oaks, drinking Gatorade and pretending I was on the injured reserve list. My daughter attempted to divert me by showing me the dollhouse she had built on three bookshelves in her bedroom. The dollhouse had one living room, one dining room, one kitchen, one bathroom, one bedroom and one projection room. "Most people," she explained, had projection rooms.

My disposition, fragile at the best of times, was not improved by the Internal Revenue Service, which claimed a payment was past due, even though we had the canceled check. No entreaty, not even a photocopy of the canceled check, could deflect the IRS computers from totting up interest and attendant penalties. Finally I typed out a note with my good left hand: "Re Yrs July 26th: Fuck you. Strong letter to follow." The feds replied almost by return mail: "We are glad to tell you that with the additional information you submitted, we are able to reduce your penalty to $0.00."

With sleep impossible, I became a walking compendium of lines from all those old Joan Crawford movies that show on television at four in the morning. "Do you like music?" Conrad Veidt asked her in *A Woman's Face*. Joan pounded away at the Steinway, not a hair of her pompadour out of place. "Some symphonies," she replied, "most concertos." It was better than Demerol. Unable to work, I busied myself taking a cram course for the New York transit patrolman's civil-service examination. I flunked Proportions and Work Schedules but received a perfect score on Judgment and Accidents. I never asked why we had this New York transit patrolman's cram course lying around the living room. Maybe it was because we had no projection room.

An advertisement invited me to hire "PARTY PEOPLE. Naked Bartender. Fighting Couple Et cetera." The mail offered a chance at a "gold mine . . . that has no parallel in the history of the written word," an opportunity to look at a transcription of an interview with Jesse James. This interview was taped in 1949, when Jesse was 102. The throb in my elbow made me impatient with the news from Chowchilla and Entebbe, Beirut and Belfast; I was drawn to humbler datelines, more eternal verities. An acre of plastic burning out of control in Santa Fe Springs, a process server in East Los Angeles nearly strangled when a servee grabbed and twisted his puka-shell necklace, a Bible station in Washington using the Scriptures to announce numbers payoffs. Each story reminded me of the first editor I ever had. "Nuns and midgets, that's the ticket," he used to say. "The story tells itself if it's got nuns and midgets."

For all those weeks in a cast, my life seemed an interminable story conference about the comic possibilities of fractures; it lacked only that perfect pitch for the ridiculous that came so easily to Mary Tyler Moore's writers. The whole experience of the broken elbow gave me more insight into the success of *The Mary Tyler Moore Show* than attending a week of production meetings would have. I watch the high-decibel confrontations on which most television shows turn and wonder whatever happened to quiet desperation. But for seven years, *Mary Tyler Moore* has looked at the mundane—the broken-elbow level of life—and found in it not only comedy but a measure of dignity as well. I remember the show when Mary implied she was taking the pill. My mother, a devout Catholic, asked me if she had heard correctly.

I nodded.

"Then it must be all right," my mother said.

1976

FRIENDS

Josh Greenfeld is a friend of mine. For years now we have talked every day on the telephone. Twice, three times, sometimes four times a day. Novelist, playwright, screenwriter, critic, journalist, columnist, diarist—Josh is all these things, and good at them, too, a jack-of-all-trades and master of more than one. I think of Josh, however, not as a compulsive scribbler, but as the Samyel Pepys of the AT&T, a telephone plugged permanently into his ear, bringing news of the venal and the absurd, for both of which he has perfect pitch, from all the far-flung outposts and hill stations of the writer's world. I tell him of a party in London, where all the glories of English letters had shown up with someone else's wife or husband, popsy or pederast, and wonder aloud how they are able to bat out a book a year, two screenplays, several introductions, the odd jeremiad for the little magazines, take a walking tour through Bosnia and a lecture tour through Tennessee, while still having the time for this elaborate sexual roundelay. "The English," Josh explains, "only fuck twice a year." I complain bitterly about an actress for whom I am writing a screenplay. "Don't worry," Josh advises, putting her in proper perspective. "She has two left tits." It is an off-the-wall, nonlinear humor that I find myself sponging up and squeezing back into my own work, without credit. Josh never complains. He scatters his wit and wisdom like so much seed into the wind, almost as if it were meant to root under someone else's by-line. We lunch and laugh, dine and laugh some more. Never, however, at Josh's house. In all the years I have known him, I have never set foot in Josh's house. The reason is his younger son, Noah. Noah is brain-damaged.

We rarely admit how many filters there are on even the closest friendship. We filter what we tell our friends, we filter what we receive from them. The quicksand of our lives is so treacherous that friendship, at times, seems an almost fatal freight. More consciously than I care to allow, I try to sieve conversations about biopsies, delirium tremens and disintegrating marriages; I want to hear secondhand, not first, when friends are removed from executive positions for "financial improprieties." There is a certain calm to be found in the lives of strangers. Years ago I sublet a tiny apartment on Gracie Square when I was in New York for a month. From the baby carriage in the vestibule and the Haitian cleaning lady who came in twice a week, from the photographs on the walls and the pill bottles in the medicine cabinet, from the appointment calendar on the bedside table and the tattered address book and the labels on the clothes left in the closet and the return addresses on the mail I forwarded, I could construct the profile of a life. Second marriage, no money, small child with medical problem, seldom seen older children from a former marriage, lapsed Catholic, unpaid alimony, garnisheed salary, shaky job, insomnia, heart trouble—a digitalis prescription filled with disturbing and increasing frequency. I knew more about these strangers who coupled and were afraid in this gloomy closet than I knew about my closest friends, and without the emotional investment. That is, until that day sometime later when I came upon the husband's obituary in the *Times*. A stroke at his desk. And a medium-sized obituary that was like a checker's report on the profile I had concocted. The accuracy of my invention seemed an indictment, an accusation: I had not lavished as much scrutiny on my friends.

Of course I know Noah. I have seen him twice, both times at the beach, and if I had to pick an adjective to describe him, it would be "beautiful." He played in the sand, crooning to himself, and except for the monotony of the croon and the fact that he acknowledged no greeting—not in itself uncommon in a small child—there was no indication that he was infected with what Josh calls, with terrifying detachment, "genetic rot." Son of a Japanese mother and a Jewish father, he seemed the perfect advertisement for interracial marriage. Josh, smart and funny; Foumi Greenfeld, a painter and writer, sensible and funny. (To Josh, after reading a piece in the *New York Times* about superstar screenwriters and their $500,000 fees, Foumi had once said, "Why you get one zero less?") Josh and I talked about Noah, but to me he seemed an abstraction. Josh called him autistic, I could only think of the startling beauty. A Mongoloid child is real, Noah was literary, the protagonist in Josh's book, *A Child Called Noah*. The story was true—the Greenfelds' growing awareness of Noah's autism and their attempts to deal with it—but to me, when a book is finished, I put it into the shelves and its characters are frozen in time. In the morning Josh would call and we would talk about Sue Mengers and Freddie Fields, about Phil Roth's new book, Henry Grunwald's future and Dick Avedon's imposter; at lunch he brought news about whom the feds had busted for tax evasion, what studio executive had just been fired and whose catamite had replaced him as vice-president in charge of production. He has a zest for gossip, an ability to fabricate from it fantasies of such breathtaking venality that he would leave me coughing with laughter. I would take a drink of water and inquire after Noah. "Someday," Josh would answer pleasantly, "I'm going to kill that kid."

Gallows humor, of course; it always made me uncomfortable. And yet, that particular minefield that was the Greenfelds' own patch of territory in Pacific Palisades was an emotional DMZ that I did not wish to reconnoiter. It was not that I rejected the possibility—no, the probability—that the beautiful child on the beach had scorched the earth around Josh and Foumi and their elder son, Karl; I just did not want to contemplate it. And so it was with the greatest reluctance several months ago that I accepted the manuscript Josh gave me. It was called *A Place for Noah* and it was a diary of the six years since the earlier book. A place for Noah—a deadening euphemism, the "place" most probably an institution. I tried to put off reading the manuscript. I was going to Europe, I had my own galleys to correct. But we both knew there was an implicit marker Josh was calling in: read it. I settled down with the manuscript Friday afternoon; by Saturday evening I was a gelatinous mess.

What strikes me now after a second close reading of *A Place for Noah* is how much Josh filtered from his friends. The Greenfelds had a second life of which I was only dimly aware, a community of parents whose only bond was the wreckage of their brain-damaged children. To institutionalize or not to institutionalize, that was the question that haunted them all. The researching of institutions was a soul-destroying look into the future. Take Letchworth Village. "The masonry is fantastic, the rolling hills impressive, but the facilities were overcrowded—with 4,000 patients—and understaffed. The place reeked institution—the smell of urine and lye; the harsh green painted walls; the dirty windows, the begrudging attitude and incompetence of uninspired civil service. First the social worker took us to one of their custodial wards: sixty old women in odd clothes sitting in a day room, all manner of freaks calling for a Hogarth, a Daumier, to sketch them. It was bath day, but the place still stunk. Half of the 'children,' as they were called, even though some of them were into their sixties and seventies, had to be fed; others weren't even toilet-trained. And there were just seven people to take care of them." This for Noah, beautiful Noah, who is now eleven years old.

Noah, who fingerpaints on the bedroom wall with his own excrement. Noah, whose occasional "Dad" or "Hi" is an oasis of speech in a desert of silence. Noah, who wets his pants and whose penis now sometimes stiffens into an erection. Noah, who is not autistic. No: that is the crutch these last six years have sawed off. "Autism" is only a word whose "Greek root oozes with scientific promise. An Orwellian word—one that cosmeticizes rather than communicates. As a writer, I should have known to be wary of so murky a word, of any attempt to conquer with language an uncharted province of science." Not autistic: brain-damaged. A short, sharp, abusing term. "Autism" belongs to those parents of retarded and brain-damaged children who "unable to face the realities and stigmas of the old words have found an elitist designation. But to me the cruelest effect of the glamorous term autism is the specious hope it promises for a miraculous cure."

Instead of specious hope, hopelessness. And with it the rages that "some days seem all that I have left." Rage at the bureaucracy of autism, psychiatrists claiming that it was an organic biochemical condition, physicians maintaining that it was psychogenically oriented, each franchise passing the malady off to the other in order to maintain its "healing monopoly" with all the concomitant largesse of government funding. Rage at the frayed nerves and the psychic strain at home. Rage at his own desperation: "I despair when

I am with him. I want to get away from him, to get him out of my life." Or again: "I wish I were still young and alone, living in a cold-water Greenwich Village apartment, dreaming of becoming a playwright." The days add up implacably into months, into years:

"August 22, 1971. 'Make arrangements for your kid before he reaches adolescence,' a friend warned, 'because after that nobody wants him. All the miracle workers give up.'

"March 28, 1972. Excrement in his pants, excrement on the bed, excrement smeared everywhere. Doing all the shit-cleaning work our tired flesh has become heir to, we began a series of mutual recriminations.

"March 1, 1973. Why hadn't I taken down the living room curtains? Noah has eaten and chewed them away.

"May 11, 1973. I drive Noah to school. I try to talk to him. I say, 'Hello, Noah.' 'We're going to school, Noah.' 'It's a nice day, Noah.' The rest of the ride is in silence.

"September 13, 1974. When Noah came home from school yesterday, he ran out into the middle of the street and lay down. Foumi tried to drag him back onto the sidewalk. He kicked her in the stomach so hard that she doubled over in pain."

I had known none of these specifics, only that Noah was a problem, poked and probed at institutions all over the state, his brain scanned, his neurological functions monitored. Prognosis: uncurable. Yet incredibly Josh was producing: a screenplay for which he was nominated for an Academy Award, a play about Martin Luther King that opened before Coretta King and an SRO crowd at Ford's Theatre in Washington, then played on Broadway and across the land. He went to Japan with Foumi for the opening of his movie, rented a tuxedo and hired a limousine to take himself to the Academy Awards. He also asked the name of my lawyer so that he could sue the producers of his play, fired his agent, sold a TV pilot, began a magazine column, ended a professional collaboration. This, not Noah, was the currency of our conversation.

Noah was a "problem," Noah was an abstract. And by thinking of him as such, I filtered out not only the lows but the highs, not only the reality of the family misery but also the reality of the family love. I did not realize that the Greenfelds had slowly, painfully come to the conclusion that there was a place for Noah, and that the place was not an institution but with them, with the family. A family can feel pain that no professional therapist could fathom, a family could also find joy where no one else could locate it—in the look of a brain-damaged child swimming, in the lope of a brain-damaged child across a palisade. "May 23, 1976. How I love Noah. A love beyond sex. A love beyond need. A love based on service. A love in fact. He can be so endearing—putting his face up to mine to be kissed. I guess every pet has his wiles. But he is my pet." Noah had hardened the bark on the Greenfeld family tree. In 1974, Karl Greenfeld, then age ten, wrote a poem:

> Noah Noah everywhere
> he goes around just like air
> And when you hear his sacred tune
> you know he'll come around the room.
> And when he comes to stay
> he will stay his way.

The Greenfelds' place for Noah is not an ideal solution. Eleven years with Noah and you learn there are no ideal solutions. Only dangers: "August 9, 1976. Every once in a while I project the future: I see Foumi at 75, Noah at 40, and myself mercifully dead."

I think I have never read a more heartbreaking line. I check my own diary entry for that same date. In the morning I saw a Clark Gable–Spencer Tracy movie that someone wanted me to remake. I had lunch with my agent to discuss my price for the screenplay (which

I never wrote), and in the afternoon I picked up the Xeroxed chapter of the novel I was writing. On the margin of the calendar I had scrawled, "Josh called." Was that the day he told me that directors are people too short to be actors? Or that the movie star had two left tits? I know I did not ask him about Noah. I wonder if I have failed him as a friend for not being more solicitous about Noah. I wonder if solicitude is the last thing he wanted, if his conversation with me and his vast network of friends is the way he keeps his sanity on those days he wishes himself mercifully dead. We are friends, but I think this is a conundrum that neither one of us can ever answer.

1978

2.

HARDWARE

upper reaches where they raced upstairs to the observation deck, finding a place along the rail there

MARVIN IN MANIALAND

The fine art of political public relations has fallen on lean times since the heyday of the Democratic Party's great press agent and ghost writer, Charley Michelson. A man who learned his literary style and political ethics at the feet of William Randolph Hearst *(père)*, Michelson spent the four decades prior to joining the Democratic fold as a top-flight journalist, building up a storehouse of information on the private lives of public men. He not only knew where all the skeletons were buried, he was not above giving the old bones a rattle every now and then. For a master stylist like Charley, language existed mainly to hang a rap on someone. For years, Republicans claimed that Michelson nailed the Depression to Herbert Hoover's hide. It is just possible that Hoover would have been stuck with the Depression even if Michelson had never existed, but it is true that Charley did enrich the language with "Hoovervilles" and "Hoover overcoats"—old newspapers worn inside a jacket to ward off the cold. In a desperate attempt to counteract Charley, the Republican National Committee went out and hired his cousin, Peter Michelson—a move that led Alva Johnston to suggest that Congress go on the road as "Charley & Pete Michelson's Greatest Deliberative Body in the World."

By Michelson's high standards, Marvin Liebman, the house flack and amiable evangelist of the Conservative Revival, is small change. No coinage of Liebman's has yet found its way into the *Dictionary of*

American Slang. Outside the pages of the *Nation* and other magazines not generally found on airport newsstands, no one has fulminated against him. Michelson's mark was as unmistakable as an ax-murderer's. Liebman's style is far more subtle. It is no mean feat to find room on the same letterhead for "Mr. Bob Feller" and "Miss Katherine Anne Porter," or to have persuaded "Dr. William Carlos Williams" to make common cause with "Miss Taylor Caldwell." But these are ploys only really appreciated by the connoisseurs. The real difference between Michelson and Liebman is the difference between a Hooverville and a Sun City. The time has changed, the audience is different. By Liebman's standards, Michelson was a piker. Charley spoke for a Senator here, a Cabinet official there. Stashed away in a New York warehouse (at a cost of $6.50 per month) are the signatures of 1,037,000 Americans who have given Liebman their proxies to speak for them—the Committee of One Million Against the Admission of Communist China to the United Nations. "If there is a China lobby," Liebman says modestly, "we're it."

Marvin (among the hippies on the Right, it is infra dig to refer to Liebman as anything but Marvin) not only speaks for lobbies, he invents them. Besides the Committee of One Million, his fertile brain over the years has hatched just about every right-wing front in memory—the Committee for Freedom of All Peoples, the American Committee for Aid to Katanga Freedom Fighters, the Committee for the Monroe Doctrine, the American Afro-Asian Educational Exchange, the American Emergency Committee for Tibetan Refugees, the Committee Against the Treaty of Moscow, the Committee for Aid to Refugee Chinese Intellectuals, the Emergency Committee for Chinese Refugees, the National Committee for Walter Judd for Vice President, the National Committee for Walter Judd as Secretary of State, the National Committee for Walter Judd for Congressman. About the last three, Liebman says: "You win a few, you lose a few."

Through this labyrinth of fronts, Liebman has been largely responsible for both the respectability of the Conservative Revival and for differentiating it from the lunatic fringe. Liebman wants no part of General Edwin Walker, Kent and Phoebe Courtney (who have been known to order their steaks "Communist blood rare") and Robert Welch (not in the least because the John Birch Society is anti-Semitic). Liebman's disapproval of these worthies is not entirely ideological. "Names like these only add animosity," he says, "and cut down on other contributions." Though he will accept money from Walker & Co. if they see fit to contribute to any of his causes, Liebman gets around listing their names on his letterheads by stating somewhere in small print that "space permits only a partial listing." It is a subtlety that Charley Michelson might have appreciated. "For want of a better name," Liebman once said, "I call this work public relations." He has since found that better name. "I am," he now says somewhat grandly, "the agitprop of the Right."

Recently, I made an appointment with Liebman to discuss the machinery of agitprop, and was directed to an old, somewhat seedy office building at the unfashionable southern end of Madison Avenue. The door of Marvin Liebman Associates was barren of all identification except a suite number. "What if someone came up here looking for the Committee of One Million and only found my name on the door," Liebman said, after introducing himself. "Nobody knows me. I'm just the guy who pulls the wires."

Depending on his mood, the speaker of those words fancies that he resembles either Sidney Lumet or Benito Mussolini. He is short, just the wrong side of chunky, has a long nose and sculptured lips, and wears thick glasses which give him a perpetually quizzical look. Though he now deals with the rich and the mighty, he makes no effort to eradicate the strains of his native Brooklyn from his voice. He laughs easily and always seems to find a way to make himself the butt of a story. A dedicated dilettante, he has written a play, published books, and tried to produce a movie. And, like most dilettantes, he is restless and easily bored. When the routine of one committee gets him down, he simply starts another to get himself interested again. "I've always been interested in causes, never politics per se," he says, and his past bears him out. Before turning Right, Liebman was both a Communist and an Irgunist. Today, he sounds as if he spent those same years down at the Trans-Lux hissing Roosevelt.

Liebman's unpretentious office was cluttered with signed photographs of the aristocracy of the Right: William F. Buckley, Jr., Captain Eddie Rickenbacker, Admiral Lewis Strauss, and former New Jersey Governor Charles Edison, son of Thomas Alva Edison and Liebman's biggest personal booster and professional supporter. On the desk, a Goldwater manifesto marked a page in a Sotheby's catalogue. On one wall hung a memorial plate with a picture of Chiang Kai-shek on it. Scotch-taped beside it was a Committee of One Million advertisement inserted by Liebman in a Paris newspaper last winter when Charles de Gaulle was getting ready to recognize Red China. A Frenchman had torn the ad out of the paper and sent it back to New York with one word scrawled on it: *"Merde."*

Liebman's immediate concern that afternoon we first met was organizing a National Goldwater Rally in Madison Square Garden. Our conversation was interrupted fitfully by telephone calls and the arrival of youthful volunteers in chinos and pimples who had come by to stamp envelopes and generally do their bit. In the outer office, Liebman's five women staff workers were on the phone drumming up funds for the Goldwater campaign. "I think the Senator is a tremendous guy," I overheard one murmur. "I do indeed. Personally, I think he's the last call for the dining car."

"A rally is a nightmare," said Liebman. "You've got to get the right chemistry. I want [former Senator] Bill Knowland as chairman. He's a great signature; he pulls people. For my second speaker, I want Congressman Don Bruce from Indiana. He's a good rally man. He's a shouter, a slogan man. It's a total community operation, a rally, and you've got to get the people shouting back 'yea' or 'nay.' " He shuddered as he recalled one of the speakers at a Young Americans for Freedom rally two years before. "I told him to give twenty slogans and sit down," he said. "But he gave this very profound speech about Gnostics and it was dis-aster."

The telephone rang. "Get an elephant and walk it around New York with a lot of signs on it," Liebman said into the receiver. "Maybe he can pull a Goldwater bandwagon or something. Hey, can an elephant walk much without getting tired? Get the band. Ink it in, but don't make a commitment." When he hung up, he said: "We all use the same bandleader—us, the ADA, everybody. He's the John Philip Sousa of the rally circuit. You gotta play something to fit the personality. If it's Congressman Bruce, 'Back Home in Indiana.' If Ronald Reagan is there, it's 'California, Here I Come.' 'The Battle Hymn of the Republic,' that's always good. It's a catchy number."

The phone rang again and Liebman put in an order for balloons and confetti. "You've got to have showbiz types," he continued after hanging up. "They intrigue people into buying tickets. If you can get Shelley Winters to come out for Goldwater, thrilling." Since this was an unlikely event, Liebman was counting on Hollywood's right-wing mainstays: John Wayne, Ronald Reagan, Walter Brennan. For a moment, he mused about another Garden rally he had organized for Dr. Fred Schwartz's Christian Anti-Communist Crusade. "Pat Boone showed up," Liebman said, "white bucks and all. He said something about having four lovely daughters that he'd rather have blown up in a nuclear war than live under Communism." Marvin shrugged. "Well," he said, "they're his kids."

When the phone rang again, I glanced at a memo Liebman was writing to Goldwater's headquarters. "It might be wise to think of the Senator's speech at this time," he had written. "Who should write it?" He also wondered who should deliver the invocation. "The thought first was to get a Negro preacher and a Negro 'Star-Spangled Banner' singer," Liebman said. "But I vetoed the idea. It would have been too patronizing, like hiring a watermelon eater. You know, they sing good, they pray nice." A more pressing problem was how to fill the Garden. "I've printed three times as many tickets as I need," Liebman explained, "and sooner or later, I'm going to have to start giving them away." With a touch of professional pride, he added: "If Barry doesn't fill the Garden, it's terribly embarrassing. For him, sure, but don't forget, also for me."

Marvin was not embarrassed. At the last minute, he slashed the price of the tickets and offered them at the Garden box office at a cut rate, but only a few in the roaring crowd of 18,000 believers actually got in on freebies. Though Liebman had talked vaguely before the rally about hiring pickets to "stir things up a little," the only marcher I saw outside the Garden was a lone Negro carrying a sign that said: "JOHN BROWN, YES, JOHN WAYNE, NO." Inside, the arena was festooned with bunting and more signs. "BISHOP LOUGH-LIN HIGH SCHOOL WILL VOTE GOLDWATER IN '68," said one, though by my calculations, the sign carriers would scarcely be eligible by '72.

Right up to the last minute, Liebman was busy changing the program. Former Senator Knowland had opted to lend his name but not his presence to the rally, and Congressman Bruce was busy elsewhere. Hollywood's faithful had all pleaded professional commitments. "You can't try and get them through their agents," Liebman had sighed earlier after one rebuff. "Agents try to keep them away from free rallies." It eventually developed that the only celebrity he could get was Constance Bennett, "so *skip it.*"

Partly out of fear of Goldwater's wrath, Liebman had shortened the program and pushed up the starting time by an hour. At a rally Liebman had organized several years before, the Senator, who was the principal speaker of the evening, had fumed backstage while the festivities dragged on toward midnight. "He finally exploded," Liebman recalled, "and said to me, 'Goddammit, are you going to get me on before sunup?'" Liebman laughed carefully. "You know, those are the only words he's ever spoken to me."

During the rally, Liebman stationed himself on the Garden floor, where he could supervise the band, keep tabs on the Goldwater Girls and try to keep things on schedule. To fill the dais, he had supplied a full complement of Conservative Republican backbenchers from Congress, all of whom were introduced in one form or another as defenders of the republic by Liebman's master of ceremonies, Congressman John Ashworth of Ohio. The major cheers were reserved for California's ultraconservative Representative James Utt, who is known variously to his disaffected constituents as "Utt the Nut" or "the Congressman from Knott's Berry Farm." Utt had warmed the hearts of the faithful not long before by implying that CBS stood for Comintern Broadcasting Company. The network, it seemed, had commented favorably on Jessica Mitford's *The American Way of Death,* and to Utt, many of whose southern California constituents are only a step away from Whispering Glades, Miss Mitford was the most dangerous fellow traveler in America.

Between such high points as Utt's arrival, Congressman Ashworth entertained the audience with drolleries about "Marquis Childlike" and "Walter Looselippmann." His introduction of William Buckley, the right-wing's premier pinup, triggered the only truly spontaneous demonstration of the evening. As

Buckley stood smiling in the $1,000 royal box, scores of youths stormed around, passing programs and placards up into the box for the dauphin's autograph. From Buckley to Barry, the program sagged. But only once—when a well-dressed, middle-aged lady spoke—did Liebman appear dismayed. "She's the only Negro on the program," he said, "and look, everybody is going to think she's white." He was right.

Finally the great moment arrived. Escorted by the Goldwater Girls, the tall, bronzed Senator strode onto the platform with his wife. The band launched into that catchy number, "The Battle Hymn of the Republic," and hundreds of red, white and blue balloons rained down on the cheering faithful. The lights in the Garden went off and spotlights played down on the standing, stomping throng. For a brief moment, Liebman was caught in a flickering spotlight. He was smiling. His evening was an artistic success.

After the rally, Liebman had invited a few friends and the hierarchy of the *National Review* up to his apartment. Marvin lives in a four-and-a-half-room aerie on the twenty-ninth floor of a high-rent West Side housing project which suggests, with its vast glassy chill, antiseptic smell and splendid isolation from the surrounding slums, nothing so much as an airport terminal somewhere in the Steppes. The decor in his own apartment can best be described as Taiwan Baroque. Everything in sight has been veneered, draped, and trick-lit beyond recognition. He has paneled his library with veneer paper, whipped windows into shuttered alcoves, turned a large closet into a small bar, dominated by a portrait of himself. The living room is hung with a small collection of Barbizon and pre-Barbizon paintings—Courbet, Diaz, and Dupres. They are offset by a bookcase full of early Christian wood carvings from Spain. "The Buckleys come in here," says Liebman, "and they want to genuflect." But the pièce de résistance of the apartment is the bedroom. The floor is covered with white vinyl tile and the bed is half-canopied with burgundy red velvet draperies, giving the general effect of a Roi Soleil boudoir. "I have come back to my roots," Liebman says delightedly. "Seventy-second Street and Palestine."

Liebman's guests that night included assorted Buckleys (not noticeably genuflecting); Frank Meyer, the *National Review*'s book editor, and his wife, Elsie, who bears a startling resemblance to Virginia Woolf; James Burnham, the quiet courtly author of *The Managerial Revolution* and now a *National Review* senior editor, and a mystified young couple who looked as if they had wandered into the wrong party. The tone of the conversation was set by William Buckley's brother John, who identified himself pleasantly as "an extremist, of course." An ex-Party member who likes to make small talk about Communism, Meyer called across the room and asked Burnham, an ex-Trotskyite, if he had ever signed an obscure Party manifesto in the thirties. Burnham said he had not. Meyer, who is extremely sensitive about whatever eminence he once had in the Party, pressed this advantage. "Of course, by my standards then, Jim, you never *were* a Communist." Burnham merely smiled.

"Score one for Frank," someone whispered.

Across the room, Priscilla Buckley, William's sister and the *National Review*'s story editor, mentioned that she would like to see *Hello, Dolly!* "But I've tried and tried," she said, "and I can't get in."

"What, what's that, Priscilla?" interrupted Meyer. "You mean you still can't get into Poland?"

"No, Frank, *Hello, Dolly!*" Somewhat disappointed, Meyer went back to musing on the decline of the Christian West.

The phone rang and Liebman went to answer it. Suddenly his voice blasted into the living room. "HELLO, GOVERNOR. YES, I THOUGHT IT WAS A GOOD RALLY, GOVERNOR, THANK YOU."

"Governor Edison," said William Buckley, adding unnecessarily: "He's deaf."

For a few moments, the living room was silent as Liebman exchanged high-pitched pleasantries with the Governor, a one-time Secretary of the Navy under Franklin Roosevelt. As we waited, I recalled something Buckley had told me a few days earlier. "Marvin's good with old people," he had said. "That's part of the reason behind his success."

Liebman arrived on the Right via that well-traveled route from the Communist Party. Son of a Brooklyn garage owner, he grew up in comfortable "middle middle-class" Jewish surroundings. His ambitions to be a writer were encouraged by one of his high school teachers, Bernard Malamud. When he was only fifteen, however, a civics teacher at Lafayette High School induced him to join the Young Communist League. "It just goes to show," he now says darkly, "that teachers can have a subversive influence." At New York University, he majored in rabble-rousing and drifted away in a year and a half. He did not really become aware of World War II until Germany invaded Russia in the spring of 1941. "When the imperialists' war became the people's war," he now says, "I wanted to do my bit." Drafted, he was assigned to Buckley Air Force Base near Denver, where he found a number of Communist soulmates. With them, Liebman made such a nuisance about Jim Crow conditions in Denver that the brass finally got him out of their hair by transferring him into a Negro unit in which he was the only white enlisted man.

After the war, Liebman became a full-fledged member of the Party. He bummed around Greenwich Village writing stories for Red magazines and took an occasional part-time job to pay the rent—which was only $11 a month. (On the impression that he was being overcharged, he later successfully petitioned the Rent Control Board to lower it to $10.) "That was the year the Village discovered marijuana," recalls Liebman. "It was Kafka and tea all year long." In 1946, Liebman married a painter named Ruth Klein; the ceremony was performed by the religious editor of the *Daily Worker*. The marriage lasted less than a year. "She was an authentic bohemian, if you will," says Liebman, "and I'm basically a middle-class guy, the classical Village bit notwithstanding." His marital troubles were complicated by his first doubts about the Party. When Party boss Earl Browder was thrown out in a palace struggle, Liebman resigned in sympathy. "Your whole life changes," says Liebman. "You feel rejected and you lose your friends because your whole social life is wrapped up in the Party."

Still very much of the Left, Liebman "fooled around with the Trotskyites" before he finally found another full-time cause—the American League for a Free Palestine a front for the terrorist Irgun organization. Though he had no previous seafaring experience, he signed on as a crew member on the S.S. *Ben Hecht,* an Irgun ship under Panamanian registry. The *Ben Hecht*'s mission was to try to take refugee European Jews through the British blockade to Palestine. ("Some people run guns," says Liebman. "I ran Jews.") Carrying Honduran papers, all twenty-five crewmen were volunteers, "soldiers of fortune, young Jews, and just plain maniacs," recalls Liebman. "One of the guys edited a magazine in the Village called *Death.*" In the Mediterranean, the *Ben Hecht* ran afoul of the British Navy and Liebman wound up in a displaced persons' camp on Cyprus. When he finally convinced the British that he was American, Liebman was released and made his way to Paris, where the Irgun paid his passage back to New York.

Liebman's experience on the *Ben Hecht* and in the DP camp gave him for the first time something really negotiable. "I became a kind of professional Jew," he now says. He worked for a number of Jewish agencies before being sent by the United Jewish Appeal to a fund-raising school, where he learned how to organize a committee and how to pressure funds out of the tight-fisted. In 1951, he went to work for Harold Oram, dean of the political fund-raisers and Liebman's professional booster. Marvin's first job there was to organize support for Rudolph Halley, the chief counsel for the Kefauver Crime Commission and a candidate for the New York City Council. The campaign began inauspiciously when Liebman neglected to proofread a mailing that went out over Halley's signature. The letters all began: "Dear Fiend."

With respectability, Liebman's dialectical parabola began. There were no causes in the middle, and to a dedicated causist like Liebman, the non-Communist liberal Left was a pallid substitute for the invigorating intrigues of the party. "Marvin was too old to be a bohemian anymore," says a friend. "He likes power and, on the Left, he was nothing, just a cog. On the Right, he could wheel and deal." Says Liebman: "I kept bumping up against my liberal friends and their stone wall of resistance kept nudging me Right. I began to see that Red-baiting was not a crime, but a proper intellectual pursuit. The former villains—Catholic priests, Republicans, even Chiang Kai-shek— why, they were among the greatest people I ever met."

As he moved Right, Liebman found a patron— Charles Edison, the handsome, white-maned turncoat New Dealer. The two men first met when Liebman organized the Committee for Aid to Chinese Refugee Intellectuals for Oram. Irgunist and aristocrat hit it off immediately. Liebman's Greenwich Village background struck a responsive chord in Edison, who in his youth had lived in the Village, founded one of the first off-Broadway theaters, and had been an intimate of Edna St. Vincent Millay. "Marvin's a guy looking for love," says Harold Oram, "and Edison was a father figure."

In 1953, Liebman dreamed up the front that was to make him: the Committee of One Million Against the Admission of Communist China to the United Nations. With the backing of Edison and millionaire Alfred Kohlberg, he got 212 businessmen, politicians, clerics, and scientists to sign a bill of particulars against UN recognition of Red China. Public response to the manifesto's message was overwhelmingly affirmative. One of the first to back it was General George Marshall, then under fire from Senator McCarthy for allegedly losing China to the Communists when he was Secretary of State. "There may have been a little guilt there," says Liebman.

For four years, Liebman ran the Committee of One Million out of Harold Oram's office, where he had risen to a vice-presidency. But when the Committee stopped being a paying account, Oram announced plans to drop it. Anxious not to let the organization die, Governor Edison gave Liebman $13,000 to set up his own office, not only to run the Committee of One Million, but as many other conservative fronts as could put into operation. Liebman has been on his own ever since.

By temperament, Liebman is an ideal propagandist: he likes to protest. "Marvin regularly spends every penny he can raise or borrow to start this thing or another," says William Buckley. "He literally didn't sleep during the Budapest crisis." Not only did Liebman not sleep, he nearly started World War III. Throughout the uprising Liebman tried to think up a stunt that would save the Hungarian rebels. The walls of his apartment were lined with charts and battle plans; drifters, college boys and conservative money men bounced in and out with offers to help. "My first idea," recalls Liebman, "was to get Ike to fly to Rome, pick up the Pope, and land in Budapest." The White House would have none of that. Undeterred, Liebman came up with his master stroke: invade. His ragtag army was a volunteer band of some 250 college students. Using money pledged by rich conservatives, General Liebman planned to charter planes in Canada, fly the volunteers to Vienna, then truck them to the border. His plan had a Machiavellian simplicity.

"The kids were all from prominent families, Ivy League types," he says. "We were hoping that once they were across the border, their families would raise hell with Washington and we'd have to send in a division to bail them out." I asked him what he had overlooked to make the plan go awry. "Midterms," he said. "The kids all had to go back to school."

Harold Oram feels that Liebman's prime asset is his uncanny sense of timing. "Marvin can always pick out the potential issue, the one that's going to count at a particular moment," says Oram. "Then he goes out and gets the line of thinking of some consummate political thinker like Walter Judd and clichés it, stereotypes it, capsulizes it." When Liebman finds an idea he can cliché, stereotype and capsulize, he sets up a committee. The front names are usually the right-wing's standard marquee personalities—Buckley, Eddie Rickenbacker, Spruille Braden. But they are only a beard for Liebman. In each of his committees, Marvin tries to stay in the background, delegating to himself the unobtrusive title of executive secretary. Once a committee is set up, the propaganda starts. Advertisements are written, speeches ghosted and mailings sent out. "I have a marvelous facility for throwing out broadsides," says Liebman. "If you read my ads, they all say exactly the same thing. You find the same clichés falling over from committee to committee. But in my heart of hearts, they're all the same."

Read at one sitting, the collected works of Marvin Liebman have the effect of verbal overkill. "DOPE," shouts one advertisement, "COMMUNIST CHINA'S ROLE IN THE INTERNATIONAL DRUG TRAFFIC." Another ad, another set of marching orders: "KATANGA IS THE HUNGARY OF 1961." In a cacaphony of silence, the headlines march by: "DEFEAT THE TREATY OF MOSCOW, SEND ARMS TO THE KATANGAN PEOPLE, JOIN THOSE AMERICANS WHO SAY NO."

Perhaps the most celebrated example of Liebman's sloganeering was his contention that Katanga was the Hungary of 1961. "Of course, that analogy is stretching it a bit," he says. "But why not call it the Hungary of 1961? It's one of the clichés, it's a good slogan. You could call Tibet the Hungary of whatever year that was or Hungary the Ethiopia of 1956. What's the difference?"

After he has written an advertisement, Liebman tries to place it either in the *New York Times* or in the *Washington Post*, "even though those are the two papers whose editorial policies are most detestable to me. But they're the ones read by the opinion makers." Copies of the ad—and requests for funds—are then disseminated through Liebman's most priceless possession: his mailing list. Since he first set up shop, Liebman has compiled a basic list of 100,000 names without which he would cease to function. It is a fundraising rule of thumb that political ad hoc committees—like the various efforts in behalf of Walter Judd—are rarely remunerative. But Liebman's list speaks with such a single mind politically—supporters of Judd, for example, would almost certainly be against the Moscow nuclear test ban treaty—that one ad hoc committee can succeed another without the time and expense of rounding up new names.

Liebman often claims that he is working for the U.S. Post Office. Of the $148,000 his office took in last year, nearly half went out in mailing costs. Yet the response on each mailing was still less than 5 percent. Nor were the monetary returns that great. Liebman takes exception with Harold Oram's "simple political axiom" that "10 percent of the people give 90 percent of the dough." Contrary to common belief, he says the bulk of right-wing money comes not from the fat cats, but from merchants, grocers and "those little old ladies in tennis shoes." The biggest names on Liebman's list seldom cough up more than $250 a year. (Even Governor Edison is good only for $500 "or maybe a grand in a good year.") Part of the reason is the proliferation of right-wing causes. "Everyone has his own pet charity now," says Liebman. Equally as important is the fact that none of Liebman's causes is tax deductible. Nor does Liebman go out of his way to hustle the big money. He often won't bother to put the touch on a mark if he can find no basis for personal rapport. "Can you imagine Marvin with H. L. Hunt?" asks William Buckley. "God, he wouldn't last two sessions with him."

Though Liebman's fee for an individual committee runs between $2,000 and $3,000 a month, many clients don't pay regularly and he almost always must use his own cash and credit to get a front started. "It's a month-to-month operation," he says. "We're never more than a month ahead at the bank." Though he pays himself only $180 a week, he has set up so many subsidiary corporations as tax devices that everything from his car to his Courbet is deductible. "It is a truism of our tax structure," he says. "Someone who has a business lives better than someone who is employed." Inevitably, Liebman's enemies spread stories about the source of his income that are often worthy of Terry Southern. One former right-wing associate straight-faced that Marvin was made a partner in a Chinese restaurant in New York as a "payoff from Chiang Kai-shek."

Success has won Liebman a passel of enemies. On the Right, the longest knives are wielded by the Birch Society and George Lincoln Rockwell's Nazi Party. "Ever since I threw the white Anglo-Saxon General Walker off the platform at the YAF rally," he says, "Rockwell's boys have been calling me 'The Kosher Konservative.'" (Rockwell, however, does afford Liebman some macabre amusement. "Did you ever see his 'Diary of Anne Fink'?" he chortles.) Other true believers resent Liebman's distaste for the right-wing evangelists like Billy James Hargis and Dr. Fred Schwartz, who, he feels, have latched onto a good deal in anti-Communism. "Intellectually, I suspect that whole revivalist crowd," he says. "They're pitchmen, medicine men." Though Liebman represented Schwartz when he came to New York with his Christian Anti-Communist Crusade, the connection was more the result of a fight with conservative columnist George Sokolsky than with any change in his opinion of Schwartz. Sokolsky was so incensed that Schwartz called his crusade "Christian" that he ordered Liebman, a close friend, not to have anything to do with him. "He told me he'd destroy me in his column if I did," Liebman says. "So I got pissed off and told Schwartz I'd be glad to work for him." The only thing that Liebman accomplished was to convince Schwartz that it was bad public relations in New York to display so prominently the word "Christian." They compromised on a new title: "The Greater New York School of Anti-Communism of the Christian Anti-Communist Crusade."

Predictably, liberal dopesters are unen[ ]astic about Liebman. Nor does Marvin help his [ ]ge on the Left when he talks about the great iss[ ] "I'm happy we have the Bomb," he once told the *New York Post*. "There have always been catastrophes available to history, like the bubonic plague, for instance. And there are little catastrophes like not being loved. People have always lived their lives under catastrophe. You can't let them make you unhappy. The Bomb is in the nature of things. I say, let's build more Bombs."

After office hours, Liebman is about as ideological as Leonard Lyons. Besides the Buckleys, who have a star quality of their own, he feels most at home with such writers and show business personalities as Hermione Gingold, playwright Muriel Resnick (*Any Wednesday*), and cartoonist Jules Feiffer and his wife, Judy. Spurred on by his artsy-craftsy friends, Liebman's own dabbling sometimes reaches frenetic proportions. His current passion is art collecting, and almost wistfully he says he would like to give up his business and become an art dealer.

But Marvin has gone through similar phases in the past. With Buckley's wife, Pat, he once took an option on the film rights of Constantine Fitzgibbon's *When the Kissing Had to Stop*, a thriller opposed to the ban-the-bombers which the Buckley clan referred to as *Off the Beach*. The project fell through when Liebman realized he didn't know how to make a movie. Though numerous book publishing ventures have left him in the hole, he now wants to publish a book on men's room *graffiti*, written by playwright Jack Richardson and photographed by Wallace Litwin, husband of Muriel Resnick and an old shipmate from the S.S. *Ben Hecht*. The whole package will be published through a new corporation, Subterranean Press. "I can run it out of my bathroom," says Liebman, with an eye out for the tax angle, "and take off 10 percent."

Liebman's cultural benders have always been viewed with a good deal of amusement by the Right's heavy thinkers, who perhaps unconsciously tend to treat him like the house mascot. The desire to dispel this slightly patronizing atmosphere, along with the onslaught of his fortieth birthday, led him a year ago to write a play. "Marvin respects people who take themselves seriously," says Judy Feiffer. "The play was his way of saying, 'Look, I'm legit.' " As a play, *Drums of Morning* reads like a dramatization of one of Liebman's advertisements. It is a doctrinaire exercise in which the nay-sayers are imprisoned on an island at the mercy of the ultimate authority, the State. Though it was scheduled for production at a New Jersey straw-hat playhouse, interest has since waned. "I wish I could say I was being persecuted for my politics," says Liebman, "but the plain fact is the play was lousy. I was forty, depressed, and wondering what I had accomplished. So I wrote the play. All it proved was that all the clichés about being forty are true."

Now over the doldrums of entering his fifth decade, Liebman is alive with new schemes to liven up the ideological war. Last spring, he acquired from the Defense Department a list of American soldiers killed in South Vietnam and began contacting their next of kin. Over their signatures, he published a full-page advertisement in the *Washington Star* (the *Washing-*

ton Post refused the ad) asking, "Why?" Why does the U.S. fight Communism in South Vietnam on one hand, and trade with the Communists on the other? Why does the U.S. authorize the cultural "exchange of ballet dancers to entertain Communist leaders in Moscow while a young American boy does the dance of death in Vietnam?"

Liebman carefully kept his name out of all the South Vietnam correspondence. All the letters to the next of kin were signed by Charles Tuthill, father of one of the dead soldiers whom Liebman picked only because he lived so close to New York. When I asked Leibman if Tuthill realized that he was being used, he replied: "Everyone is used in one way or another. If anybody chooses to make political capital out of this, okay. If the Republicans have any brains, it will be used." Still, he denied any partisan intent: "It would break faith with Mr. Tuthill." I asked if this wasn't disingenuous. "Sometimes to maintain a posture of honesty in this world or in this business is disingenuous," he answered. "I'm just utilizing an apparatus and some professional skills to do something I want to do. I'm taking a citizen action. It's all for the good, the true and the beautiful."

In the cause of the good, the true and the beautiful, Liebman doesn't miss an opportunity to round up a new recruit. Recently, he was asked to forward his "simplest publication against the recognition of Communist China" to Linda Schersand, a California sixth-grader who had requested the material to prepare for a school debate on the subject. "My dear Linda," wrote Liebman. "We are enclosing a little book which was published by some of our friends in Hong Kong. It tells of the adventures of a little girl in Communist China. We hope it may be helpful to you. Good luck on your debate." The title of the book was *Alice in Manialand*.

1964

81

INDUCTION DAY

Wednesday is induction day in Oakland. It was shortly before six o'clock on this particular Wednesday in March when I passed the toll station on the Bay Bridge from San Francisco and headed for the induction center. On the seat beside me was a leaflet from the Peace and Freedom Party saying that Richard Kunst, a twenty-four-year-old graduate student in Chinese language and literature at Berkeley, was going to refuse induction that morning. He had decided to become a "non-cooperator with the Selective Service System," the leaflet said, "in order to resist American militarism in Vietnam and the system of conscription which is its mainstay." The leaflet called for a support demonstration "to encourage other inductees arriving at the Induction Center to join in saying 'NO' to the system which oppresses them."

Oakland is not one of the more inspiring cities in America—"There is no 'there' there when you get there," Gertrude Stein once said—and the induction center is in one of its less inspiring sections. It occupies four floors in a drably anonymous nine-story building that is surrounded by cheap hotels, a bowling-supply store, sheet-music shops, and $3 income-tax advisers. The center handles inductees and enlistees from all over northern California and western Nevada. The building was still locked by the time I parked my car, but the first inductees had already begun to arrive. They milled in small groups on the sidewalk, strangers all, yawning, not talking to one another. Most carried airlines bags and some slumped on the sidewalk, their backs leaning against the building, and stared vacantly into space. I remember the day I was inducted. At the time it seemed the most desolate day of my life.

Diagonally across the street, by the garage the police use as their command post for possible induction disturbances, four prowl cars were parked by the curb. One of them glided across the street as the first demonstrator arrived. She was a middle-aged woman in a cloth coat and she began passing out pamphlets that asked: "Why are we fighting in Vietnam? Because big corporations in the United States have billions of dollars invested abroad which would be lost if these revolutions succeed. Anti-Communism means risking your life to protect the property of the rich at the expense of the poor." The police car followed slowly behind the woman. She reached into her bag and drew out an enormous fruitcake wrapped in tinfoil. She offered some to the policeman. He seemed nonplused. "Too many calories, I'm afraid," he said.

The inductees watched the scene in silence. The woman named the son of a prominent national figure and asked why he had not been drafted. "Because he's a fairy, lady," one of the inductees said. The group around him began to laugh, and with wrists limp, they minced and simpered along the sidewalk. "Oh, to be a queen for today," one of them said. Most of the young men just watched phlegmatically. Some stuffed leaflets into their pockets. A youth crossed the street carrying a large placard that said, "What are you dying in Vietnam for?" An inductee sidled up to him. "For you, jerk," he said.

At precisely half past six, as the doors to the induction center opened, the installation commander walked around the corner. The draftees parted to let him past. His name was Clyde A. Cortez, he was an Army lieutenant colonel, and on his uniform jacket were stepped row after row of decorations, campaign ribbons, combat stars and clusters. I asked Colonel Cortez if I could go inside to see how the Army handled a refusal to report for induction. He brooded for a moment. "Why not?" he said finally. Just inside the front door was taped a sign forbidding the carrying of placards of any description and the distribution of seditious pamphlets and leaflets. "If they got any, we give them a receipt for it and they can pick it up when they leave," Colonel Cortez said. He was a stocky, swarthy Latin and he spoke in a slow military drawl. "It's their private property, you know."

I asked if he anticipated any trouble. "No, just another Wednesday," he said. He pointed across the street. "This Oakland police force, they're good people, a real bunch of professionals." He looked at my notebook. "You people are always writing about these demonstrators," he said reproachfully. "If you want to write about something, you should write about these Salvation Army ladies come down here every Wednesday. They're real fine people. They give these boys shaving kits, you know, toothpaste and razor blades. Nothing but name brands."

One of Colonel Cortez's officers explained to me that each draft resister is informed that under the Universal Military Training and Service Act he is subject to five years in prison and a $10,000 fine if he refuses induction. If he still refuses, he is asked to sign a statement that says, "I refuse to be inducted into the armed forces of the United States." I asked what would happen if an inductee would not sign. "I guess you'd have to say he was uncooperative," Colonel Cortez said. "But we don't arrest people or anything like that. We just forward his papers to the appropriate authorities."

Shortly before seven Richard Kunst entered the induction center. He was a handsome young man with a trim blond beard. He had his wife and a friend with him. Kunst's wife was a quiet, attractive young woman with a ban-the-bomb emblem pinned to her coat. It was several moments before anyone took any notice of Kunst. He finally spoke to a sergeant, who waved his thumb over his shoulder and mumbled,

cold." His bunkmate looks embarrassed and pretends not to hear.

The men are restricted to Building 590. They shine their boots and polish their brass, the witless Army pursuits for passing the time. There is little camaraderie. It is the first barracks I have ever been in without seeing a single deck of cards, a single pair of dice. The men are strangers brought together for two days before once again finding the bonhomie of a unit. Resignation and uncertainty are the only common denominators, and they blur the men together into a kind of facelessness. The feeling is heightened through the afternoon and evening by the squawk box, which calls out a series of the strangely deracinated names common to Army personnel rosters: "Jonsurd . . . Sugdennis . . . Fernander." Many seem anxious to be on their way. "I want to get out with the guys," I hear one boy say.

"But, man, they're going to be shooting at you," someone says.

"Yeah, but at least I'll be with people I know."

I take a tour of Building 590. There are television sets, a pool table, Ping-Pong. Beside a writing table is a rack of religious literature—*The Serviceman: Patriotism and Morale; Has the New Liturgy Killed Personal Piety?* (The answer: "Truth on both sides.") By the shipping station there is a duffel bag tagged simply, AWOL. Dozens of vending machines disgorge an endless variety of coffee, milk, soft drinks, ice cream, sandwiches, pastry, Nalley's Hot Tamales, Nalley's Hot Enchiladas, Nalley's Chili Con Carne. In the latrine, men have written all over the walls the date of their departure, the date of their return. There is only one attempt at gallows humor: "Jonnie Rae Smith, Vietnam, Leave 5 June 1967—Return?" The lights go off and I make my way back through the aisles. I have seen too many war movies, too many opening scenes in which the camera pans over the platoon as the audience picks out the ones who are not going to make it through the last reel. I cannot help myself as I pass the men lying listlessly in their bunks. "That one," I say to myself, "that one."

I stretch out on a bunk. Around me men doze. A transistor radio picks up an acid-rock station in San Francisco, and the strains of "Acapulco Gold" filter softly through the bay. Across the aisle a boy endlessly packs and repacks his duffel bag. His bunkmate has six rolls of toilet paper and he tries to make room for them. He discards his low quarters and a dozen old copies of *Playboy,* from which he methodically cuts the foldout Playmates, wrapping them in a plastic bag and then placing them neatly in his duffel. In the bunk beneath me, three young privates discuss the ethics of sleeping with one's sister-in-law and compare the merits of the women of Roanoke and the women of Wheeling. "Those girls in Wheeling ain't very good-lookers," says one, "but they sure got shapes on them."

Sleep comes, and then at 0430 the great exhaust fan goes on and a sergeant walks through the bay. "Time, gentlemen," he says softly. "It's time." The men of Group 20 pick up their hand baggage and fall in by the door of Building 590. A sleepy Air Force enlisted man tells them that their buses will take them to Travis Air Force Base, halfway between Oakland and Sacramento, where a World Airways Boeing 707, Flight No. W239, will fly them, via Anchorage, Alaska, and Yokota Air Base, Japan, to their destination, Bien Hoa, South Vietnam. The total flying time will be nineteen hours. There will be in-flight movies and five stewardesses.

I find a seat in the last bus. Dawn is just beginning to pinken the sky. In the seat ahead of me, a PFC in the infantry attempts to make conversation with a sergeant in the medics. "Don't pick up any dead bodies, Sergeant," the PFC says. "I hear they're booby-trapped."

"I won't be picking any up, son," the sergeant says. "I'll be back in the lab cutting them."

He looks out the window and the PFC tries to laugh. "If you see me coming through, handle me gentle, Sergeant."

It is shortly after six when Group 20 arrives at Travis. Thirty minutes later, Flight No. W239 is called. The last man aboard slaps his hand on the ground. At 0708, the 707 is airborne. Afterward, driving to Sacramento, I turn on the 8 A.M. news. An infantry company has been slaughtered in the central highlands. I remember what the post commandant told me about the men who process back through Oakland on their way home from Vietnam. "One thing we do give them a steak," he said. "We give them a ticket d they can have that steak any time they want it. orning, noon or night."

1967

MAYE & LEROY

I'll call her Maye. She came from Barstow, a town in the California desert, a pit stop midway between Los Angeles and Las Vegas. Maye had lived there for five years. Her father had come from Arkansas when she was fifteen to work as a civilian at George Air Force Base, and then one morning he put his lunch pail into his secondhand Buick Riviera and drove off and never came home. There was nothing much for Maye and her mother to do but stay in Barstow. Maye ran the cosmetics counter at a store she insisted on calling "the five-and-dime," mainly because of a tuneless song lyric she had made up and which she sang constantly. "All the time at the five-and-dime, All the time at the five-and-dime."

The first day I met Maye she was crying. It was at the U.S. Army's Rest and Recreation Center at Fort De Russy in Honolulu. Because of its proximity to the U.S. mainland, Hawaii is the most favored R & R location for American servicemen stationed in Vietnam. Every month some 9,000 troops, both officers and enlisted men, fly in from Saigon and Danang and Bien Hoa for five-day leaves in the islands; over 80 percent of them are met there by wives or other members of their families. Maye had come from Barstow to meet her husband, a corporal whom I'll c Leroy. She and Leroy had been married for only ni months and Maye hoped he would get transferred ou of his infantry company and into the Engineers. Ler had been a night man at a Barstow gas station before he got drafted and Maye wanted him to learn a trade in the Army. She was not quite sure what trade he would learn in the Corps of Engineers, but she had once had a date with a civilian hydraulics specialist at George Air Force Base and he had said that the possibilities in engineering were unlimited. It had been six months since she had seen Leroy, but now there was a mixup and Maye's face was puffy with tears. Leroy had missed his scheduled flight and the chaplain at Fort De Russy had told her that if there was space available, he would arrive the next day.

"Will he still get the five days?" Maye said. "I mean, this is a once in a lifetime for us, being in Honolulu and all, and they won't take away a day 'cause he missed his plane, will they?"

"No, ma'am, you'll have a regular five-day vacation," the chaplain said.

Maye was a heavy-set girl with a kind of pellagra-haunted, dust-bowl face. She was wearing a muumuu and sandals, and her hair was bouffant and tinted with gold. She was staying in a small hotel off Waikiki and she was worried about what Leroy would think of the accommodations. "There's a lot of coloreds here," she said. "Leroy don't like coloreds much."

We ambled for a while down Waikiki. The streets were crowded with vacationing college students, and Maye seemed vaguely pleased by their limber, golden good looks. "I bet they're the type that come to Honolulu every summer," she said without resentment. She bought a Frostee Freeze and when she turned away from the counter, she bumped into a colleg boy wearing a fraternity sweat shirt. On the front of the shirt was stenciled, KILLER—KAPPA SIG, and on the back the phrase, HIRE THE MORALLY HANDICAPPED.

"I like your shirt," Maye said.

Killer, the Kappa Sig, ignored her, and for a long time Maye sat silently, running her tongue over the frozen chocolate. "A lot of wives, they brought their magazines out," she said finally. "Not me, I can't imagine reading on vacation. I'm having too good a time."

There was a message for Maye when she got back to her hotel. Leroy would definitely be in the next day. Maye counted the money she had left. She had arrived in Honolulu with $78 in cash—"Fourteen a day and eight for mad money," she said—but in less than twenty-four hours she had already spent a third of it. She decided, however, to buy some pink hair rollers and another muumuu. "If anything happens when Lee gets here, it's a very useful dress," she giggled. "I mean, girls do get pregnant."

The next morning I drove Maye over to Fort De Russy. She was wearing her new muumuu and her hair was in rollers covered by a lemon chiffon scarf. "Lee and I will probably go out tonight and I want my hair to look nice for him," she said. There was a newscast on the car radio about Vietnam and Maye turned it off. "I don't want to even think about it," she said. "I want this to be the nicest trip we'll ever have."

There was a few minutes' wait at Fort De Russy before the buses with the R & R troops arrived from the airport. A large, jovial Negro chaplain circulated among the clustered wives and said, "Get your eyeballs in shape for looking now. Remember, no tears. You're the first civilized folks these boys have seen in a long time, so look pretty." Maye knotted the chiffon scarf tight under her chin; the woman on the bench next to her kneaded a pair of rosary beads. "She must be a Roman Candle," Maye whispered. Finally the first bus pulled through the gates. Leroy was the last man off the third bus. He was a slight, sandy-haired boy with sunken cheeks and he was carrying a cardboard box on which was lettered, PURCHASED— GUAM—ONE GALLON DISTILLED SPIRITS. Maye held back her tears and threw her arms around his neck.

"Hi, honey," she said.

"Hi, honey," Leroy said.

"You look thin," Maye said.

Leroy shrugged.

"You got your transfer in for Engineers?" Maye said.

There was a brief orientation before the troops were released. "You are at all times prey to subversive elements," the orientation officer said. "These subversives will try to induce you to desert. If you become suspicious of any subversive elements, contact the proper military authorities and safeguard your country."

I did not see Maye and Leroy for five days, until the night that Leroy went back to Vietnam. I drove them out to the airport and tried not to listen to the swallowed sobs in the back seat. Leroy's plane was scheduled to leave at midnight, and until the boarding call came, the wives and husbands stood by the gate clinging to each other, not saying much, trying not to cry. Then the boarding announcement came and the men filed through the gate toward the Pan-American jet clipper *Crystal Palace*. Maye raced upstairs to the observation deck, finding a place along the rail there

94

with the other women, some gaunt, some heavy, heartland faces bloated with tears, dresses out of date, shoes out of style, and they waited and watched the plane doors close, waited as the big jet trundled ponderously down the runway, waited until its night lights disappeared finally in the black Pacific sky. It was only then that the big tears came, the muted keening there under the big yellow neon sign that said ALOHA.

It was a scene that I had preferred to forget and I was more or less successful until a postal card arrived this morning postmarked Barstow. It was from Maye. She said she was pregnant—"Hawaiian nights!!!" she wrote—and that Leroy was due home for Thanksgiving and that she would remember five days in Honolulu for the rest of her life.

1968

SANCTUARY

The day after Christmas the grandstands for the Tournament of Roses Parade were going up along Orange Grove Boulevard in Pasadena. It was a bright crisp day, unusually cold for southern California, and the bunting and the banners were snapping in the breeze. Orange Grove Boulevard is where the rich used to live, second- and third-generation money from the East in an atmosphere so sedate, it was once said, that the only sound was the hardening of arteries. But now the rambling prairie houses have given way to garden apartments with heated swimming pools and lanai privileges, and farther along Orange Grove the faces

95

turn from suburban white to ghetto black and there are no more lanais. It was in a Quaker meeting hall in this fading section of Pasadena that three young fugitives from the armed services, Army Pvt Timothy Springer, twenty, Marine Pvt Neil Blanton, nineteen, and Marine PFC Steve Davis, twenty, sought and found sanctuary during the Christmas season.

Under medieval law, a fugitive who found refuge in a church was immune from arrest. Though this tradition has no legal validity today, the Resistance, a New Left group pledged to aid draft resisters and AWOL's from the military, has persuaded several churches in Los Angeles to offer sanctuary as a protest against the war in Vietnam. One of these was the Orange Grove Meeting of the Society of Friends. Shepherded by the Resistance, the three boys moved into the Quaker hall the week before Christmas, though not without some debate among the parishioners. The Resistance had vowed to stay with the three until they were arrested, and some members of the meeting were concerned about the prospect of drugs on church property and the possibility, as one put it, that "the boys and girls might sleep too close together in the hall." Once approval was granted, the three notified the Shore Patrol that they were resigning from the military. Aware of the image problem, military authorities proceeded cautiously. A spokesman announced that the Shore Patrol would not arrest the youths immediately, "because it is Christmas and they are in a church."

The morning I drove out to Pasadena a barefoot young blond girl was sitting on the steps of the meeting hall, playing a guitar. Inside, fifteen or twenty members of the Resistance, some of them with children, were lounging and sleeping in the social room. Most of them were wearing buttons that said CELEBRATE LIFE; BRAHMS, NOT BOMBS; and GOD IS AN UNDEFINED TERM. There was turkey soup and hot chocolate and a communal cigarette bowl. On a bulletin board was tacked a child's drawing of a peace symbol, around which someone had scrawled, "Jesus wore long hair." At a table an intense young woman was addressing Christmas cards; every person on her list was in a federal prison. "I bet you didn't know we had political prisoners in this country," she said. "Quakers, Jehovah's Witnesses, draft resisters, I just tell them we care, we're working, and we love them." Into each envelope she put a flower petal.

The three boys had been AWOL long enough to let their hair grow long, and one of them had cultivated a scraggly red beard. As I talked to them, what struck me most was the banality of their situation. They seemed to have wandered into the minefield of protest by accident. None of them, in fact, had been drafted; all three had enlisted. "The draft was on my tail," Springer said. "I was told if I enlisted and got into communications, I wouldn't be carrying a gun." Blanton, whose father is a career officer in the Air Force, had a fight with his family. "They sort of disowned me," he said. "It was important to make my parents proud of me, so I joined the Marine Corps." Davis had a desultory college career. "All I learned at the University of Florida," he said, "was that drinking beer was a bummer." He told me that he had been driving what proved to be a stolen car and that an arrangement had been made whereby charges would be dropped in exchange for his enlistment in the Marines. "I didn't dig jail then, like I do now," he said.

Inchoate rebels with an inchoate dislike of the military. When the opportunity presented itself, they just took off. It is possible now, however, for the ordinary AWOL to become a passionate protester. It lends a rationale to rudimentary doubts, to impulsive action. For the AWOL, the Resistance is like an extralegal USO. Under its aegis, ill-formed ideas are sharpened into manifestos. I listened while the three youths talked about militarism and becoming cogs in the government's killing machine. I asked why they had not gone to Canada. It was a copout, they answered; only by taking a public stand, by facing court-martial, dishonorable discharge and up to five years in a military stockade would they draw attention to the evils of the system. And besides, Davis said, "if Canada is a bummer, you're stuck there for the rest of your life."

It is easy to say that the three have neither the intellectual gifts to capitalize on their situation nor the resources to extricate themselves from it. As it happens, I agree with George Orwell that "the only 'ism' that has justified itself is pessimism," but I was absurdly touched by them as I sat in the lengthening afternoon and listened to them talk about five thousand years of history and the perfectibility of man. Each seemed to have a success to report; a right-wing father who had seen the light, a trio of officers in some urban jail who now refuse to guard draft resisters. I wished I could share their optimism. In any case, I had seen the inside of a military stockade and I wished the boys well.

1969

APOSTASY

"It is well," Robert E. Lee said, "that war is so terrible—we would grow too fond of it." Perhaps the only redeeming feature of the war in Vietnam was that there was so little of which to grow fond. Its actions do not fly from regimental battle standards nor are they taught in the classrooms at West Point; statues of its heroes do not adorn town squares nor are shopping malls and housing developments named after them. Its victories and defeats are not commemorated in song. Even those who have written about Vietnam seem to have been confounded by the war. The fiction has been without energy and the nonfiction drenched in either superiority or guilt, and tending to promote the notion—a rather comforting notion, in retrospect—that it was the best and the brightest who turned us into winners and losers. Now there is Philip Caputo's *A Rumor of War*. To call it the best book about Vietnam is to trivialize it. Heartbreaking, terrifying and enraging, it belongs to the literature of men at arms.

The task Caputo has set for himself is deceptively simple. His book, he maintains, "has nothing to do with politics, power, strategy, influence, national interests or foreign policy; nor is it an indictment of the great men who led us into Indochina and whose mistakes were paid for with the blood of some quite ordinary men . . . it is simply a story about war, about the things men do in war and the things war does to them." In this assessment of his own work, Caputo is wrong, for by trying not to indict, he has produced an indictment that is all the more damning, a document that will make the strongest among us weep.

First there is Philip Caputo himself, a lower middle-class Italian Catholic from the suburbs of Chicago, educated by the Jesuits and imbued with the ideals of Kennedy's Camelot. In the early sixties he joined the Marines and was commissioned a second lieutenant. He believed in the righteousness of any cause he was ordered to defend and that in the Marines he would be given the opportunity to prove what boys in their twenties wanted proof of—their courage, manhood and toughness. He landed in Vietnam in March 1965 with the first ground combat unit sent to Indochina; ten years later he returned, as a prematurely old correspondent for the *Chicago Tribune,* to see the fall of Saigon. One of the first to fight in that "splendid little war" (as one of his fellow officers called it in 1965), he was also one of the last to be evacuated.

Then there were the men of Caputo's platoon. "They were to a man thoroughly American, in their virtues as well as their flaws: idealistic, insolent, generous, direct, violent and provincial in the sense that they believed the ground they stood on was now and forever a part of the United States simply because they stood on it. Most of them came from the ragged fringes of the Great American Dream, from city slums and dirt farms and Appalachian mining towns. With depressing frequency, the words '2 yrs high school' appeared in the square labeled EDUCATION in their service record books, and under FATHER'S ADDRESS, a number had written 'Unknown.' They were volunteers, but I wondered for how many enlisting had been truly voluntary. The threat of the draft came with their eighteenth birthdays, and they had no hopes of getting student deferments like the upper middle-class boys who would later revile them as killers . . ."

They learned to hate before they became killers, and what they learned to hate first was the land. No one has ever described the look and the feel and the texture of Vietnam better than Caputo. The siege heat was a vile and malevolent thing. During the monsoon the rain thudded against Marine bodies like an avalanche of cold, wet steel balls. The jungle was blank and implacable, its very impenetrability the source of its power to cause fear. Rock apes crashed through the night, poisonous kraits slithered underfoot and pigs truffled among napalm-charred corpses, feasting, as it were, on roast people. Malaria, blackwater fever, dysentery and leeches were constant companions. The one smell that permeated Vietnam was the smell of human excrement. "The water loosened everyone's bowels . . . and what with waste matter caking to anal hairs and no baths and constant sweating and uniforms stiff and white with dried sweat, it got so we could not stand our own smell."

It was a war with rules no one understood. Ethics "seemed to be a matter of distance and technology." An unarmed Vietnamese could not be shot unless he was running; it was as if the act of running for one's life certified a political allegiance. Villages could be napalmed but not fired by ground troops with phosphorescent grenades. "Without a front, flanks or rear, we fought a formless war against a formless enemy who evaporated like the morning jungle mists."

As men began to die, Lieutenant Caputo lost his faith. The dead on both sides were reduced to exposed viscera and splattered brains and bits of skin and cartilage floating in crimson puddles. "The body, which is supposed to be the earthly home of the immortal soul . . . is in fact only a fragile case stuffed full of disgusting matter. . . . The sight of mutilation did more than cause me physical revulsion; it burst the religious myths of my Catholic childhood. I could not look at those men and still believe that their souls had 'passed on' to another existence." Fear became a virus and survival the new religion. It was the dawn of creation in the Indochinese bush, an ethical as well as a geographical wilderness, and some of the men of Charlie Company, 1st Battalion, 3d Marines, "acquired a contempt for human life and a predilection for taking it."

The war settled into a savage ritual of tit for tat and Caputo, a man with a taste for the moral distinctions made by the classics of English literature, grew as numb as his men, unable either to condemn or condone. Vietnam simply *was,* and convictions departed with faith. "Everything rotted and corroded quickly over there: bodies, boot leather, canvas, metal, morals. . . . Our humanity rubbed off us as the protective bluing rubbed off the barrels of our rifles." Ruthlessness was a virtue, retribution a necessity. Villages where the Viet Cong staged ambushes were razed unquestioningly and both sides shot prisoners without mercy. "The comradeship that was the war's only redeeming quality caused some of the worst crimes. . . . The hair-trigger alertness, the stress of guerrilla fighting, the feeling that the enemy was everywhere created emotional pressures which built to such a point that a trivial provocation could make these men explode with the blind destructiveness of a mortar shell."

Not until Caputo was transferred back to regimental headquarters did he begin to meditate on the war. One of his ancillary duties was as Regimental Casualty Reporting Officer or, as he categorized himself, "The Officer in Charge of the Dead." Like a bookkeeper of death, he kept up-to-the-minute records on acetate charts of both friendly and hostile KIA's, WIA's and DOW's (dead-of-wounds). The terminology of death was so antiseptic as to make the dead as meaningless to Caputo as names in a telephone book: a man shot through the guts was labeled "GSW [gunshot wound] abdomen, through-and-through," shrapnel wounds were called "multiple fragment lacerations" and the phrase for dismemberment was "traumatic amputation." The arithmetic of the body count and the kill ratio was like a metastasizing cancer: Caputo's own company commander offered any man with a confirmed VC kill an extra beer ration and the time off to drink it. "This is the level to which we had sunk from the lofty idealism of the year before. We were going to kill people for a few cans of beer. . . ."

For the Officer in Charge of the Dead, the rear was a grotesque parody of civilian life. There were football pools and volleyball matches and horseshoe pitches. One officer practiced calling square-dance tunes and another devised a new form of poetry based on the stringing together of random words from the dictionary. To improve the martial spirit of rear-echelon Marines, Caputo was ordered to put on display the rotting, stinking bodies of Viet Cong KIA's; still later the same bodies were hauled out again for the benefit of visiting dignitaries from Saigon. Boredom gave way to incipient madness, and as the names of dead friends from his old unit came across Caputo's desk, the madness turned into an irrational hatred of the Viet Cong. Finally Caputo asked to be transferred back into the line. "Revenge was one of the reasons I volunteered. . . . I wanted the chance to kill somebody."

Once more in command of a platoon, Caputo became indifferent to death. "I ceased to fear death because I ceased to care about it. . . . I would die as casually as a beetle is crushed under a boot heel, and perhaps it was the recognition of my insectlike pettiness that made me stop caring. I was a beetle. . . . My death would not alter a thing. I had never felt an emotion more sublime or liberating than that indifference. . . ." In other words, First Lieutenant Philip Caputo, USMCR, exhilarated by combat, as Robert E. Lee knew a man could become, relieved of faith, fear and convictions, became a human time bomb, tick, tick, ticking away.

The explosion when it came resulted in the death of two young Vietnamese barely more than boys. They may have been Viet Cong supporters, they may only have been in the wrong place at the wrong time. Philip Caputo was charged with premeditated murder. The legal machinery that finally aborted his court-martial could stand as a metaphor for the war in Vietnam itself. Caputo was not allowed to use the war as an extenuating circumstance; rather he was charged as if he had shot down two innocent bystanders during a bank stickup in Los Angeles. In his pretrial depositions, he never perjured himself, but he learned "about the wide gulf that separates facts from the truth. . . . The war in general and U.S. military policies in particular were ultimately to blame for the deaths of Le Du and Le Dung. That was the truth and it was that truth which the whole proceeding was designed to conceal."

The charges of murder were ultimately dropped. Caputo was shipped home and honorably discharged. He married, fathered children, was active in the antiwar movement. He became a journalist, was a member of a *Chicago Tribune* team that won a Pulitzer Prize for investigative reporting, won another prize covering wars in the Middle East, went back to Saigon for the end. He is as much a casualty of the war as if he had lost an arm or a leg.

I cannot begin to tell you how much I was affected by *A Rumor of War*. Never have Vietnam's ambivalent realities been so vividly captured. Here was "an experience as fascinating as it was repulsive, as exhilarating as it was sad, as tender as it was cruel . . . where the communion between men [was] as profound as between any lovers." There were moments when the book brought tears to my eyes and there were moments when I wanted to form my own platoon, and the names I wanted in that platoon were Kennedy and Nixon and Kissinger and Rusk and McNamara. I wanted them to smell their own diseased bowels and I wanted them to see one of their own sheared off at the genitals by a Bouncing Betty land mine, and I wondered if at the end of a year in the jungle the survivors of that malignant platoon would still mouth those "patriotic ideas about duty, honor and sacrifice, the myths," as Caputo says, "with which old men send young men off to get killed and maimed."

These are not the thoughts, however, that ultimately make *A Rumor of War* a dangerous and even subversive book. Caputo's book is the first to insist—and the insistence is all the more powerful because it is implicit—that the reader ask himself the questions: How would I have acted? To what lengths would I have gone to survive? The sense of self is assaulted, overcome, subverted, leaving the reader to contemplate the deadening possibility that his own moral safety net might have a hole in it. It is a terrifying thought, and *A Rumor of War* is a terrifying book.

1977

QUEBEC ZERO

It is eighty-six miles from Malmstrom Air Force Base to Quebec Zero, and in the winter, with ice glazing the roads and snow drifting over the Montana range country and the Rockies hidden under a coverlet of clouds, the easiest way to get there is by helicopter. It was cold and crowded in the chopper. There were two other crews besides the three men I was with, one bound for Romeo Zero, the other for Tango Zero, and what struck me about them first was how young they were. Some were boys barely into their twenties, the oldest a year or two younger than I am. Age is not something I brood over, but theirs was a responsibility I did not wish to have on my own shoulders, for entombed out there in steel and concrete capsules sixty feet beneath the rolling prairie, they would, if they were ever called upon to do so, blow the world to pieces.

I had arrived at Malmstrom the day before, driven past the enormous sign at the gate that said PEACE . . . IS OUR PROFESSION. Malmstrom is the headquarters of the Strategic Air Command's 341st Strategic Missile Wing, and for hundreds of square miles around the base, an area the size of several New England states, the wheatland is planted with the wing's own special crop, two hundred nuclear Minuteman I and II missiles, each sheathed in its own individual silo and rooted deep beneath the surface of the plain. Twenty-four hours a day the missiles are on alert, electronically trained on targets thousands of miles distant. The purpose of my visit was to spend a twenty-four-hour tour of duty with one of the crews that control each ten Minutemen, to see what it was like, how it worked on the mind, to have World War III only an arm's length away.

The command capsule I was assigned to was designated Quebec Zero ("Quebec" being the letter "Q" in the military phonetic alphabet), its missiles Quebec eleven through twenty. The crew commander was a short, smiling thirty-three-year-old Texan, Captain James W. Wilson; his alternate, Captain Laster B. Meads, twenty-nine, was a large, slow-talking North Carolinian. The third crew member was First Lieutenant Charles L. Thysell, a twenty-four-year-old Minnesotan who, in his spare time, under the auspices of the Air Force, was studying for a master's degree. We were briefed early in the morning with the nineteen other crews in the wing going on alert that day. Watches were synchronized, weather information given, and after I was asked to leave the room, there was an EWO check. I asked one of the officers what EWO meant. "Emergency war orders," he said.

The helicopter got lost on our way to Quebec Zero. There are no markings on the endless range, nothing but plowed-under wheat fields and an occasional herd of Black Angus cattle huddled against the cold. We circled low over the blast doors of a missile silo to get our bearings. It was innocuous-looking, almost flush with the ground, easy to miss from the air. I tried to visualize the doors opening and the missile lumbering off into space toward its target. Later I asked Wilson if he knew where the missile was headed. "As far as I'm concerned it's just sitting on target," he said. "I don't need to know what that target is, and I don't care." There seemed to be a clear psychological advantage in thinking that at the end of the Minuteman's long arc lay only an abstraction known as "the target."

It was nearly an hour before we got to Quebec Zero.

Though it is surrounded by fertile Montana wheat fields, there is not a blade of grass within the fenced-in area. If grass does begin to grow, Wilson explained, it is killed immediately, thus precluding the danger that a grass fire could flash down into the capsule. The one building within the enclosure is painted a bilious military green and contains a kitchen, a dining area, a lounge with television set and nine bedrooms for the capsule crew and other personnel. Wilson and Thysell were to pull the first shift. Each strapped on a snub-nosed .38 and then they took the elevator down into the capsule. Because of the exchange of classified orders and information, I was not allowed to witness the changeover of old and new crews, and so I went into the dining room to get lunch. Not until the second cup of coffee did it occur to me that one of the reasons that crew members carried sidearms was to use on each other in the event that either went berserk below.

Shortly after noon I went down into the command capsule. It sits to the left of the elevator behind a huge six-and-a-half-ton blast door. The room is approximately fifty feet long by thirty feet wide, divided down the middle by a bank of computers and electronic encoding and encrypting devices. At right angles to each other, some fifteen feet apart, are the two consoles where the commander and his deputy sit. On the deputy's console is a bank of green, amber, red and white lights which constantly tell the status of each of the ten missiles commanded by the capsule. Every few seconds the missiles are electronically interrogated. A slight beeping noise and a blinking light on the deputy's panel signal a change in status or a minor malfunction. When this happens, the deputy dials the missile electronically. Seconds later an electronic printer spits out a series of numbers detailing the fault. Except for major maintenance, faults are corrected automatically. The missiles seem to have an independent existence, keyed only to a series of cryptic legends printed on the deputy's console: INHIBIT, HOLD, NO-

GO, SECURITY FAULT, WARHEAD ALARM, STATUS CHANGE. And then, from the top, the cold, logical progression: STRATEGIC ALERT, ENABLED, LAUNCH COMMAND, LAUNCH IN PROGRESS, MISSILE AWAY.

It is MISSILE AWAY that is the first and last reason for Quebec Zero. The means to carry out this command are located in a small red safe, roughly eight inches square, above the deputy's console. The safe is secured by two ordinary combination locks, which change as the crews change. Each crew member brings his own lock on duty, adjusted to his own secret combination. When he goes down into the capsule, he fastens that lock to the strongbox. The fact that each crew member knows the combination of only his own lock is a fail-safe to prevent any one man from breaking into the strongbox, for inside are the keys with which the missiles are armed and launched.

For my benefit, Wilson and Thysell outlined the steps following a presidential strike order, relayed through SAC. The entire procedure takes less than three minutes. First the crew members decode and authenticate the order, using classified documents. Then they go through a launch checklist. When this is completed, they unlock the safe. Inside are the keys and additional coded documents to further validate the go-code message. "If these check out," Wilson said matter-of-factly, "then I'm going to war." Each man inserts a key in his console. The keys must be turned simultaneously, and since the consoles are so far apart, it is physically impossible for one man to turn both at once. The turning of the keys activates the missiles and is known as "one launch vote." Before the missiles can be fired, however, this same procedure must be repeated by another capsule in the squadron, Romeo Zero, say, or Tango Zero. Only with the receipt of this "second launch vote" are the missiles actually blasted from their silos. "So you see, nothing can go wrong," Wilson said. "Four guys in two different capsules have to go nuts at the same time. I've heard the odds against that are something like one in eight million."

Somehow I did not find the odds appealing, nor did it seem entirely plausible that only an insane man would want to turn the keys. Perhaps what surprised me most was the discovery that the fail-safe was actually less elaborate than I had imagined: that four men, whatever their mental state, could launch a flight of nuclear missiles without any outside orders. I asked if the President could rescind a launch order after the missiles were airborne, if there was a mechanism that could destroy them before they reached their target. Wilson shook his head. "Once they're gone, they're gone," he said. "Goodbye."

I did not know whether to be chilled or reassured that awe had vanished, that life in the capsule could settle into a routine. Perhaps ennui was the most effective safeguard against mental hazard. The minutes ticked away. Every four hours one of the crew went topside to get some sleep. Lights blinked, gauges quivered, the console beeped, the speaker warbled. "Oil Burner 4 low level route closed to all SAC aircraft. . . . Change frequency to 06320 Echo 1." A fault light flashed, and the printer spewed forth numbers: "306, 320, 322, 336." The effect was dehumanizing. I count myself a stable person, but as the hours wore on, I could not take my eyes off the red strongbox. I had an insane urge to break into the safe, take a key and turn it in the keyhole. I wanted to see what would happen.

The night seemed endless. I went topside and slept a troubled sleep. When I went back down into the capsule at 4 A.M., the conversation turned prosaic. There among the computers and switches we talked about barbecued chicken and French toast with boysenberry sauce. I watched the clock. And then it was time to go. The new crew had arrived. I went outside with Wilson and watched him burn the secret codes and messages in a small incinerator. We waited in the thin, cold sunlight for the helicopter, stamping our feet on the hard, brown turf. I had a plane to catch, and I did not shower or shave before I got on it. I wanted to go home.

1967

PORT CHICAGO

A dog sat scratching itself in the middle of Main Street the afternoon I drove into Port Chicago, past the trailer camp on the outskirts of town and the pastel bungalows with peeling paint and flaking plaster. There was a Greyhound depot on Main Street and a barbershop that had gone out of business and Dee's Bargain Shop, where the window display was a collection of unmatched plates and plastic drinking glasses and broken coffeepots and mended irons. HELLO, PAL, said the faded lettering on the marquee of the crumbling Port Chicago Theater. YES, WE ARE OPEN EVERY NIGHT. In the lobby of the theater there was a hand-lettered billboard announcing that the day's double feature was *Blood Bath* and *Queen of Blood*. It was hard to believe that Port Chicago lay on a finger of San Francisco Bay, twenty miles from the Golden Gate. It has the feeling of the dust bowl, a forgotten hamlet on an unremembered side road from an age we would like to forget. It is a town to come from, a place to get out of—which is exactly what the United States Navy is trying to persuade the 3,200 inhabitants of Port Chicago to do.

The reason for the Navy's urgency is that Port Chicago is the principal munitions supply dump for the Vietnam war. Each month, 100,000 tons of shells and rockets and bombs are disgorged from the magazine at the U.S. Naval Weapons Station in the hills above Port Chicago and shipped to the loading piers less than a mile from Main Street. Seven days a week the ships load, and when the three piers are filled to capacity, there are six ships carrying 24 million pounds of munitions sitting at the docks. The specter that haunts the Navy is that of explosion. It is no idle nightmare. On a hot July night in 1944, the S.S. *Quinault Victory* and the S.S. *E. A. Bryan* lay loading at Pier One. Suddenly, within five seconds of each other, the two ships exploded. Towns fifty miles away felt the shock waves of the blast, and windows were shattered twenty miles distant. When the flames finally subsided, the bodies of 322 stevedores and crew members were dug from what was left of Pier One. Only three and a half million pounds of explosives were involved in the 1944 explosion; today, with seven times that much on the docks at any given time, the Navy claims that an accident would make Port Chicago a coffin.

I drove the few miles from Port Chicago to the Naval Weapons Station. The setting is ironically pastoral. A windmill flopped aimlessly in the breeze. Cattle grazed, and bales of hay punctuated the sun-burnt hills that contain hundreds of thousands of tons of death. The public-affairs officer at the base told me that the Navy had petitioned Congress four times since 1964 to allow the purchase of Port Chicago. Now, with Port Chicago shipping 75 percent of the ammunition used in Vietnam, Congress was listening for the first time. The House Armed Services Committee has passed a proposal condemning the town and allocating $19.8 million for the purchase of all its property. This amounts to somewhat more than the appraised value of the town. Having seen Port Chicago, I thought it a more than generous offer. It was favored by the larger property owners, who, because of the past disaster and the present danger, can find no one except the government willing to buy their land. The Navy has no plans for the town. It will raze the buildings and lease out the land for crops and grazing. "For nineteen million dollars," the public-affairs officer said, "we can remove thirty-two hundred people from a lethal area. It's as simple as that."

And yet it was not as simple as that, as I discovered when I visited the office of Congressman Jerome Waldie, who represents the district encompassing Port Chicago. Many of the townspeople are elderly and live on fixed incomes, and moving would be a severe economic hardship. A poll taken in the town has revealed that 76 percent of the people there do not want to leave Port Chicago. Even more troubling is the fact that the Navy has been less than honest in its dealings with Congress. The piers violate the Navy's own minimum safety regulations. They are too close together and several hundred feet too short, so that if one ship explodes, there is a distinct possibility of a chain reaction that would blow up every ship docked along the piers. Congressman Waldie has proposed that instead of buying Port Chicago, the Navy move the piers to nearby Roe Island, which would give them the two-mile safety zone they now so ardently desire. The Navy had ridiculed Waldie's plan as "unfeasible." But in 1965 the Navy came up with the exact same proposal, a fact that it deliberately withheld from Congress during the recent Port Chicago hearings. "The fulfillment of this item," the then Navy Secretary wrote in 1965, "would relieve the Navy of unfavorable publicity and liability in the future. It will fulfill the moral obligation to the community of Port Chicago." The plan, however, was vetoed by the Pentagon on the grounds that it would cost five times as much to move the piers to Roe Island as it would to raze Port Chicago.

I went back to Port Chicago with ambivalent feelings. I suppose I had expected the names of the *Qui-*

nault Victory and the *E. A. Bryan* to be as indelibly imprinted on the consciousness of Port Chicago as the *Enola Gay* is on the consciousness of Hiroshima. Yet I could find no one in the town who could identify the two ships. In fact, at that moment the townspeople seemed more concerned with the three peace demonstrators whom I saw sitting outside the gate to the piers, sharing a bottle of Bubble Up and carrying a weathered wooden sign that said LET VIETNAM BE.

"That kind of help we don't need," an old man on Main Street told me. I asked if there was not a hazard in staying in Port Chicago. "It's a hazard living anyplace," he said.

Before I left town I sat in Fink's Silver Pitcher on Main Street, having a beer. It is a seedy tavern with dirty cartoons pasted on the mirror behind the bar. A stevedore who lived in one of the outlying towns was talking to an elderly Port Chicagoan. "The Navy's giving you a good deal," the stevedore said. "What do you want to live in this dump for?"

The native son looked out the window at Main Street for a long time before he gave his answer. "It's home, I guess," he said finally.

1967

KING TIGER

It had been nearly a year since I last saw Reies Lopez Tijerina, and under the hot lights of the Los Angeles Sports Arena, he seemed strangely out of place, a white face among the black, a wide peasant face that belonged to the piñon, the sage and the cottonwood of northern New Mexico and not the garbage and rats of the urban slum. But in the hierarchy of protest there are no strangers, and now he was one with the black leaders gathered in the arena to ritualize the incarceration of a Negro militant accused of killing a policeman. He was escorted to the stage by a bodyguard of Brown Berets, Mexican youths with sunglasses and oddly delicate beards, and he embraced Stokely Carmichael and Rap Brown before he began to speak.

He had once been a fire-and-brimstone lay preacher and he was still a spellbinder, but now he was learned in a new rhetoric, the metaphors of long hot summers, past, present and to come. "The brown and the black are here to fight the same enemy, and this enemy, the United States Government, is trying to oppress the whole world. The white U.S. Government does not want us to criticize him, but I will, because I see nothing good in him. I ask the Government to repent, to join the black man and the Indian. They know we are going to defend our rights, even if there is some blood spilled. The she dog, after she has had some pups, will not run from anybody, and we in New Mexico will not run from anybody. I say, 'Black Power, yes.' The black, the brown and the Indios have been selected by the forces of nature to march together, fight together, even die together."

Viva," came the shout. *"Viva Tijerina!"*

The predominantly black audience waved posters and damned the police. Some members recited their litany of violence. "Army .45 will stop all jive," they said. "Buckshots will down the cops." It could not have been a more vivid contrast to the first time I heard the words *"Viva Tijerina"* last summer outside the courthouse in old Santa Fe. There, amidst the sun-baked adobe, time seemed to have stopped. The somnolent town belonged to another place, another era, another culture. Standing under the hot afternoon sun, several hundred Spanish Americans, their faces burnt and seamed with toil, repeated the chant over and over. Police eyed them warily. The passageway leading to the second-floor courtroom was blocked by a state police lieutenant impassively holding a loaded shotgun at port arms. One of his troopers frisked me and then passed me to another, who patted me down a second time, even removing the eraser from my automatic pencil to examine the contents inside. The precautions were for the arraignment of Reies Lopez Tijerina on charges of kidnapping and assault with intent to commit murder.

He called himself *Rey Tigre*, or King Tiger, and his dream was nothing less than the establishment of an independent nation, an *alianza* of free city-states in the harsh, unyielding mountains of northern New Mexico. Basic to his plan was the return to the people of their ancient Spanish land grants. In the sixteenth century the conquistadors wrested the land from the Indians, and after being given title by Spain, passed it on through generation after generation of their descendants. Theoretically, the grants were respected when New Mexico became part of the United States, but in truth the Spanish Americans, their power by now diffuse and diluted, were systematically stripped of lands and privileges that had been theirs for centuries. With a veneer of legality, the railroads took rights-of-way, the government formed national parks. Other tales of gringo plundering are less savory. There is the story of the territorial governor who pardoned a murderer, his quid pro quo being 45,000 acres of an old land grant, and it is told in one village how God-fearing parishioners released title to their grant after their priests threatened to excommunicate anyone who did not contribute to the building of a new church.

I wanted to see the country and drove north from Santa Fe. Buttes and mesas and canyons, all in reds and browns and golds, stretched as far as the eye could see. It was a landscape of hope, but in the villages all I heard was a chronicle of despair. I drove to adobe hamlets over rutted dirt roads that were rendered impassable by the slightest rain. In one village I was told that the children had missed half their school sessions the winter before because snow had closed the roads. Of the 23,000 people in one northern county, 11,000 were on some kind of relief. In Mora and Taos counties nearly half the families existed on less than $2,000 a year. "A modern house," a state welfare worker told me, "is a house with indoor plumbing."

Forgotten by the state, old resentments still smoldering, the descendants of the conquistadors turned to Tijerina, who at the very least, whatever the plausibility of his dream, articulated their discontent. Dirt poor and land hungry, this onetime itinerant cotton picker-turned-revolutionary roamed the high country, a peasant Don Quixote in search of windmills at which to tilt. Once he served "eviction" notices on the current owners of 594,000 land-grant acres. Another time he and several hundred followers laid claim to a national park, formed their own government, and "arrested" U.S. Forest Rangers for trespassing before they themselves were run off the land. Then one day last June, Don Quixote became El Cid. With a score of his followers he slipped into the sleepy, bedraggled village of Tierra Amarilla, seventy miles north of Santa Fe. In a blaze of gunfire, they stormed the county courthouse. They pumped shells into the walls, critically wounded two lawmen, and released ten of their cohorts from jail. Then the raiders melted away into the hills from which they came.

The National Guard was mobilized, tanks rumbled north, the entire state police force was alerted. It made no difference that Tijerina was finally apprehended lying on the floor in the back of a car, complaining of a stomachache. The peculiar alchemy that makes a "personality" had already taken place. Tijerina's release on bond—his trial for the raid is still pending—was all that was needed to keep the mixture brewing.

For months now I have watched the legend grow. Tijerina came from New Mexico and traversed California, speaking at its campuses, hammering home his points on television, attracting the underground press, the New Left and the entrepreneurs of protest. I could see why. His quest, absurd and gallant, had the potential for reconverting the fallen-away, bringing back into the mainstream of dissidence those people who had grown guiltily ambivalent about the general momentum of chaos building up in the nation's cities.

Tijerina had become a curiosity, a symbol of revolt. The goals of his revolution, never very clear, seemed to have vaporized. Now, this Sunday at the Sports Arena, Tijerina was talking about his "mutual-assistance treaty" with the leading black militant organizations: "The two peoples agree to take the same position as to the crimes and sins of the Government of the United States of America." He was talking about the war in Vietnam: "I will not fight against our colored brothers in Vietnam. I would rather spend five years in the penitentiary than do this." He was talking about the power potential of the Spanish-American people.

As the cheers reverberated, a black militant told the audience, "While we're *talking* revolution, he's *making* revolution in New Mexico." More cheers. I asked one of the black leaders what the "alliance" was expected to accomplish. He shrugged and smiled. "Those who know don't say," he said. "Those who say don't know." The afternoon suddenly depressed me and I left the Sports Arena. I feared that what had started as a cause had become a commodity.

1968

APOLLO 204

There was a time when I might not have noticed the newspaper item, but today I did: the target date for the Jupiter shoot was 1972. On that frigid, distant planet 480 million miles from the sun, NASA scientists said they hoped to find some of the original material that went into its creation. There was no mention of astronauts Grissom, White and Chaffee. The moon might have been made of green cheese. The space program seemed back on its well-oiled tracks, breezy, confident, impenetrable. And yet, it would never be quite the same for any of us.

Two days before Apollo 204 burned on its launching pad at Cape Kennedy, I drove out to the North American Aviation plant in Downey, California, where the capsule was designed. I had been assigned to do a story on the first Apollo shot and I wanted to see the equipment. It was raining that day, the kind of torrential monsoon that afflicts southern California those few days a year when the sky opens. Now, weeks later, I can remember everything that happened that Wednesday, what I had for lunch, the kind of beer I drank. I got annoyed at the security guard because he made me park so far from the administration building, and I somehow faulted North American for being located just down the street from the "largest Chrysler-Plymouth dealer in Southern California," a man whose insistent huckstering is drilled into the brain every hour of the television day and night. I remember thinking as I walked through the rain, irritated, soaked, a cold coming on, that I had never thought much of the astronauts anyway.

As a journalist, I am inhibited by the fact that I don't much like to ask questions. I have never been able to ask anyone how much money he makes or how long he and his wife have been sleeping in separate bedrooms. I rely upon having my ignorance chipped away by observation. But my ignorance about the space program was so vast that day that I was forced, haltingly, afraid of making a fool out of myself, to make the requisite queries. The answers are recorded in my notebook and I am not sure that I could tell you what they mean. There are references to "thrust" and "psi" and "O-g." The engineer to whom I talked was infinitely patient, with a broad, open Irish face, and I can remember thinking how our prejudices are programmed, how I had never expected to find an Irish engineer; a German surely, a Scandinavian or a Jew perhaps, but not a man named McCarthy. He talked about skiing and he talked about Mars as if they were equally plausible. Mars was the next great space adventure, he said, and then he was talking about the snow at Mammoth. It was as if the moon had already been conquered. The Mars target date was 1985, the round trip would take two years, with a ten-day layover on the planet. I brought the subject back to the moon. "You can run a Greyhound bus line up there," he said. "Let the men dig rocks while they wait to come back."

His confidence was contagious. It is always easier to think of the project beyond the one immediately at hand. And yet there was a question I had to ask. What if something went wrong? In the back of every reporter's mind lurks the malignant knowledge that disaster is good copy. It is not something that he wishes to happen. It is simply a contingency not to be over-looked, a fact of the profession, as death is for the pathologist. Perhaps I had expected a nervous clearing of the throat or a darting of the eyes, but it was a question the engineers had of course heard many times before. There was, I was told, a 99 percent survival factor. The odds seemed attractive, and I believed in them.

Before I left, I was shown a full-size mockup of the Apollo capsule. I was allowed to crawl inside, and for some twenty minutes I was strapped horizontally into what would have been White's center seat. After a few moments I felt a tightening in my legs and a small but persistent pain at the tip of my spine. The muscles in the back of my neck started to constrict and the veins in my temple to throb. Above my head was a dizzying array of dials, switches, gauges and tape re-corders. I wondered how the astronauts could func-tion in such an uncomfortable environment and was told that at zero gravity, when the body is weightless, there is no pressure to compress the muscles. I began to absorb the trivia of flight. I added three ounces of hot water to the dehydrated crab Newburg and learned that the beef and gravy tastes better eaten dry, like jerky. I checked the food locker and the suction vac-uum cleaner and the waste storage compartments. I zipped myself into the sleeping hammock anchored under the captain's couch and found myself lapsing into the jargon of space, talking about "emergency egress." I learned that the astronauts did not shave because there was no way to capture their whiskers, which in the weightless atmosphere floated around the cabin like so many tiny glass slivers. I was impatient about the moon and preferred talk of Mars.

And then two days later, at 6:31:03 P.M., there was a spark, and fourteen seconds later it was all over. I was on the Hollywood Freeway when I heard the news on my car radio and in that moment I remem-bered something I had been told at Downey. I had remarked that the capsule seemed small, and an engineer had replied, "There's seventy-eight cubic feet per man. The average male coffin only has twenty-eight." Egocentrically, I felt closer to the accident because *I* had sat in the center seat and *I* had convinced myself that the major problem remaining in lunar exploration was how to capture chin whiskers. Death on the launching pad, where there were so many grander possibilities for space immortality, was as if Achilles had fallen down the cellar stairs.

I did not care to admit that there was another reason why the accident so moved me. For me anyway, and I wonder how general the feeling was, the bloom had worn off the space program. We had become indifferent to the astronauts, so sure of their capabilities that all the suspense had drained out of the adventure. How many of us could name the two men who had flown the last Gemini mission? When was the last time we gathered around a television set to watch the drama of a countdown? The only spaceman I could remember was Charles Conrad, and only because he was a class ahead of me at college.

There was something too perfect, too anesthetizing about the astronauts. We had stopped thinking of them as mortals. They seemed unreal, knights of some dull lunar Round Table. It was easy to take an insidious delight in the rumors, true or untrue, that their wives did not like each other, that one was a philanderer and another drank too much, because the malicious stories invested them with a humanity they otherwise seemed to lack. With their magazine contract, their motel, their bank, their political candidacies, they had made space seem less an adventure than a parlay. They were not in the mold of Lindbergh, lonely men making solitary decisions, pitting their will against the universe. Most of their decisions were made for them. A hand in the control booth pushes a button and the rocket blasts off; a computer in Houston tells them when and where to come down.

It seemed the ultimate triumph of technology over

man. The countdown, the blast-off, the predicted number of orbits, the splashdown, the ritual aboard the carrier—it had become so we were scarcely aware it was happening. What the fire aboard Apollo 204 touched was a sense of guilt that made the space program more real than it had been since the people of Perth turned on their lights. Death had proved what we had chosen to forget—that the astronauts were as vulnerable as the rest of us.

1967

MEMENTO DELANO

It was a long time before I returned to Delano. I passed it a number of times on my way to Sacramento, where I have family, but I never had the urge to stop. It was not a place of old friends and warm memories. It was a place where I had been and a place I was glad to leave. There was something sad and brooding about it, an endless, unfinished chapter straddling Highway 99. I remembered the last time I had been there. It was four years ago, in March 1967, and I stopped only by accident. I was driving from Sacramento to Los Angeles, that interminable drive, like driving four hundred miles on a pool table, comforted only by the car radio and the valley deejays' version of hard rock—a little Burt Bacharach, a touch of the Fifth Dimension. There was no traffic, the speedometer needle kept inching up. I had no intention of stopping in Delano, but just outside the city limits, I noticed that I needed gas. As I cruised onto the freeway off-ramp, I noticed the blinking red light of the Highway Patrol.

The officer was very young, twenty-two at the outside, with one of those OCS haircuts, all skin on the sides, a part and two inches on the top. He was wearing smoked sunglasses and a lot of Mennen's Skin Bracer. He was very courteous.

"You were going eighty-five in a seventy zone," the patrolman said.

There was no argument. I sat in the front seat of his patrol car and gave him my driver's license. He asked my occupation. I told him. He put his pen down.

"You know about this grape strike here? That's a good story."

I told him I was in the process of writing it. For what magazine, he wanted to know. He was interested now. He had inserted the carbon paper, but still had not made a mark on the ticket. I told him the name of the magazine.

"Is that a liberal magazine or a conservative magazine?"

"They let you think pretty much what you want."

It seemed to satisfy him. He carefully put his pen back into his shirt pocket and closed the flap over it.

"You ever met this Cesar Chavez?"

"Yes."

He was closing his summons book. "He a Communist?"

"No."

The youth was silent for a moment. Then he unbuttoned his shirt flap and took out his pen. He reopened his summons book. "You were doing eighty-five in a seventy zone," he said.

In a sense, after four years, this brief encounter with the California Highway Patrol remains my most vivid impression of Delano. When asked "What was it like?" or "What does it all mean?" it is with difficulty that I can recall anything else. There are other things I remember, of course, but they are all equally tangential to what was happening. In no sense could they be used to make a point, to show a moral. I remember a cool night in the foothills of the Sierra when a panicky young farm worker was casually seduced by a California golden girl. I remember the boy still desperately picking on his guitar even as he was being led off to the bedroom and I remember that the next morning when the girl knocked on my door to wake me up she wasn't wearing any clothes. I remember a grower named Jack Pandol, whom I liked personally better than anyone I met in Delano, telling me that he really had very little in common with his brother-in-law, who was also a farmer, and when I asked why, he said simply, "He's in alfalfa. I'm in grapes."

I did not sense then, as I do now, the gulf between all I heard and read about the issues—the "story"—and what strikes me now increasingly as the "real," those moments that have no function in the "story," but which seem in retrospect more interesting, more imaginatively to the point, more evocative of how we live and what we feel. Jack Pandol's story about his alfalfa-growing brother-in-law was real and said more about what it was like to be a grower than all the cant I heard and all the account books I read that hot summer. There was in it the sense of being alone, of embattlement, the feeling that if he didn't have much in common with his brother-in-law, he was going to have even less in common with Chavez. And the California golden girl's seduction of the young farm worker was real. It is clear to me now that no amount of good faith on her part could bridge the chasm of social and sexual custom between them. She worked hard and loyally for Chavez, but in the end I think she had even less communion with the *campesinos* than Pandol.

I think I became further estranged from the events in Delano by the promiscuity of the attention lavished on Chavez. The insatiable appetites of instant communication have necessitated a whole new set of media ground rules, predicated not only on the recording of fact but also on the projection of glamour and image and promise. The result of this cultural nymphomania is that we have become a nation of ten-minute celebrities. People, issues and causes hit the charts like rock groups, and with approximately as much staying power. For all the wrong reasons, Chavez had all the right credentials—mysticism, nonviolence, the nobility of the soil. But distastefully implicit in instant apotheosis is the notion of causes lost; saints generally fail and when they do not, the constant scrutiny of public attention causes a certain moral devaluation. Enthusiasm for a cause is generally in inverse proportion to actual involvement. One could fete grape workers, as the rich and beautiful once did on a Long Island estate, without thinking about, if indeed one even knew about, the Suffolk County potato workers only a few miles away living in conditions equally as wretched as any pickers in the Great Central Valley of California.

And so I followed the strike from afar. Desultorily I kept a file, neatly packaging the headlines in a series of folders. *Note & file:* Chavez boycotts table grapes nationally; *cross-reference:* Lindsay administration halts purchase of grapes by New York city institutions; *cross-reference:* Pentagon increases grape purchases to help growers. *Note & file:* Chavez embarks on a penitential fast; *cross-reference:* Robert Kennedy and Cesar Chavez—who stands to gain the most? *Note & file:* 1969—large crop, depressed prices, boycott; *cross-reference:* strike speeds automation. *Note & file:* 1970—short crop, recession, boycott. *Note & file:* July 29, 1970—Delano growers capitulate, sign three-year contract with Chavez. "We are happy peace has come to this valley," says a growers' spokesman. "It has been a mutual victory."

"Mutual victory"—the phrase had the hollow sound of rhetoric and too often the territory behind rhetoric is mined with equivocation. I wondered who, if anyone, really was victorious in Delano, wondered if victory was tinctured with ambiguity. And so for the first time in four years I returned to Delano, goaded there by the instinctive feeling that there are no solutions, only at best amelioration, and never ultimate answers, final truths.

I've never talked to Cesar Chavez. But you know, I've been around longer than he has and I think I know these people better than he does. Maybe he'd learn something if he talked to me.
    Former U.S. Senator George Murphy (R., Cal.), May 1969

It was Robert Kennedy who legitimized Chavez. Prior to 1966, when the U.S. Senate Subcommittee on Migratory Labor held hearings in the valley, no Democrat would touch the Chavez movement. It had always been necessary to attract a few Southern votes in order for prolabor legislation to pass in the Congress, and Southern agrarians would not toss a bone toward labor unless farm workers were excluded from all provisions of any proposed bill. Robert Kennedy was no stranger either to expedience or to good politics and, along with most of organized labor, saw little to be gained by an identification with Chavez. But he was persuaded to attend the hearings in March 1966 by one of his aides, Peter Edelman, acting in concert with a handful of union officials alive to the drama in Delano. Even while flying to California, Kennedy was reluctant to get involved, demanding of his staff, "Why am I going?" He finally showed up at the hearings a day late. The effect was electric, a perfect meeting of complementary mystiques. Kennedy—ruthless, arrogant, a predator in the corridors of power. And Chavez—nonviolent, Christian, mystical, not without a moral imperative of his own.

For the next two years, it was almost impossible to think of Chavez except in conjunction with Robert Kennedy. The Kennedys sponged up ideas, and implicit in Chavez was the inexorable strength of an idea whose time had come. Kennedy's real concern for the farm workers helped soften his image as a self-serving

126

keeper of his brother's flame and in turn plugged Chavez into the power outlets of Washington and New York. For the first time Chavez became fashionable, a national figure registering on the nation's moral thermometer. Robert Kennedy and Cesar Chavez—the names seemed wired into the same circuitry, the one a spokesman, the other a symbol for the constituency of the dispossessed.

Whatever the readings on fame's Geiger counter, it was a bad time in Delano. The strike, in 1968, was mired in quicksand. An attempt to organize the grape ranches of the Coachella Valley had failed miserably. The threat of violence was in the air. A newspaper in India reported a $10,000 bounty on Chavez's head. However unsubstantiated the rumor, bounty spelled contract, and contract spelled hit. Bodyguards dogged Chavez's footsteps and a German shepherd watchdog patrolled his door. And then Robert Kennedy was killed the same day that Chavez had dispatched platoons into the barrios of East Los Angeles to round up votes for his benefactor in the California Democratic primary. Chavez showed up at Kennedy's funeral at St. Patrick's Cathedral in New York characteristically late, dressed in a sweater. He marched to an empty pew and stood throughout the ceremony, to the mounting annoyance of a group of U.S. Senators whose view he was blocking.

The strike had begun to lose its momentum the year before. Perelli-Minetti was the last Delano grower to sign with Chavez, and even that was by default. The grower had originally settled with the Teamsters, an agreement bitterly assailed by Chavez as a sweetheart contract, and it was only after the two unions had arbitrated their jurisdictions that UFWOC inherited the Perelli-Minetti workers. Chavez's next target was the Guimarra Vineyards, the largest table-grape growers in America, themselves controlling 10 percent of the annual crop. His strategy was a San Joaquin Valley version of the domino theory: knock over Guimarra and the other growers had to fall in line. But the Guimarras were a rough bunch of boys, a network of Sicilian fathers and brothers and sons and sons-in-law not especially known for their enlightened views about the labor movement. Even their lawyer was one of their own, John Guimarra, Jr., then not thirty, a Stanford Law School graduate who gave up an Orange County law practice to come home as the family's counsel and spokesman.

The strike against Guimarra proved one thing—there wasn't a picket line in the world that could force a grower to agree to a contract. It was next to impossible to certify a strike. Workers who were pulled out were readily replaced by scabs and green-carders—foreign nationals (in this case Mexicans) with U.S. work permits, or green cards. The pickers were usually out of town working at another farm before the applicable state agencies even arrived to verify their departure. Though green-carders were legally enjoined against working in a strike situation, they were free to work if no strike had been certified. And in the conflicting claims as to the number of workers who actually walked out at a struck farm, I am inclined for one reason to lean more toward the grower's figure than the union's: it simply defied all logic for a picker to go out on strike. However grandiose (by grower standards) a picker's hourly wage, his annual income was barely at subsistence level, if indeed that high. Given that picking is one of the most miserable jobs known to man, it is usually—for whatever social or cultural reasons—the best a picker can hold. So no matter how much he favored the union, he would have had to be a sainted fanatic to go on strike and further heighten both his own and his family's level of misery.

Against Guimarra, Chavez needed another edge and he fell back on the boycott he had used so successfully against Schenley and Di Giorgio. Both these concerns were public corporations, however, susceptible to stockholder pressure, and both had a line of consumer products that could be successfully boycotted. Table grapes were another thing altogether. There was no label identification; a bunch of grapes was a bunch of grapes. The problem did not seem to deter Chavez. He seems to regard a boycott almost as a religious experience. "It's like quicksand," he says. "It's irreversible. Once it gets going, it creates a life of its own. It reaches a point where nothing can stop it. It's like trying to fight the wind."

At first the Guimarras were equal to the blow. When UFWOC prevailed on stores to stop buying the Guimarra label, the firm began borrowing labels from other growers and using them in place of its own. Even a rebuke from the Food and Drug Administration charging that label switching was contrary to federal regulations did not deter the grower. By the end of 1967, Guimarra was using, by union count, 105 different labels. In retaliation, UFWOC early in 1968 extended its boycott beyond Guimarra to include every California grower of table grapes.

As the growers dug in, there was within the union a certain impatience, a certain fraying of the precepts of nonviolence. The imperceptible erosion of the growers' position was not particularly heady to union militants steeped in the literature of the headlines, the combat communiqués from the core cities. There was a new truculence in the air; packing crates were burned, tires slashed, scabs roughed up. Chavez was not unaware of the nascent violence. Late in February 1968, he quietly began a penitential fast to redirect the movement back onto its nonviolent course. Only on the sixth day of the fast did he alert aides to what he was doing. No one had to be apprised of its exploitative potential. The circus aspect of the next seventeen days (the fast lasted twenty-three days) dismayed a number of Chavez's staunchest supporters who, while not doubting his intentions, nevertheless deplored the manner in which union aides pandered to the media that flocked to Delano. If not actively choreographing the fast, UFWOC officials did little to discourage the faithful who seemed to equate it with the Second Coming. Tents were pitched for farm workers maintaining a vigil for Chavez, and old women crawled on their knees from the highway to the quarters where he was lodged for the duration of the fast.

Whatever its indulgences, the fast was like a hypodermic full of pure adrenaline pumped into the union. It seemed to find new resolve, new strength. But the fast had also endangered Chavez's always perilous health. One of his legs is shorter than the other, one side of his pelvis smaller. Six months after his fast, his energies depleted, Chavez was hospitalized. His condition was diagnosed as a degenerating spinal disc. For months he remained virtually an invalid, resisting treatment. Then early in 1969, Senator Edward Kennedy, at his own expense, sent Dr. Janet Travell, the back specialist who had treated John Kennedy, to Delano to look at Chavez. Dr. Travell concluded that Chavez's problem was not spinal but the result of muscular breakdown in his back. Her treatment (among other things, she prescribed a rocking chair) gradually freed Chavez from his bed. Without pain for the first time in nearly a dozen years, he could turn his full attention to a strike that by mid-1969 seemed endless.

In John Guimarra, Jr., the growers had their most impressive spokesman. In contrast to the primitives of the elder generation, his normality seemed practically epicene. Not for him any vulgar Red-baiting; even the ritualistic evocation of outside agitation was toned down. The 1968 election gave the growers a friendly administration in Washington and an almost immediate by-product was a substantial jump in the Pentagon's purchase of table grapes. Pentagon spokesmen indignantly denied that the increased purchases were meant to undercut the boycott, claiming instead that military *chefs de cuisine* had merely whipped up a number of new grape delicacies. The growers even developed a degree of media sophistication of their own. The California Table Grape

Growers Association hired J. Walter Thompson, the nation's largest advertising agency, to come up with a campaign extolling table grapes (it seemed impossible for a while to pick up a service magazine without the eyes feasting on some alchemy of grapes and sour cream and brown sugar) and also engaged Whitaker & Baxter, a public-relations firm specializing in political causes (it handled the American Medical Association's effort against Medicare), to produce material countering the boycott. The gist of this campaign was that Chavez was being kept alive not so much by fuzzy-minded urban liberals boycotting grapes as by the greed of the AFL-CIO. Organized labor, according to this argument, had developed with age a severe case of varicose veins. While union membership continues to increase, the percentage of the population it represents decreases; there are fewer blue-collar workers, while white-collar workers are difficult to organize. Therefore the attraction of the nation's two million farm workers. UFWOC's dues are $3.50 a month, $7,000,000 a month if all two million workers are organized, $84,000,000 a year in the coffers of the AFL-CIO.

The beauty of such an argument is that innuendo does the work. But beyond the rhetoric, the growers were hurting. In New York, the world's largest market for table grapes, the boycott had cut the number of railroad boxcars unloaded in 1968 by a third; in Baltimore by nearly half. Many supermarket chains simply refused to carry California table grapes. In some instances, their motives were not altogether humanitarian. Union locals hinted broadly that, unless grapes came out of the stores, butchers and retail clerks would not cross UFWOC picket lines. Not long after the NLRB put a stop to such intimidation, fires were discovered in at least three New York A&P's, cause in each instance unknown, although it was the considered opinion of the city's chief fire marshal that the boycott might have been a contributing factor. If a message was intended, it was received loud and clear. Across the country, grapes disappeared from the shelves.

The success of the boycott was enhanced by the uncertain state of the economy. Agriculture is a carnivorous business. Farmers feed on the misfortunes of their own; a disastrous frost in Arizona profits the growers of the same crop in the San Joaquin Valley. Crops are subject to roller-coaster fluctuations. The large harvest in 1969 depressed grape prices; the short crop in 1970 was more susceptible to strike and boycott. What the Nixon economists called a "seasonal adjustment" was a full-fledged recession and it was bleeding growers as it bled the rest of the country. The grape business was plagued by bankruptcies. Money was short, interest was high. Farmers were paying 9 and 10 percent for bank loans to start their crop; the shakier the grower's finances, the higher the interest he had to pay.

His predicament, however, was not designed to elicit much sympathy. Though growers might claim that they were getting stuck with someone else's check, the bill for a hundred years of often malevolent paternalism was now being called in. If that bill seemed inflated by a surcharge of moral indignation, one had only to remember how long past due it was. The growers had finally run afoul of the times. Halfway around the world, the nation was involved in a hated, pernicious war. It was a house divided, doubting itself, forced to examine charges that it was racist both at home and abroad. It was difficult to conjure up a charismatic grower; the words just did not adhere. A man with thousands of acres worth millions of dollars simply did not have the emotional appeal of a faceless crowd of brown-skinned men, women and children eking out a fetid existence, crammed into substandard housing, isolated by language and custom from a community that scorned them. Never mind that the grower was mortgaged to the eyeballs, strangling on 9 and 10 percent interest payments. In the summer of 1970, high interest rates did not sing like food stamps.

The first break came from a handful of growers in the Coachella Valley. They signed with UFWOC and boxes of their grapes, adorned with the union's black-eagle emblem, were exempted from the boycott. After the May harvest, the union growers found their grapes bringing 25¢ to $1 more per box than those of the boycotted farmers. The lesson was not lost on the Delano growers. Late one night in July, John Guimarra, Jr., made his move. From a pay telephone at a dance he was attending in Bakersfield, he called Jerome Cohen, UFWOC's lawyer, in Delano. He told Cohen that he was flying out of Bakersfield at nine the next morning on a mission that could have "drastic consequences" for the grape industry; he asked if he could meet with Chavez before he made this "major move." (He did not mention what this major move was, and when I asked him six months later, he still refused. "It's water under the bridge," Guimarra said.) Cohen got hold of Chavez, who had been making a speech that night in San Rafael. Tired though he was, Chavez agreed to an immediate meeting. At 2 A.M., the parties met at the Stardust Motel in Delano and negotiated for the next six hours. Early Sunday morning they had reached tentative agreement. That same day Guimarra presented the agreement to the other Delano growers. I asked him how they had reacted. "Well, we had already stuck our foot in the water and I guess they thought it wouldn't hurt to see where negotiations led," Guimarra recalled. "But I wouldn't say any of the growers jumped up and down and said, 'Gee, hand me a contract.' "

Three days later, the twenty-six Delano growers signed a contract with UFWOC. The agreement called for $1.80 an hour, plus 20¢ per box incentive pay the first year, escalating to $2.10 an hour the third. Outwardly there was a sense of collective relief that after five years hostilities had ended. But there were still some residual hard feelings. Most centered on the

133

stipulation that Chavez would supply every worker from a union hiring hall. Privately there was not a grower in Delano who thought UFWOC could deliver a full crew in time for the harvest. (The question was academic that first summer, as the harvest was already underway when the contract was signed and growers had full crews in the fields.) If UFWOC has not supplied enough workers by the start of the harvest, the contract allows growers to hire pickers on their own. But farmers fear that if they are forced to wait that long, their crops might start to rot. I asked John Guimarra, Jr., what action he would take in this eventuality.

"I'll burn your book," he replied without hesitation.*

That was the end of the grape strike. The lettuce strike in Salinas had already begun. Even as the conflict in Delano was winding down, Chavez had informed the lettuce growers in the Salinas Valley that he wished to organize their field workers. With almost indecent haste, the Salinas growers responded by soliciting the Teamsters, and twenty-four hours before the Delano contract was signed, they announced an agreement allowing the Teamsters to represent their field hands. Whatever the Teamsters were, what they were not was a union run by a radical Mexican mystic, and to the growers this was a most seductive enticement.

Since Chavez and the Teamsters had agreed three years before not to poach on each other's territory, the Salinas announcement was tantamount to a declaration of war. Late in August, Chavez struck the Salinas ranches. On the first day of the strike, between five and seven thousand workers walked off the job. The mood at UFWOC was euphoric. Never before

---

* The book referred to is *Delano: The Story of the California Grape Strike*, which was published in 1967. This piece appeared as an afterword in a new edition of that book, published in 1971.

had Chavez been able to pull workers out of the fields in any substantial numbers. The effect on the growers was immediate. Railroad carloads of lettuce shipped out of Salinas slipped from a normal 250 a day to as low as thirty-five. In some areas the wholesale price of lettuce soared from $1.75 a crate to $6; in Los Angeles supermarkets the retail price rose 10¢ a head in a single day. Grower losses mounted to $500,000 a day. The numbers were enough to convince a few of the larger Salinas growers to sign with UFWOC. "The Teamsters had our contract," said a spokesman for Inter-Harvest, a subsidiary of United Fruit, "but UFWOC had our workers."

The majority of Salinas growers did not see it that way. In vain they tried to get an injunction against the strike, claiming they were the victims of a jurisdictional dispute between UFWOC and the Teamsters; a judge in Santa Maria ruled against the injunction on the grounds that there was insufficient evidence that the Teamsters actually had the support of the field workers. The Teamsters seemed to be schizophrenic about the whole thing. On the one hand, Teamster antipathy toward Chavez and his "smelly hippies" had long been documented; on the other, the Teamsters could count. The Teamster solution was to renege on its contracts with the growers and turn them over to UFWOC. The growers would have none of it; a marriage of convenience was still a marriage. It was an unprecedented situation—management holding to the sanctity of contracts for workers the union no longer wanted to represent. Not quite sure what to do, the Teamsters bent a few UFWOC skulls to keep in practice and talked a lot about law and order. Nor did the uncompromising majesty of the law make it seem any less droll. Less than three weeks after the Santa Maria decision, a judge in Salinas, ruling on virtually the same evidence, issued a permanent injunction against all UFWOC strike activity in the Salinas area.

Chavez's response was immediate. Hardly were his picket lines withdrawn than he ordered a nationwide boycott of all non-UFWOC lettuce in California and Arizona. Almost predictably hewing to the script of Delano, the first two growers to yield, Freshpict and Pic 'N Pac, were both subsidiaries of large consumer corporations (Purex and S.S. Pierce) concerned that a boycott might spread to their more visible packaged products on supermarket shelves. The other Salinas growers had no such concerns and, except for one defection, stood firm. In Salinas's least dreary restaurant, Caesar Salad was renamed Salinas Valley Salad (it was an affront to the palate under any name). Ironically, Chavez's most prominent foe in Salinas, Bud Antle, Inc., was not really a particular UFWOC target. In a situation almost unique in California, Bud Antle's lettuce workers had been under union contract since 1961. Not that Bud Antle's intentions in allowing the organization of their field workers were entirely altruistic. Nine years before, the Teamsters had lent the financially straitened company $1,000,000 and the quid pro quo was a union contract for, among others, the lettuce workers. Though he frequently alluded to the Teamster loan, Chavez had no real wish to challenge the contract. But in an across-the-board boycott, things get broken; it was the classic case of the omelet and the egg.

The boycott against Bud Antle landed Chavez in jail for the first time in his organizing career. Under court injunction to end the boycott against the firm, Chavez refused. Three weeks before Christmas 1970, a Salinas judge ordered him into jail until he did so. However legally impeccable the court order, the jailing of Chavez backfired emotionally against the growers. In plain terms, the lettuce boycott had been up to this point a flop. Five grinding years of strike and boycott against the grape growers had simply run down the batteries of Chavez's supporters. His incarceration, however, was an instant recharge. A vigil was set up outside the Salinas county jail. The star names pilgrimaged to Salinas, led by the widows Coretta King and Ethel Kennedy, whose very presence was a stark reminder of those insane few months in 1968 when martyrdom seemed the only resolution to the nation's problems. On Christmas Eve, Chavez was released from jail pending a hearing on his case by a higher tribunal. But his jailing had given the boycott so much momentum that the Teamsters announced a boycott of their own, a boycott against the loading or unloading of any UFWOC-picked crops, at least until UFWOC called off its campaign against Bud Antle. The permutations seemed limitless. It was as if the lessons of Delano were written on the wind.

FACTS:
There are five million Mexican Americans in the United States. They are the nation's second largest minority. Almost 90 percent live in the five south-western states of Arizona, California, Colorado, New Mexico and Texas. They comprise 15 percent of the population of Texas, 10 percent of the population of California and 28 percent of the population of New Mexico. More than one-third live in "official" poverty on incomes of less than $3,000 a year. Their birth rate is twice the national average, and the mortality rate for infants less than a year old is twice that of Anglos. Their median age is eleven years less than that of the Anglo; 42 percent of the Mexican-American population is under the age of fifteen. They average approximately eight years of schooling, four years fewer than the Anglos. Half of all Mexican Americans who enter high school drop out before finishing. The Mexican-American unemployment rate is twice that of Anglos, and almost 80 percent work at unskilled or semiskilled jobs.

The harvest from the grape strike is like a short crop in a good year. Because of Chavez and Chavez alone, it is now possible to predict that all farm labor will be organized in the foreseeable future. Perhaps not by UFWOC. Old habits die hard, and for growers a farm union is hard enough to swallow without Chavez as a chaser. Most would cheerfully sign their workers over to something like the International Ladies Garment Workers Union if they thought it was the only way to thwart him. Even grower associations are now calling for farm labor to come under the umbrella of the National Labor Relations Board, and the sound of their platitudes is heard in the land: "It is time that farm workers be allowed to join the 1970's. Too long have they been cut off from the mainstream of the American labor movement." (Applause.) Six years ago this might have been enough to buy off a strike. Not now. Success has made Chavez very sophisticated and he is in no hurry to embrace the NLRB. As amended by the Taft-Hartley and Landrum-Griffin acts, the NLRB now prohibits the two major weapons in Chavez's arsenel—secondary boycotts and organizational strikes. He is very much aware that since the passage of these two amendments no large group of unskilled labor has been organized. Until adjustments can be made, inclusion under the NLRB is a lollipop Chavez would just as soon forswear.

And yet beyond UFWOC's demonstrable success, beyond its cool reading of the times, there is little room for euphoria. The nagging thought persists that the strike in Delano was irrelevant except as an abstraction. Victory there was like administering sedatives to a terminal-cancer patient, a mercy, a kindness, death-easing rather than life-saving, a victory finally important less for its fulfilled intentions than for what, unintended, it presaged. Higher wages, a fund of new members, greater independence from management— these traditional benchmarks of labor achievement do not really apply to Delano. In the narrowest sense, a union of farm workers can only lighten its members' burden of misery. The figures are simply too relentless. Nearly 700,000 workers earned wages in California's fields and vineyards in 1967 (the most recent year for which comprehensive statistics are available), and while they earned $1.78 an hour on the farm, their average annual income for *all* work, both farm and nonfarm, was only $1,709. And though the 700,000 included foremen, crew leaders, supervisors and other year-round employees, only 31,000 earned as much as $5,000 that year in farm work.

There is simply too little future in farm work. While farms grow bigger and productivity increases, the number of farm workers steadily declines. Four percent of California's growers own nearly 70 percent of the farm land; eight percent hire over 70 percent of the farm labor. Over the last twenty-five years, the number of farms in California has been cut by more than half. Cities roll past the suburbs into the country, swallowing up small farms that historically soaked up the glut in the labor market, farms far more valuable to the grower as subdivisions than they ever were as acreage. Two years ago, less than two percent of the wine grapes in Fresno County were harvested by machine; the estimate for 1971 is more than 30 percent. In three years the Fresno County Economic Opportunities Commission predicts that 65 percent of the wine and raisin grapes in the San Joaquin Valley will be picked mechanically. Even table grapes could be picked automatically were consumers willing to buy them in boxes, like strawberries, instead of insisting on the esthetic appeal of bunches. It is estimated that mechanical pickers will cost Fresno County farm workers nearly $2 million in wages during 1971 and that by 1973 some 4,500 heads of families will be displaced by machines.

Growers recite these figures as if they were graven on stone. There is little doubt that Chavez has speeded up the wheels of automation, but the implication is that no one ever dreamed of it until he came along; indeed that, were it not for Chavez, no machine ever developed, no matter how economical, could ever separate a grower from his beloved workers. Engagingly enough, the growers really believe it.

The curious thing about Cesar Chavez is that he is as little understood by those who canonize him as by those who would condemn him. To the saint-makers, Chavez seemed the perfect candidate. His crusade was devoid of the ambiguities of urban conflict. With the farm workers there were no nagging worries about the mugging down the block, the rape across the street, the car boosted in front of the house. It was a cause populated by simple Mexican peasants with noble agrarian ideas, not by surly unemployables with low IQ's and Molotov cocktails.

All that is missing in this fancy is any apprehension of where the real importance of Cesar Chavez lies. The saintly virtues he had aplenty; it is doubtful that the media would have been attracted to him were it not for those virtues, and without the attention of the media the strike could not have survived. But Chavez also had the virtues of the labor leader, less applauded publicly perhaps, but no less admirable in the rough going—a will of iron, a certain deviousness, an ability to hang tough in the clinches. Together these twin disciplines kept what often seemed a hopeless struggle alive for six years, six years that kindled an idea that made the idealized nuances of Delano pale by comparison.

For the ultimate impact of Delano will be felt not so much on the farm as in the city. In the vineyards, Chavez fertilized an ethnic and cultural pride ungerminated for generations, but it was in the barrio that this new sense of racial identity flourished as if in a hothouse. Once four-fifths of the Mexican-American population lived in the rural outback, but as the farm worker became a technological as well as a social victim, his young deserted the hoe for the car wash. Today that same four-fifths float through the urban barrio like travelers without passports, politically impoverished, spiritually disenfranchised. State and municipal governments have so carefully charted the electoral maps that it is impossible for a Mexican American to get elected without Anglo sufferance. California's only Mexican-American congressman depends on Anglo suburbs for more than half his support and in the state legislature the gerrymandering is even more effective; there was in 1971 only one Mexican assemblyman and no state senator. It was a system that placed high premium on the Tio Taco, or Uncle Tom.

But since Delano there is an impatience in the barrio with the old formulas and old deals and old alliances, a dissatisfaction with a diet of crumbs, a mood—more than surly, if not yet militant—undermining and finally beginning to crack the ghetto's historic inertia. Drive down Whittier Boulevard in East Los Angeles, a slum in the Southern California manner, street after street of tiny bungalows and parched lawns and old cars, a grid of monotony. The signs are unnoticed at first, catching the eye only after the second or third sighting, whitewashed on fences and abandoned storefronts, the paint splattered and uneven, signs painted on the run in the dark of night, *"Es mejor morir de pie que vivir de rodillas"*—"Better to die standing than live on your knees." The words are those of Emiliano Zapata, but the spirit that wrote them there was fired by Cesar Chavez.

It is with the young that the new mood is most prevalent. On the streets they sell orange posters that say nothing more than *"La Raza."* At Lincoln High School in East Los Angeles, students walked out on strike as a protest against overcrowding and neglect, a strike that challenged the passivity of their elders as much as it did the apathy of the Anglo community. Go to any protest meeting in East Los Angeles and the doors are guarded by an indigenous force of young vigilantes called the Brown Berets. ("We needed a gimmick, we needed a name," one of their leaders told a reporter from *Time*. "We thought of calling ourselves the Young Citizens for Community Action, but that didn't sound right. We tried Young Chicanos, but that didn't work either. We thought of wearing big sombreros, but we figured people would just laugh at us. So we hit on the beret and someone said, 'Why not the Brown Berets?' And it clicked with all of us.")

The pride that Chavez helped awaken took on a

different tone in the barrio than in the vineyards. The farm workers' movement was essentially nonviolent, an effort based on keeping and exhibiting the moral advantage. But in East Los Angeles today the tendency is to pick up life's lessons less from Gandhi than from the blacks. Traditionally, brown and black have been hostile, each grappling for that single spot on the bottom rung of the social ladder. To the Mexican American the Anglo world held out the bangle of assimilation, a bribe to the few that kept the many docile. Denied to blacks, assimilation for years robbed the Chicano community of a nucleus of leadership. Today the forfeiture of this newly acquired cultural awareness seems to the young Chicano a prohibitive price to pay. The new courses in social bribery are taught by the blacks.

What the barrio is learning from the blacks is the political sex appeal of violence. Three times in the past year, East Los Angeles has erupted. The body count is still low, less than the fingers on one hand, hardly enough to merit a headline outside Los Angeles County. The official riposte is a call for more law and order. The charges of police brutality clash with the accusations of outside agitation. But beyond the rhetoric there is new attention focused on the ghetto. The vocabulary of the dispossessed is threat and riot, the Esperanto of a crisis-reacting society, italicizing the poverty and discrimination and social deprivation in a way that no funded study or government commission ever could.

Like Malcolm X and Martin Luther King, Jr., Cesar Chavez stands astride history less for what he accomplished than for what he is. Like them, he has forged "in the smithy of his soul," in Joyce's phrase, the "uncreated conscience" of a people. He is the manifestation of *la raza,* less the saint his admirers make him out to be than a moral obsessive, drilling into the decay of a system that has become a mortuary of hopes. We are a nation with a notoriously short attention span, needing saints but building them into a planned obsolescence. The man who survives this curse of instant apotheosis becomes, like Cesar Chavez, acutely uncomfortable to have around, a visionary ever demanding our enlistment as he tries to force the stronghold of forgotten possibilities. He demands only that we be better. It is a simple demand, and a terrifying one.

There is something exquisite about rural California in January. It is the month of the rains, a clear, cold, almost refrigerated rain, invigorating as an amphetamine. The hills are so green they seem carpeted in Astroturf. Peacocks preen by the side of the road. The wail of a train whistle, almost unheard since childhood, pierces the valley. In Delano there was a semblance of peace. On Main Street the bumper stickers that once said "Boycott Grapes" or "Buy California Grapes" were faded and peeling, like scar tissue from a fight everyone said they wished to forget. Out past the Voice of America transmitters on the Garces Highway, hard by the municipal dump, UFWOC has a new headquarters complex called Forty Acres. There is a gas station and an office and miscellaneous dilapidated buildings. What struck me most was how quiet it was. Underneath that vast empty sky at Forty Acres, even the lettuce strike was discussed with as little fervor as the weather. It was as if after five years of continuous combat everyone had come down with an attack of rhetorical laryngitis. Downtown there is talk of diversification, of attracting industry to Delano, of an industrial park. I was told about the labor pool— 20 percent unemployment in the winter—and how a one-crop town needs to get into other things. The Chamber of Commerce and the city council have established the Delano Economic Expansion Project (DEEP) to lure industry into the area, and hired the former manager of the Hanford (California) Chamber of Commerce to head it up. "One thing Cesar Chavez did for us," he says. "In Hanford I spent a whole lot of time trying to get people to know where Hanford is. In Delano I haven't had to do that." There was one other thing I noticed in Delano. I didn't know if it was a DEEP project or not. The sign on the outskirts of town used to say, "Hungry? Tired? Car Trouble? Need Gas? Stop in Delano." There is a new sign now out on Highway 99. It says, "DELANO. WELCOME ANY-TIME."

1971

3.

TINSEL

SNEAK

There was never any doubt that the Studio would hold its first preview of *Dr. Dolittle* in Minneapolis. Fox considered the Minnesota capital its lucky city; Robert Wise's production of *The Sound of Music* was first sneaked there and, with the enormous success of that picture, the studio superstitiously kept bringing its major road-show attractions to Minneapolis for their first unveiling before a paid theater audience. With so much money at stake—the budget of *Dr. Dolittle* was close to $18 million—the Studio was unwilling to hold a sneak anywhere around Los Angeles, reasoning that it could get a truer audience reaction in the hinterlands, far from the film-wise and preview-hardened viewers who haunt screenings in and around Hollywood. The plan originally had been to go to Minneapolis on Friday, September 8, and to Tulsa the following evening, but early that week the Tulsa screening was canceled. "If the picture plays, we don't have to go to Tulsa," Richard Fleischer said. "If it doesn't play, why go to Tulsa the next night and get kicked in the ass again? You make some changes, then you go to Tulsa."

Because of the magnitude of *Dr. Dolittle*, the Minneapolis screening attracted twenty-eight Studio personnel from New York and Los Angeles. The major contingent from Los Angeles was booked on Western Airlines Flight 502, leaving at 8:30 A.M. on September 8. Arthur Jacobs, accompanied by Natalie Trundy, arrived at International Airport nearly an hour before flight time. He was tieless and wearing a dark blazer and he lingered around the escalator coming up from the check-in counters on the ground floor, greeting members of the Fox party as they arrived. His salutation never varied. "I'm not nervous," Jacobs said. "I'm not going to Minneapolis. I'm just here to wave you all goodbye."

"Oh, Arthur," Natalie Trundy said. "Calm down."

"Calm down," Jacobs said. "*Calm down.* You treat me like one of the dogs." He turned to Fleischer. "We've got poodles. She treats me like a poodle."

"You're a very nice-looking poodle, Arthur," Fleischer said.

They milled around the gate, waiting for Flight 502 to be called, Jacobs, Natalie Trundy, Fleischer, Mort Abrahams, Herbert Ross, the choreographer on *Dr. Dolittle,* and Warren Cowan, who was once a partner of Jacobs's in a public-relations firm and whose company, Rogers, Cowan & Brenner, was handling the publicity and promotion for *Dolittle*. At last the flight was called. As Jacobs and Natalie Trundy walked up the ramp, Jacobs turned to Fleischer and said, "I just don't want to go to Minneapolis. Let's go to Vegas instead."

"It would be less of a gamble," Fleischer said.

Jacobs and Natalie Trundy took two seats at the rear of the first-class compartment. Cowan, a short, pudgy man with constantly moving eyes and a voice that sounds somewhat like Daffy Duck's, sat by himself in front of them and spread the New York and Los Angeles papers on his lap. Jacobs could not keep still. "We land at noon," he shouted up the aisle. "At twelve-thirty, we visit the public library. At one o'clock, the museum."

No one laughed except Fleischer, who tried to humor Jacobs. "At one-thirty, the textile factory," Fleischer said.

"And then we have a rest period between eight and eleven this evening," Jacobs said. This was the time scheduled for the screening.

"What I like about you, Arthur, is your calm," Fleischer said.

"Why should I be nervous?" Jacobs said. "It's only eighteen million dollars."

The trip to Minneapolis was uneventful. Most of the Fox people slept, except for Jacobs, who kept prowling the aisle looking for someone to talk to. It had just been anounced in the trade press that week that Rex Harrison had bowed out of the musical production of *Goodbye, Mr. Chips* which Gower Champion was scheduled to direct and Jacobs to produce for release by M-G-M. "It was all set," Jacobs said sadly. "Gower and I even went to Paris to see Rex. We drive out to his house in the country and he meets us at the door. 'Marvelous day,' he says. You know the way he talks." Jacobs put on his Rex Harrison voice. " 'Marvelous day. Bloody Mary, anyone, Bloody Mary.' He gets us the Bloody Marys and then he says, 'Now let me tell you why I'm not going to do *Mr. Chips.*' That's the first we heard about it. It was all set. Well, Gower looks at me, picks up his attach2e case and says, 'Sorry, I'm going to the airport, I'm going home.' " Jacobs gazed out the window at the clouds. "It was all set," he said. *"All set."*

The Fox party was met at the airport in Minneapolis by Perry Lieber, of the publicity department, who had flown in from Los Angeles the day before to supervise the preview arrangements. Lieber approached the task as if it were—and indeed he seemed to equate it with—the annual pilgrimage of the English royal family from Buckingham Palace to Balmoral. There were none of the ordinary traveler's mundane worries about luggage, accommodations and transportation. Lieber had checked the entire twenty-eight-man Studio contingent into the Radisson Hotel, ordered a fleet of limousines to transport each planeload of Fox people to the hotel, and arranged that all baggage be picked up at the airport and sent immediately to the proper rooms and suites. He gathered baggage tags and dispensed them to waiting functionaries and gave each new arrival an envelope containing his room key and a card listing that person's flight arrangements to New York or Los Angeles the next day, as well as the time that a limousine would pick him up at the hotel for the trip out to the airport.

Jacobs took his envelope and gave it to Natalie Trundy. For a moment, he peered intently at Lieber's tie pin, a musical staff on which the words "The Sound of Music" were written in sharps and flats. "You've got the wrong picture," he said.

"Are you kidding?" Lieber replied boisterously. "This is my lucky tie pin. You know how *Sound of Music* did and we previewed that here."

Warren Cowan shook his head slowly. "This has got to be the most superstitious movie company in the world," he said.

"If they're so superstitious," Fleischer said, "then why didn't they get Bob Wise to direct this picture?"

Outside the airport, standing beside a limousine, Natalie Trundy pulled out a Kodak Instamatic and began snapping pictures of the Fox party. She was dressed all in white and was wearing pale yellow sunglasses. She aimed her camera at Cowan, but her flashbulb misfired and she asked for one more shot.

"Oh, for God's sake, Natalie" Jacobs said. "Let's get going."

Cowan sat on the jump seat and opened a copy of the *Minneapolis Tribune* to the theater section, where the Studio had placed a teaser advertisement that did not give the name of the picture. The advertisement was headlined "Hollywood Red Carpet Preview."

"They're charging two sixty a ticket," Cowan said. "That's a mistake. You want to get the kids at a preview of a picture like this, and at two sixty a head, it's too steep."

"They should have made it two bucks a couple," Jacobs agreed miserably. At this point, he seemed to see disaster in everything. "To get the Friday night dates."

"It's a mistake," Cowan repeated softly.

As the limousine sped toward downtown Minneapolis, the chauffeur began to issue statistics about the city. "There are fifty-eight lakes and parks within the city limits," he said. No one paid any attention. Jacobs put out one brown cigarettello and lit another.

"Are you going to stand or sit in the theater tonight?" he asked Fleischer.

The director stared out the window at the early autumn foliage. "I'm going to lie down," he said. He patted Jacobs on the knee. "It's only a preview, Arthur," he said.

"Of an eighteen-million-dollar picture," Jacobs said.

Lunch was served in the Flame Room of the Radisson. It was after three o'clock and the dining room was deserted, but the kitchen had been kept open for the Fox group. Many had not yet arrived and others were up in their rooms napping. Jacobs had changed into a dark suit and he bounded from table to table.

"Don't forget, we're due at the art museum at three-thirty," he said.

"Arthur's making jokes," Lionel Newman said. The head of the Studio's music department, Newman had arranged the score and conducted it on the sound track. He had arrived in Minneapolis the day before with a Studio sound engineer to help set up the theater for the preview. "Arthur, as a comic, you're a lard-ass."

Jacobs looked chagrined.

"You know what I call this hotel?" Newman said. "Menopause Manor." He smiled at the waitress. "That's okay, honey, I don't mean you. But you got to admit, there's one or two old people staying here. I mean, this hotel talks about the swinging sixties, they don't mean the year, they mean the Geritol set."

Suddenly Jacobs raised his arm and shouted, "The Brinkmans." Standing in the doorway of the Flame Room, with his wife Yvonne, was Leslie Bricusse, the tall, bespectacled young English writer who had written the screenplay, music and lyrics for *Dr. Dolittle*. Jacobs was beside himself. "The Brinkmans are here," he cried to Fleischer. "Brinkmans" was his nickname for the Bricusses. "Did you see them?"

"He could hardly miss, Arthur," Newman said. "You make it seem like the start of World War III."

"Sit over here, Leslie," Jacobs said. He snapped his fingers for the waitress, who was standing right behind him. "We need chairs. Leslie, you want a sandwich, coffee, a drink?"

The Bricusses were pummeled by the Fox people and diffidently gave their order to the waitress. Yvonne Bricusse, a handsome, dark-haired English actress, slipped into a banquette alongside Natalie Trundy, who kissed her on the cheek. She poured herself a cup of coffee.

"What are you wearing to the opening?" Natalie Trundy said.

"New York?" Yvonne Bricusse said.

"Mmmmm," Natalie Trundy said.

"A heavenly thing," Yvonne Bricusse said. "Leslie bought it for me. Autumn colors, sort of. Burnt orange, with a bow here." She patted her bosom.

"Divine," Natalie Trundy said. "How about Los Angeles?"

"Nothing yet," Yvonne Bricusse said, sipping her coffee. "I thought I'd get something made. What do you think of Don Feld?" Feld is a motion-picture costume designer.

"Heavenly," Natalie Trundy said. She reached over with her fork and speared a piece of steak off Jacobs's plate. "A lot of feathers, though."

Yvonne Bricusse brooded for a moment. "Mmmmm," she said. "I know what you mean. He *does* like feathers." She stirred a spoon lazily in her coffee cup. "What about you?"

"In the works," Natalie Trundy said. "They're on the drawing boards, New York, London, Los Angeles, all the openings." She fluttered her arms like a ballerina. "I'm going to *float*. I haven't even talked about colors yet. I want to see how they look on the board."

That evening, before the preview, Richard Zanuck hosted a party for the Fox group at the Minneapolis Press Club on the second floor of the Radisson. Zanuck had just that day returned from Europe, a combination business and pleasure trip to London and Paris, then a week vacationing in the South of France with David and Helen Gurley Brown. He looked tanned and healthy. "I'm still on Paris time," he said, dipping a cocktail frankfurter into some mustard. "Stopped off in New York this morning to see a rough cut of *The Incident*, then back onto a plane out here."

"You can sleep tomorrow," Arthur Jacobs said.

Zanuck shook his head. "I'm going back to Los Angeles at six-thirty in the morning."

"Why?" Jacobs said.

"I want to go to the Rams game tomorrow night," Zanuck said.

Jacobs looked incredulous. He filtered through the room, stopping at each little group. "Dick's leaving for L.A. tomorrow at six-thirty. In the morning. You know why? He wants to go to the Rams game."

At 7:45, Perry Lieber beat on the side of a glass with a fork. He told the assembled group that the preview started at eight sharp and that after the picture there would a supper served in Richard Zanuck's suite on the twelfth floor. The picture was playing just down the street from the hotel at the Mann Theater, one of a chain owned by a Minnesota theater magnate named Ted Mann. Fox had rented the theater for the night, paying off Universal Pictures, one of whose roadshow films, *Thoroughly Modern Millie*, was playing there. Three rows of seats had been roped off for the Fox contingent, along with three other seats in the back of the house for Jacobs, Mort Abrahams and Natalie Trundy. Jacobs had specially requested these seats because he is a pacer and wanted to be free to walk around the theater without disturbing anyone. As Jacobs walked into the lobby of the theater, his eye caught a large display for *Camelot,* the Warner Brothers-Seven Arts musical that was to be the Christmas presentation at another Mann house. He stopped in his tracks.

"Oh, my God," he said. He looked at the people spilling into the theater. "Oh, my God, *Camelot.* That's what they'll think they're going to see. Oh, my God."

The house lights went down at 8:13. The audience was composed mainly of young marrieds and the middle-aged. There were almost no children present. Zanuck sat in an aisle seat, with Barbara McLean, the head of the Studio's cutting department, beside him, a pad on her lap, ready to take notes. The overture was played and then a title card flashed on the screen that said, "Equatorial Africa, 1845." The card dissolved into a prologue and Rex Harrison, in frock coat and top hat, rode onto the screen on top of a giraffe. There was no murmur of recognition from the audience. Some of the Studio party began to shift uneasily in their seats. The prologue lasted only a few moments. Harrison, as Dr. Dolittle, the man who could talk to the animals, slipped off the back of the giraffe to treat a crocodile ailing with a toothache. He tied a piece of string to the aching tooth and then tied the other end of the string to the tail of an elephant. At a signal from Dr. Dolittle, the elephant pulled on the cord and the tooth snapped out of the crocodile's mouth. Harrison patted the crocodile on the snout, put its huge molar in his waistcoat pocket, climbed on the back of a passing rhinoceros, and rode through the jungle out of camera range. There was not a whisper out of the audience as the prologue dissolved into the cartoon credits. At the appearance of the title *Dr. Dolittle*, there was a smatter of applause from the Studio contingent, but the clapping was not taken up by those who had paid $2.60 a ticket.

Throughout the first half of the film, the audience was equally unresponsive. Even at the end of the musical numbers, there was only a ripple of approval. At the intermission, David Brown hurried out into the lobby. "I want to hear the comments," he said. The noise in the lobby was muted. Most of the people just sipped soft drinks and talked quietly among themselves. Several of the Fox people blatantly eavesdropped on their conversations. Jacobs stood by one of the doors, his eyes darting wildly. Natalie Trundy leaned against him, her eyes brimming with tears, kneading a Kleenex between her fingers. In the center of the lobby, a circle of Studio executives surrounded Richard Zanuck.

"This is a real dead-ass audience," Zanuck said. "But you've got to remember, this isn't *Sound of Music* or *My Fair Lady*. The audience hasn't been conditioned to the songs for five years like they are with a hit musical."

"This is an original score," Stan Hough said.

Zanuck nodded his vigorously. "And an original screenplay," he said. The muscles in his jaw popped in and out feverishly. "My God, these people didn't know what they were going to see when they came into the theater. The first thing they see is a guy riding a giraffe."

"It's not like *Sound of Music,*" Hough said.

"Or *My Fair Lady*," Zanuck said. "Those songs were famous before they even began shooting the picture."

The second half of the picture did not play much better than the first. There was only sporadic laughter and desultory applause for the production numbers. When the house lights finally came on, the only prolonged clapping came from the three rows where the Studio people were sitting. In the lobby, ushers passed out preview cards. Tables had been set up and pencils provided for the members of the audience to fill in their reactions. These cards were more detailed than most preview questionnaires. "PLEASE RATE THE PICTURE," the cards read. "Excellent. Good. Fair." In another section, the questionnaire asked:

How would you rate the performance of the following?
> *Rex Harrison*
> *Samantha Eggar*
> *Anthony Newley*
> *Richard Attenborough*

Which scenes did you like the most?

Which scenes, if any, did you dislike?

WE DON'T WANT TO KNOW YOUR NAME, BUT WE WOULD LIKE TO KNOW THE FOLLOWING FACTS ABOUT YOU:

A. Male—Female

B. Check Age Group You Are in—
> Between 12 and 17
> Between 18 and 30
> Between 31 and 45
> Over 45

THANK YOU VERY MUCH FOR YOUR COURTESY AND COOPERATION.

Jacobs wandered through the lobby. His eyes were bloodshot. Natalie Trundy trailed after him. She had stopped crying, but her eyes were red-rimmed.

"I hear the cards are 75 percent excellent," Jacobs said to no one in particular. He watched a woman chewing on a small yellow pencil as she perused her card. The woman wrote something down, erased it, then wrote something else. Jacobs tried to look over her shoulder, but when she saw him, the woman shielded her comments with her hand.

156

Ted Ashley, the president of Ashley-Famous Artists, Rex Harrison's agents, came up and clapped Jacobs on the back. "Arthur, you've got yourself a picture here," Ashley said. Jacobs waited for him to say something else, but Ashley just slapped him on the back again and went over to talk to Zanuck.

"The audience was kind of quiet," Zanuck said.

Ted Mann, the theater owner, a large blocky man at one of whose theaters *Dr. Dolittle* was going to play when it opened in Minneapolis, elbowed his way to Zanuck's side. "I want you to know, Dick, a year's run," he said. "A year minimum."

"I thought the audience was a little quiet," Zanuck repeated.

"Yes, it was, Dick," Mann said. "But it's the kids who are going to make this picture, and we didn't have many kids here tonight." Mann seemed to search for the proper words. "You've got to realize," he said, "that what we had here tonight was your typically sophisticated Friday night Minneapolis audience."

Zanuck seemed not to hear. "There weren't conditioned to it like *Sound of Music*," he said.

"That's my point, my point exactly," Mann said. "But they'll be hearing this score for the next four months until the picture opens. By the time December rolls around, they'll know what they're going to see, don't you worry about that, don't you worry at all."

Jacobs looked over at Zanuck. "Over 50 percent excellent," he said.

The theater emptied and the Fox party slowly walked back to the Radisson half a block away. There was little enthusiasm as they rode up the elevator to the party in Zanuck's Villa Suite. The suite was enormous, on two levels, with a large living room and two bedrooms on the balcony above it. A bar had been set up on the balcony and a buffet beside it. The food had not yet arrived. There were only two large bowls of popcorn which were quickly emptied. The room was quiet, with only a slight hum of conversation. Jacobs, Abrahams, Bricusse, Natalie Trundy and Barbara

McLean sat around a coffee table totting up the cards, stacking them into piles of "Excellent," "Good" and "Fair." There were 175 cards in all—101 "Excellent," 47 "Good" and 27 "Fair." One viewer had written "Miserable" and another noted that Rex Harrison played Dr. Dolittle "like a male Mary Poppins." Two women objected to a scene with white mice and five to another scene in which Anthony Newley drinks whiskey out of a bottle.

"Those broads are all over forty-five, right?" Jacobs said.

"The 'Fairs' are all over forty-five," Abrahams said.

Ted Mann peered down at the cards. "You've got to realize that this was a typically sophisticated Friday night Minneapolis audience," he repeated.

"What we needed was a lot of kids," Natalie Trundy said. She dabbed at her eyes with a handkerchief and asked someone to bring her a Scotch on the rocks.

It was obvious that the Studio was distressed by the results of the preview. It was not just that the cards were bad—though with $18 million riding on the film, they were considerably less favorable than the Studio might have liked. But what disturbed them even more was the muted reaction of the audience during the screening of the picture.

"I think it's damn silly to come all the way to Minneapolis and then not tell people what they're going to see," Zanuck said. "It's all right to have a sneak in Los Angeles. But you come this goddam far to get away from that inside audience. So tell them what they're going to see. Get the kids out."

Richard Fleischer nursed a drink, stirring it slowly with his finger. "That's right, Dick," he said. "Tell them in the ads." He moved his hand as if he were reading from an advertisement. " '*Dr. Dolittle*—the story of a man who loved animals.' "

"Right," Zanuck said. "They know what they're seeing, they'll break the goddam doors down." He

158

gave his glass to Linda Harrison and asked her to get him another drink. "When we run it next, in San Francisco, maybe, we'll tell them what they're going to see. No goddam teaser ads."

"I'd be mystified," Fleischer said, "if I came into the theater and didn't know what the picture was and the first scene was a guy riding a giraffe."

Jonas Rosenfield, the Studio's vice-president in charge of publicity, who had come from New York for the screening, edged up beside Zanuck. "It's all true," he said. "But we've all got to admit that this was an invaluable preview. We know now how to promote this picture to make it the big success we still know it's going to be."

"This is what previews are for," Owen McLean said.

"Right," Stan Hough said. "This is what we come to Minneapolis for, to find out things like this."

Waiters arrived and laid out a supper of filet mignon on hamburger rolls. Calls were placed to Harrison in France, where he was making another Studio picture, *A Flea in Her Ear,* and to Darryl Zanuck in New York.

When the call to Darryl Zanuck came through, Richard Zanuck and David Brown went into a bedroom and closed the door. The party seemed to settle in. Jacobs still went through the cards, one by one.

"No kids," he said. "Everyone is over thirty."

"It's the kids who'll make this picture a hit," Harry Sokolov said.

In a corner of the room, Owen McLean sat down on a couch beside David Raphel, the Studio's vice-president in charge of foreign sales. "Well, David," McLean said, "what did you think?"

Raphel, a distinguished-looking middle-aged man with a slight foreign accent, wiped a piece of hamburger bun from his lips. "A very useful preview," he said carefully. "This picture will take very special handling to make it the success we all know it's going to be. We mustn't forget the older people. They're the repeaters. The children won't get there unless their grandparents take them. The grandparents, they're the repeaters. Look at *The Sound of Music*."

"There are people who've seen *Sound of Music* a hundred times," McLean said.

"My point," Raphel said. "My point exactly."

Slowly the party began to break up. It was after one A.M. and a number of Studio people were leaving for Los Angeles at 6:30 the next morning. At the door of Zanuck's suite, Ted Ashley shook hands with Jacobs.

"You've got yourself a picture, Arthur," Ashley said. "It's all up there on the screen."

"It'll work," Jacobs said. "Cut a few things, switch a few things."

"It's going to be great, Arthur," Rosenfield said. He patted Jacobs on the arm. "None of us has any doubts about that."

Zanuck's suite cleared by 1:30 in the morning. At 4 A.M. he called Harry Sokolov and told him to round up Hough, McLean and David Brown for a meeting in his room. They convened in Zanuck's suite at 4:45 A.M., and for the next hour Zanuck went over the picture reel by reel. Before the meeting broke up, shortly before six, it was tentatively agreed to cut the prologue. A decision was deferred on whether to cut any of the musical numbers. Arthur Jacobs was not present at this meeting.

1969

PAULINE

Some facts: A year or so ago I was asked to review Pauline Kael's *Raising Kane,* an arrogantly silly book that made me giggle and hoot as much as any I had ever read about Hollywood. But because I had a picture coming out later that year and because Ms. Kael is the film critic of the *New Yorker,* my worst instinct prevailed and I passed on the assignment. It was an ignoble thing to do, and thus when, shortly before the same picture was released, I was asked to review Ms. Kael's new book *Deeper into Movies,* I agreed, on the condition that I could review her entire oeuvre. A few weeks later, that picture opened in New York and Ms. Kael disliked it as thoroughly as I had *Raising Kane.* That, for those who wish to get off here, is the record.

In fact, I met Ms. Kael once and found her enormously engaging. It was at a party at my agent's house in New York on Academy Award night. She was perched in front of the television set, a tiny, birdlike woman in a Pucci knockdown and orthopedic shoes, giving the raspberry to each award. William Friedkin was a "corrupt director," Gene Hackman would be "ruined" by his Oscar. There was a refreshing directness about her. "Who are you?" she asked me. I told her. "I liked your book," she said. The book was called *The Studio,* and was a nonfiction account of a year in which I had the run of Twentieth Century-Fox. "Where's Joan?" she asked. "I want to meet her."

I was not wild about introducing Ms. Kael to my wife, Joan Didion. She had despised Joan's novel, *Play It as It Lays* (Wilfrid Sheed had reported her reading it aloud derisively on the beaches of Long Island), as she was later to despise the film made from the book, and Joan in turn had hammered Kael over the years, suggesting among other things "vocational guidance." They circled each other warily, Ms. Kael from the Napa Valley, my wife from the Sacramento Valley, and they hit upon their rhythm—Valley talk. They talked about ranches and pickups and whiskey on the floorboards and the Silverado Trail, two tough little numbers, each with the instincts of a mongoose and an amiable contempt for the other's work, putting on a good old girl number. It was a funny act to watch and I liked her.

I even liked talking to her about movies. In general, I like fewer films than she does, but arguing opinions about movies is like arguing about God, politics or sex, a stimulating but ultimately windy exercise. With that rather substantial caveat, I often find Kael enjoyable to read. She is as passionate about movies as anyone who has ever written about them, and it is from this passion that all her other virtues derive. She is funny, quirky, bright, encyclopedic, healthily mean-spirited, combative, malevolent, contentious and often right. She is also often ludicrous, and this too derives from that same passion. At times she seems less a critic than a den mother, swatting her favorites gently when they get out of line, lavishing them with attention, smothering them with superlatives for their successes. How was one to react to her contention that the opening of *Last Tango in Paris* was a cultural landmark comparable to the first performance of *Le Sacre du Printemps?* Such maternal excess scars her work, and worse. In her rhapsodies to the stylish and efficient potboilers of the young Coppola and the boyish Spielberg, her search for cosmology in the entertaining rubbish of *Jaws* and *The Godfathers*, Kael exhibits a passion so sexual in its underpinning that it becomes embarrassing.

If Kael looks better than she actually is, it is in no small part due to the quality of the competition. The nature of the film critic is to pump himself up. One critic's cant is another's Kant; the game is less one of taste than of ego and exhibitionism. It is exhibitionism, however, at a dispiriting level. One does not set out in life to become a movie critic; it is where one ends up. A truce is made with life, an armistice with ambition: it is far easier for the manqué litterateur to explain why he has not made a movie than why he has not written a book. Stanley Kauffmann, erstwhile actor, editor, playwright, drama critic, filmmaker, novelist—a Renaissance failure, as it were—is smarmy, Judith Crist unreadable, the news-magazine reviewers would-be screenwriters with an eye for the main chance. John Simon has limitless venom, but he sprays it around so indiscriminately that it becomes antitoxic and he rather sweet. And what can one say about a man who ruts after fame so promiscuously that he debated Jacqueline Susann on television and allowed himself to be interviewed for the woman's page of the *New York Times* as Daniel Ellsberg's wife's former boy friend? How perverted the lust for celebrity when one can portray oneself publicly as the Eddie Fisher of the Pentagon Papers.

Which leaves Kael. Reading her on film is like reading Lysenko on genetics—fascinating, unless you know something about genetics. The Rosetta Stone of her work is *Raising Kane,* which combines the Herman Mankiewicz-Orson Welles shooting script of *Citizen Kane* with a commentary by Kael on the making of the picture. *Raising Kane* reads as if it were not so much written as chattered in a movie queue by one of those film buffs who has seen everything and understood nothing. It is a pastiche of morgue clips, selective interviewing and gussied-up gossip speciously fobbed off as film erudition. It abounds in lists of old movies—*The Moon's Our Home* and *He Married His Wife* and *Easy Living* and *Midnight* and *Mississippi* and *Million Dollar Legs*—that seem dropped in only to impress the muddle-headed: if she has seen that many films she must be getting at something. The ploy belongs to the idiot savant, and recurs constantly in Kael's work; she needs only the faintest cue to swing into *She Done Him Wrong, I'm No Angel, Top Hat, Swing Time, The Lady Eve*—usually by way of showing them superior to the latest Fellini or Resnais.

Raising Kane is also suffused with that protocol of banality that flourishes west of Central Park—Hollywood the Destroyer. In the case of Herman Mankiewicz, it was not true; he flowered in Hollywood as he never had in New York. In the case of other writers, it is ridiculous. There is first of all the assumption that if these writers had not been working for Sam Goldwyn or Irving Thalberg they would have been writing *Moby Dick* or *Long Day's Journey into Night*. Then there were the writers who were not destroyed—Faulkner, Hellman, O'Hara, Behrman, West, Kaufman—writers who took the money and ran. The writers who fell apart in Hollywood would have fallen apart in Zabar's; the flaw was in them, not the community, but this is hard for the determinist movie critic to accept.

All this was by way of decorating Kael's thesis that Herman Mankiewicz was at least equally responsible with Welles for *Citizen Kane*. What seems to bother Kael is Welles's contention that "cinema is the work of one single person." There in a nutshell is the auteur theory, a theory that seems designed to inflate the already swollen vanity of film directors while enraging just about everyone else. Perhaps if the auteur theory were less Frenchified and more in the American grain, it might be more acceptable. The chairman of the board theory, say, or the senior partner theory. All it means is that someone is in charge, and that someone, that senior partner, is generally the director. I do not think that Kael would dispute the notion that there is not a page in the *New Yorker* that does not reflect the personality, taste and interests of its editor, William Shawn, even though he rarely writes a word that is in it. This, of course, is what Welles meant, as anyone who has ever worked on a film would understand. Unless one is courting disaster, the final choices must ultimately reside in the hands of one man. Read the script of *Citizen Kane* and see: ten directors could have shot it word for word; nine would have botched it, the tenth was a genius.

In her zeal to show Welles as a thief stealing credit from Mankiewicz, Kael has indulged in some highly suspect, not to say slovenly, reporting. As Peter Bogdanovich pointed out in *Esquire*, Kael simply ignored any indication that Welles had anything to do with the script of *Citizen Kane*, despite evidence that his participation was, to say the least, active. That is the way the Pentagon operates; the government has no monopoly on the selective truth.

But it is when Kael gets into the actual filming of *Kane* that she becomes particularly inane. "There's the scene of Welles eating in the newspaper office," she writes, "which was obviously caught by the camera crew, and which, to be a 'good sport,' he had to use." I thought I was hallucinating the first time I read that sentence, and now, every time I break it down and parse it, new questions arise. Where was the camera? Were Welles's meals usually lit? Was it his habit to dine in the middle of a setup? When did the crew have its own lunch break? Did the crew usually stand discreetly out of camera range and watch Welles gobble? Was Welles a noted "good sport"? Is Pauline Kael trying to tell us that *Citizen Kane* was cinema verité?

It is this implacable ignorance of the mechanics of filmmaking that prevails in all of Kael's books. Yet she is never called on it. The reason, of course, is that her audience knows even less of these mechanics than she does, and professional film people do not wish to incur her displeasure by calling attention to it. She seems to believe that films are made by a consortium of independent contractors—the writer writes, the cutter cuts, the actor acts, the cameraman photographs. In effect she is always blaming the cellist for the tuba solo. She cannot seem to get it through her skull that if Conrad Hall shoots that "fancy bleak cinematography" she so despises, it is because his director, Richard Brooks, wants it. To be sure, the error is not Kael's alone. Few critics understand the roles of chance, compromise, accident and contingency in the day-by-day of a picture. One prominent critic evoked Eric Rohmer when a scene in a picture on which I worked was filmed entirely as a reaction shot. The reason for the reaction shot was that we were behind schedule, the location had to be abandoned and the actor in the scene showed up too drunk to say his lines.

The entire process of directing eludes Kael. She perceives it as flashy "technique" and tricky "camera angles," which quite rightly she considers the last refuge of the charlatan. She understands what writers do, but she thinks they do it alone: she cannot seem to understand that good directors direct the writer the same way they direct the actors or the cameraman. Generally they pick their projects and hire their writers. I cannot imagine Kael sitting down with William Shawn after seeing a movie and discussing what they are going to say about it, but that is what a story conference is all about. When Kael talks about the screenplay of *Sunday, Bloody Sunday* being successful because scenarist Penelope Gilliatt kept her "self-respect as a writer," she's talking gibberish. If a writer is not in control in the story conference and behind the camera and in the cutting room, if there is another writer banging away on the set, as there was on *Sunday, Bloody Sunday,* "self-respect" is beside the point. Robert Benton and David Newman, the scenarists of *Bonnie and Clyde,* may, as Kael says, "be good enough to join that category of unmentionable men who do what directors are glorified for." That is a very nice compliment, but it does tend to glide over the really unmentionable Robert Towne, who rewrote *Bonnie and Clyde,* as well as the picture's producer, Warren Beatty, and director, Arthur Penn, who hired and guided him through the rewrite.

This insensitivity to the way movies are made eventually corrodes Kael's real virtues. "Coherence and wit and feeling" are what she most wants to see in a film. Almost alone among the major critics she sees "escapism" as a "function of art," and, "in terms of modern big city life and small town boredom, it may be a major factor in keeping us sane." Most invigoratingly, she has postulated a theory of movies as "trash art," an idea, considering the maniac economics of the movie business, that may be the only viable way to view the form. So far, so good. But with the years, Kael's crotchets have become rigidified. By temperament out of the Preston Sturges 1930's, she seems almost an exile in the sixties and seventies. Anomie, acidie and alienation are personally repellent to her. She often complains of pictures that make her feel "slugged and depressed," and bingo, we are into *Million Dollar Legs* again. She eviscerates Fellini, Resnais and Antonioni for their concern with the morally languid upper-middle class (that she liked *L'Avventura* seems almost an exercise in aberrant behavior). Part West Side radical, part populist Western xenophobe, she sniffs out fashionable "anti-Americanism" like a lady from the DAR, and God help the trendy foreigner or American living abroad (e.g., Richard Lester, who directed *Petulia*) who she thinks is spitting on the flag.

Kael makes rather casual use of the word fascist. Sam Peckinpah's *The Straw Dogs* is a "fascist work of art" and action pictures in general are "better suited to fascism . . . than to democracy." About *The Great Waldo Pepper,* she writes: "I can't tell if Americans will like this movie, but I think Hitler would have drunk a toast to it." This is sleazy, a crotchet that needs a biopsy, "fascism" used in the way Joe

McCarthy tossed around "Communism" a generation ago. "If thought corrupts language," George Orwell wrote, "language can also corrupt thought."

What seems eccentric or idiosyncratic in the course of one Kael review or even one Kael book finally becomes alarming over six books and some seven hundred reviews. She is fluent in the more evasive verb tenses, e.g., "M-G-M's lawyers *must have taken* a dim view of this. A smaller company . . . *might have encouraged* him." After a little of this fishiness, one begins to smell the taint in Kael's famous style, with all its spontaneity and populist energy. The style begins to seem, based as it is largely on parenthetical innuendo and cleverly buried qualifiers, less energetic and spontaneous than merely shifty, and quite calculated. When Kael tells us that "Jean Renoir is the only proof that it is possible to be great and sane in movies, and he hasn't worked often in recent years," we are meant to infer that Renoir's greatness and sanity render him unemployable. In fact, Renoir is almost eighty and an invalid. And when she tells us, about Sidney Lumet doing *The Group*, that "it's doubtful that he ever read any Mary McCarthy," we are meant to read "doubtful that he ever" as "certain that he'd never." Rich with subjunctives, slippery with "presumably's," it is a rancid technique; others less charitable than I might—to borrow a verb tense from the progenitrix—even call it dishonest.

And even I might go that far when it comes to Kael's creative viewing. In her review of *Jeremiah Johnson*, she wrote: "When the Crows, recognizing Jeremiah's courage, end their war against him, and the chief gives him the peace sign, Jeremiah signals him back, giving him the finger." Not in the print I saw he didn't—Robert Redford returned the peace signal—and when I checked with the director's office I was told that no scene was ever written or shot in which Jeremiah gave the Crow the finger. But the imaginary finger was necessary for Kael to make her point. "In that gesture," she wrote, "the moviemakers load him with guilt for what the white Americans have done to the Indians, and at the same time ask us to laugh at the gesture." *Jeremiah Johnson*, she concluded, seemed to have been made "by vultures." Perhaps it was only reviewed by one.

When language degenerates, what is it worth? Like the reporter who sits in the hotel bar and fashions energetic and colorful dispatches about street life in the far country, Kael counts on a reader who will accept her version as filed. Here a little fudging about the temple bells, there a description of the parrot bazaar too picturesque to pass up, never mind that the parrot bazaar is shuttered. Robert Redford giving the finger to the Crow, Orson Welles stealing a credit, who will ever know the difference? What is regrettable is that not too many of Pauline Kael's readers will, and what is more regrettable still is that Pauline Kael knows it.

1973

GONE HOLLYWOOD

I once heard a screenwriter accepting an Academy Award say, rather sententiously, "In the beginning was the Word." Actually the line is not accurate. Actually, in Hollywood, that line would go through a step outline, treatment, three drafts, polish, additional dialogue and an arbitration by the Writers Guild. Actually the line would come out, "In the beginning were the Writers."

In the beginning, my wife and I were the writers on

169

our last picture and remained so through three drafts, an arbitration, a threatened breach-of-contract suit and a sizable legal (read "cash") settlement for agreeing not to file that suit, which we never had any intentions of doing in the first place. As closely as I can figure, we were followed on the picture, officially and unofficially, by fourteen writers. The film is called *A Star Is Born* and stars Barbara Streisand and Kris Kristofferson, and I can pinpoint the exact moment when it was conceived. It was at one o'clock in the afternoon on the first day of July 1973, when I turned to my wife, while passing the Aloha Tower in downtown Honolulu on our way to the airport, and said sixteen words I would often later regret: "James Taylor and Carly Simon in a rock-and-roll version of *A Star Is Born*."

It was a project that had everything. (A project is a property with one "element," although not a "bankable" element. A bankable element is a star or a director, and once there is a bankable element, a project becomes a "go-project." A writer is a non-bankable element but is nonetheless essential, as the screenplay is the bait to land the fish, or the bankable element.) With two previous Oscar-nominated versions, *A Star Is Born* had "title identification" and a story so well known that its last line, "Hello, everyone, this is Mrs. Norman Maine," had passed into the repertoire of every gay cabaret act in the land. Furthermore, the prospects for a hit sound-track album were so great, according to the Warner Bros. music people, that anything the picture brought in would be gravy. And if the music people were higher on Carly Simon, whose career was soaring, than they were on James Taylor, whose career then was not, they at least gave us a line we could incorporate into the screenplay: "Don't worry about James if you don't use him, we can always find something for him to do, maybe a house in Malibu." In fact, the project had only one drawback, about which we kept a discreet silence: we had never seen *A Star Is Born* in any of its prior incarnations. Nor had we any intention of seeing *A Star Is Born,* or of reading the scripts, treatments, synopses or memorandums pertaining to any previous version. We were only interested in a movie about the rock-and-roll business, but the only way we could get a studio to underwrite the screenplay was to dress it up in what they perceived as an old but very well-cut suit of clothes. As long as there was a superficial resemblance to that classic story we had never seen, we would not be in breach of contract.

That there was an element of hustle in all of this is a given. Hustle is a basic ingredient of a screenwriter's life. Writing for the screen is not done in a vacuum but more or less at the whim of agents, stars, directors, producers, studio executives and the wives, husbands, lovers, mistresses and assorted rough trade of all the above. "The screenplay is written by a salaried writer under the supervision of a producer," Raymond Chandler once wrote, "by an employee without power or decision over the uses of his craft, without ownership of it, and however extravagantly paid, almost without honor for it." It is useful to remember here that most producers used to be agents and theirs is a world that has only one frame of critical reference: "piece of shit." The highest praise this world can bestow on a screenplay is, "It's not your run-of-the-mill piece of shit," which usually means that McQueen is reading it, at which point it either becomes a go-project or reverts back to just another piece of shit.

This basically excremental view of screenwriting sets the tone for the studios' financial dealings with writers. The business-affairs lawyers who make a studio's deals have all the ethics and charm of Meyer Lansky or Abbadabba Berman, the man who fixed the numbers racket and who was usually described as the Mob's "strange genius." It thus behooves a writer to have a banker's familiarity with such niceties of deal making as cutoffs and conversions and change-of-elements ("the worst clause in this business," my agent says) and pari passu and the most-favored-nation clause and gross players and cross-collateralization and definition and first position and point reduction and abatement and rolling break. ("You can chase rolling break around the world and never see it," was another piece of wisdom imparted by my agent, making it sound like the perfect wave.) These are all points designed to deprive the writer legally of what his contract otherwise stipulates he is getting. The general view is that screenwriters are overpaid, but at least half of what they ask for they will see only under conditions so arcane as to relegate full payment to cloud-cuckooland.

Part of what a writer gets paid for is not to remind a "pay-or-play" star or director (pay-or-play means the element gets paid whether the go-project goes or not) that he was the only one there when the pages were blank. The moment when the star and the director begin to talk about "my film" and "my concept," the writer is on his way out the door. He becomes an embarrassment to these conceptualizers; his presence casts a pall over "their" film. A number of pay-or-play elements have their won security-blanket rewriters, who come in without credit to restitch the last sequence on *The Missouri Breaks* or pull together *The Marathon Man,* punch up *The Bad News Bears* or hold Robert Redford's hand on *All the President's Men*. This is how movies are written. It is a business, and for every writer who doesn't like it, there are a thousand ready to take his place.

If in Hollywood the screenwriter is viewed as an overpaid purveyor of ordure, in other precincts he is labeled as Gone Hollywood. I have never been quite clear what Going Hollywood meant exactly, except that as a unique selling proposition it's a lot sexier than Going University of Iowa Writers' Workshop. There is something wonderfully Calvinistic about the concept, especially as it is most firmly held by those most insane to Go—the dreary cineasts who spend every waking hour in a darkened theater, emerging only to write about The Film in a language said to be

172

English. They bewail the fact that Hollywood is a business run by businessmen for a profit (an *aperTcu* akin to discovering that the Pacific is an ocean), yet for all their *ars gratia artis*-prop, every mail brings their scripts and treatments to some despised mogul's desk. The ecology of Hollywood eludes them. It never seems to occur to these film buffs that the wretched De Laurentiis *Mandingo* pays for the De Laurentiis Altman, that the Irwin Allen disaster epic underwrites the small Paul Mazursky film.

No one, however, makes us write movies. We do it because we like the action, even playing against a heavy deck, and because writing screenplays, especially before the pay-or-play money becomes oppressive, is a lot of fun. The possibilities are infinite; it is only the probabilities that are finite. We started *A Star Is Born* by going on the road with rock groups, three weeks of one-night stands in the armpit auditoria and cities of the land. The trip was a blur. In Chicago a groupie talked about mainlining adrenaline. "It only makes you scared," she said, "for twenty minutes." In a dressing room in Cleveland, one of the Led Zeppelin had penciled on the wall, "Call KL5-2033 for good head." I called KL5-2033 (no other identification given) and KL5-2033 asked my room number at the Hollenden House, any friend of the Zeppelin was a friend of hers. In a motel in Johnstown, Pennsylvania, I spent the better part of an afternoon listening to Uriah Heep's bass player debate the pros and cons of a fretless neck on a Gibson; I was in Buffalo before I learned that a Gibson was a guitar. From Buffalo, the itinerary to Allentown, Pennsylvania, involved two Allegheny flights and a three-hour layover in Pittsburgh. The producer didn't like any of the above elements, so we are perhaps the only people in the world ever to take a Cadillac limousine from Buffalo to Allentown, total cost $435, with a chauffeur who looked as if he had been the wheelman on most of the important Mafia hits in upstate New York. He wore a black chauffeur suit with red piping, red, white and

173

blue high-heel clogs, and stuck in his waistband was the kind of .357 magnum cannon that Clint Eastwood used in *Dirty Harry*.

The first draft of *A Star Is Born* included in one way or another all these people, and it took six months to write. It took one more draft and another six months to make us thoroughly sick of the project. I recall the second six months only as an endless argument, carried on over commissary lunches and studio meetings, usually about who the pay-or-play elements should be. I could never understand why our opinions were so desperately sought, since we had only to voice them to have them ignored. Our first choice to direct was Warren Beatty, whom the studio did not see as a director, our second Mike Nichols, whom the studio did not see as a director on this picture, and after that we kept our mouths shut. Our agents sent the script to Peter Bogdanovich, for which transgression we fired them; his opinion of the script matched ours of his pictures. A director finally came aboard, but as he was going through a messy divorce and as he was trying to put his mother into a tax-shelter condominium in Florida and as he was interviewing UCLA housekeepers who didn't wear brassieres and as he had a number of other projects in various stages of development, his time was fragmented. When the studio would not make him pay-or-play, he left. *A Star Is Born* was becoming a career, and we asked our lawyer to get us out.

Enter Barbra Streisand. We had met her several years before at a dinner party given by her agent, Sue Mengers. When we were introduced, she had said, "Hello," and then without pausing for breath, "What do you think of fidelity in marriage?" The question apparently had a point, for some months later we were asked to write a picture for her on marital infidelity. We didn't, but here she was again, with the muscle to move out the original producer and replace him with her lover, Jon Peters. Venality forced us to reconsider our intention to quit; with Barbra Streisand involved, we knew we weren't going to get poor.

Our relationship with Streisand and Peters was extremely cordial. We drank a lot of wine and blew a few cools and our daughter played with Barbra's son. I wasn't crazy about their playing in the cage with the pet lion cub, but I figured what the hell, this was Hollywood. We also saw *A Star Is Born* for the first time. But Barbra was working on another picture and when it was finished she wanted to take a long vacation. We were also hearing talk about "my film" and "my concept." Barbra and Jon saw the picture as being about their own somewhat turbulent love affair, which didn't leave much room for existential ironies. She also thought the man had the better part, which was true. As her company was now financing the picture, it began to look like a long summer. Two weeks after Barbra Streisand came in, we again asked our lawyer for an out.

Enter Catch-22. We couldn't just quit, because we then would have been in breach of contract and lost our "points," or percentage of the profits and we regarded those points as our combat pay, our veterans' benefits. Nor could we be fired, because then we would have left with our points intact, and the business people would have none of that. They wanted us to give some of our points back, which we refused to do until it was stipulated that we could leave without being in breach. It took eight weeks to negotiate this point, eight weeks during which we wrote a third draft, although we were not in contact, on advice of our lawyer, with anyone actually involved in the making of the film. Finally, almost fifteen months to the day after I uttered those sixteen words while passing the Aloha Tower in downtown Honolulu, a settlement was signed and we were out of *A Star Is Born*.

This story has a postscript. A year, ten writers and another legal action after we left *A Star Is Born*, the president of Warner Bros. asked our agent if we would consider returning to repair the damage. The price discussed for four weeks was the same as our original fee for fifteen months. For two heady days we paid off our mortgage, priced a Mercedes and laid away our daughter's tuition to Radcliffe. Then we said no. We never knew how firm the offer was, but in any case *A Star Is Born* was a part of our life that was over and going back would have served no purpose. Now, a year after that, we are back in the movie business again, this time with an original story. The other day I told it to a producer friend. "That," he said, "is not a piece of shit."

1976

STUNTS

WIDE SHOT—STUDIO GATE

The peppermint-striped wooden barrier drops down just as the yellow Morgan starts through. It does so just in time to miss the windshield, but it catches MEL, MARTY *and* DOM's *waving arms as they drive through.* MEL, MARTY *and* DOM *hang from the suspended barrier as the driverless car continues on into the studio.*

A simple shot. Involving, in the jargon of the trade, a "jerk-off." Quite literally, MEL, MARTY and DOM will be "jerked" from the yellow Morgan as the wooden barrier theoretically "hits" them, jerked by three thick cables strung from a three-ton crane high above the shot, out of camera range. MEL, MARTY and DOM are Mel Brooks, Marty Feldman and Dom DeLuise, but MEL, MARTY and DOM will not be jerked off. They are too expensive, too valuable, impossible to replace in this second week of shooting on Mel Brooks's new $6-million comedy, *Silent Movie*. MEL, MARTY and DOM will do the approach shots, the close-ups and the reaction shots, but the actual jerk-off will be performed by three stunt doubles.

At the gate location for *Silent Movie* there was that sense of chaotic tedium endemic to movie sets. A sizzling January sun baked the crew as it set up the shot. Dress extras played gin rummy and backgammon and read the trades. Printed T-shirts seemed the uniform of the day: an art deco "Chicago Exposition—1933," a macho "VD Hot Line—623-8143" and the burgundy-colored soother worn by the writer, star, director and resident genius of the picture, "Hi, I'm Mel. Trust me."

Max Kleven was not wearing a "Trust me" T-shirt. A tall, slender Norwegian, forty-two years old, twenty-two years a stunt man, Kleven was *Silent Movie*'s stunt coordinator and second unit director, the man who "gaffed," or set up, the stunts, picked the stunt men, and who would, in the event of injury, step in for stunt retakes. Kleven invariably refers to stunts, no matter how dangerous, as "gags." As stunt coordinator, he stands by the camera during the shot. "If you're in the shot," he says, "you can't tell if it's a good gag or not."

The three men Kleven had picked for stunt doubles—Billy Shannon, Jimmy Shepherd and Orwin Harvey (who would double, respectively, for MEL, MARTY and DOM)—were selected not only for their abilities as stunt men but also because with a hairpiece here and a putty nose or chin there, each would pass for his star in that fleeting instant before a wide-angle long shot of a stunt became a close-up of a principal. All four had long experience in falling down hard: Kleven was a competitive ski jumper before becoming a stunt man, Harvey a circus high diver and Shannon and Shepherd were both on the rodeo circuit. Because the film is silent, and therefore dependent on rough-house visuals, Kleven had hired his three stunt doubles for the picture's entire fifteen-week shooting schedule. "They're here for the duration," Kleven said. "But the duration is a day-to-day thing. If they get hurt . . ." He shrugged. "But you're only hurt if you break something. If it's a bruise, a Jacuzzi will fix you up."

As they waited for the take, the three stunt men went over the yellow Morgan carefully, looking for obstructions that might impede their hasty exit from the tiny car, ordering the removal of a protruding elbow rest in the back seat. The back of each man's costume was slit open to expose the harness to which the cables from the crane were attached. To cushion the fall, each stunt man had devised his own layer of protective padding—jockstrap and cup, hip and thigh pads, rib pads, a foam-rubber corset, shoulder pads. Finally, an extra-thick elbow pad for the "quitting arm," the arm that each man would throw out of the yellow Morgan to break his fall when he landed.

At last the shot was ready. The three stunt men jammed themselves into the Morgan, which had a license plate that read FUNN. Over a bullhorn, the assistant director shouted, "You guys should be waving and smiling at the guard before the gate hits you." As the cable was attached to his harness, Shepherd smiled wanly and said, "I don't know why I'm nervous, I've already got the job." One of the crew laughed. "You mean, 'Who do I have to fuck to get off this picture.' "

The set quieted. Brooks called, "Action." The Morgan wheeled toward the barrier. The cables jerked. All three stunt men went flying from the car, Shannon and Shepherd hit the asphalt and bounced up quickly. Not Harvey. He lay on the ground for a moment and then groggily got to his feet. He was a large, heavyset man and he had been crammed down too deep in the little car. The cable had yanked him wrong and he had landed on his back and cracked his head on the pavement. A lump the size of an egg was forming on the top of his skull. A studio nurse put an ice pack on it. He checked his teeth, worked his jaw, tried to move his back around. Cast and crew were solicitous for a moment, then seemed to ignore him. It reminded me of that moment after an injury on a football field: run the next play, pretend it didn't happen. Harvey was through for the day.

In his portable dressing room, Kleven padded up to replace Harvey in the next take. He added one piece of equipment Harvey had neglected—a protective skullcap inside his hat. "It's one of those days," Kleven said. "The shot's important, but you're important, too." Finally ready, he walked over to the Morgan. He checked the angle of his fall, kicked some pebbles out of the way, made sure the three cables weren't crossed. He got into the car. "I'm going to be sitting so light in here," he said, "a butterfly could knock me out." Again the camera rolled, the cables jerked, the stunt men went flying. All three were on their feet immediately. "Print it," Mel Brooks said. "That was swell. Anyone dead?"

There were no further stunts scheduled for the day. Back in the dressing room, Kleven peeled off his padding. I have written a number of pictures, but usually when the stunt men were doing their stuff, I was off typing in a hotel. This was the first time I realized how dangerous their work is. Falling off a burning oil derrick, crashing a diesel rig, fighting on top of a snow-covered moving train—this was the nine-to-five routine of a stunt man's life. Everything was timing, measuring, anticipation. Play the gag, don't let the gag play you. "It's a hiring-your-body kind of job," Max Kleven said. "There's not that much finesse to it. You just have to fall right."

Kleven was eighteen when he came to the U.S. from Norway. "I worked to get out," he said. "I wanted to come to a place where things were easier." A skier since the age of four, he jumped competitively and perfected his English. A ski jump in a television beer commercial was his entrée into stunt work. The jump was performed in the heat of summer with straw serving as snow; it gave Kleven an SAG card (all stunt men are members of the Screen Actors Guild) and film to show to stunt coordinators.

The time was the early fifties, when the cowboy was the king of television and a talent for falling off a horse was in great demand. It is a talent best perfected in a sandy riverbed with a veteran stunt man as an instructor. "I don't recommend a couple of kids going out and falling off horses," Kleven says. "Someone is going to get hurt."

The basic implement in falling off a horse professionally is an L-shaped iron bar, called a step, which replaces the off-camera stirrup. The step enables the stunt man to push off the horse without getting his foot caught in the stirrup. With time, the step, endless practice and a lot of nerve, Kleven learned the basic "saddle fall," the "header" (a push-off and roll forward), and the "horse fall" (horse and rider both going down on cue). The toughest of all was the "fall and drag," where the stunt man does a saddle fall and then is dragged by a rig attached from the step to his leg until he hits a quick-release button.

Horse work led to "high work" (falling from great heights—a cliff or a window) and ultimately to "car work." At six feet two, Kleven is the perfect height for a stunt man. "I can double from six feet to six four," he says. "I don't know how some of the little guys make a living. There's not that many small stars, so they only get the nondescript gags." From cheap television series like *Rin Tin Tin* and *Rescue 8*, Kleven progressed to *Naked City* and finally to features: *The Anderson Tapes, Hard Times, Rollerball*. The stunt man became a stunt coordinator and then a second unit director, designing and directing the more complicated and time-consuming stunts after the stars had completed their close-ups.

Kleven's bible is *The Stuntman Book*. It contains eight-by-ten glossies of all two hundred full-time stunt men and women, plus a list of available equipment owned by stunt people for lease to film companies. The equipment ranges from airplanes and camera-mounted motorcycles to fire suits, high-fall pads, "seventeen jerk-off vests with all necessary traps," and "breakaway tongues for wrecking any type of horse-drawn vehicle." The book also has a minimum price list for "stunts performed under the best of conditions": a car turnover—$600; a wagon wreck—$600; fall from a bucking horse—$300; rearing a horse—$172.50; high falls—$12 per foot up to thirty feet. The stunt man is paid for every take, unless he is responsible for ruining the shot; then he gives a free stunt. And for each frill or refinement on a stunt, he negotiates a higher price on the spot. "You do a horse fall in Central Park, it's going to cost more than out here," Kleven says. "There's not that many cowboys in New York City."

Kleven is interested in appearing in hit pictures. One of his most dangerous stunts was driving an explosive-triggered Cadillac off a pier at eighty mph, bailing into a trail car and out of camera range just as the Cadillac shot over the end of the pier and blew up. "It was a terrific gag, but it was a lousy movie and no one ever saw it. That's the trouble. You can do your best gags in pictures that are down the toilet. I'm like everyone else. I want to do hits. I want my work seen."

I wanted to ask him if he was ever afraid, but I didn't. Fear seemed such a given that it was an irrelevant question. In effect, what a stunt man does for a living is not so much drive a dynamite-laden car off a dock as keep fear in check. There are less noble ways to face a day. And so instead I asked him if he had ever broken anything. He looked at me a long time before he answered. "Yeah, I broke something, but I don't want to talk about it," Max Kleven said.

"There's some guys who sit around and do nothing but talk about the bones they broke. I'm not into that Evel Knievel shit. I'm here twenty-two years later and everything is functioning and that's my claim to fame."

1976

TINSEL

The only time I ever met Joseph E. Levine he told me it was snowing in Russia and then left the room. It did not occur to me to mention that it was also snowing outside on Sixth Avenue, because one had the sense that Levine was perhaps the only man in the world not a general to whom snow in Russia was a matter of life or death. I never asked any of his subalterns the significance of the Soviet snow; one became used to cryptic utterance in the Levine organization. "You're hot now," one of his supernumeraries told my wife and me when we checked into Levine's offices to write a screenplay, "but in six months the bloom will be off the rose."

We were shooting. We were behind schedule. We were over budget. Nearly a quarter of a million dollars over budget. The studio was furious. They had held up our final screenplay payment and were threatening to take away our points, or percentage of the profits. We were speaking through lawyers. Studio bookkeepers and accountants combed the books. Talk of injunction was in the air, a showdown meeting arranged.

The studio vice-president wore blue suede Gucci loafers and a white suit with a belt in the back. he was surrounded by his accountants. He liked to scream. He screamed that we were amateurs. He screamed that only an amateur would rent a house at the beach for $1,000 a day just to shoot its exterior.

It was a puzzling assertion. In fact the producer had made a good deal for the house, renting it, for both interiors and exteriors, for an entire week at only $1,250.

"A thousand dollars a day," the vice-president screamed insistently.

"Who told you that?"

"William."

"Who is William?"

The accountants began to shift uneasily.

"My wife's hairdresser," the vice-president said.

Writing films is a good deal like writing for *Time* magazine, except that the pay is better. The film writer is first of all *hired,* and as an employee, no matter how grandiose his salary, he must tailor his ideas to those of his employer. He can wheedle, cajole, or even scream, but if he fails to persuade his employer, he either goes along or gets out. If he gets out, he is easily replaced. On a recent Barbra Streisand picture, there was one credited writer, but five others, including two Academy Award winners, worked on the screenplay. Now these six people didn't meet at lunch one day and decide to make a film, you do the plot, you do the humor, you do the flashbacks, and I'll do the polish. They were all hired, their brains picked by the producer and the director, and then discarded. In the wisdom of the Writers Guild, one of these six received a solo credit, but the fingerprints of the other five are smudged all over the finished film.

*   *   *

The first film script I wrote, in the summer of 1964, was called *Show Me a Hero,* as in Scott Fitzgerald's "Show me a hero and I will write you a tragedy." It was a measure of the script's worth that neither was it a tragedy nor was the protagonist a hero; she was a heroine. The subject of the yarn—it could not properly be called anything else—was topical: a woman who had become a national figure because of her undying love and loyalty to a husband withering away in a Communist prison on a trumped-up charge of espionage. A reporter from a magazine called *Tempo* (I had once worked for *Time* and written for *Life*) is sent to find out what makes this symbol of the good, the true and the beautiful rise above the nation's prevailing moral inertia. (Remember, this was years before the POW wives and Mrs. Commander Lloyd Bucher.) Things are not what they seem. The heroine is a pawn in a right-wing plot. The heroine moreover is living a lie; she never loved her husband. And the husband indeed was a spy, a task he undertook when he discovered that the heroine did not love him. (Not only was he a spy, it turns out, but a setup deliberately blown by his superiors so that a prisoner exchange could be effected with his Communist captors, exchanging him for a famous Red agent who had agreed to double for the CIA behind the Iron Curtain; the famous Red agent, however, had undergone a change of heart and hung himself in his American prison cell rather than turn traitor. This was a subplot.) The young reporter, sickened by these revelations, declares his love *in camera* to the heroine. The heroine reciprocates carnally in a midwinter tryst in either a cottage on Fire Island or a suite at the Radisson Hotel in Minneapolis, a plot point to be worked out later. The military-industrial complex uncovers the illicit romance. The heroine declares herself sick of sham and says she will publicly avow her love for the young reporter. The inhabitant of the Oval Office indicates with all the wisdom of his years that such an avowal of infidelity would be a source of great disillusion to what, in 1964, was not yet known as the Silent Majority. At precisely that moment, the heroine's husband is released from his Communist hell. Love or Duty, which will the heroine choose?

The young reporter says, "I love you, Marjorie," for that is the heroine's name.

And the heroine says, "Oh, Joe," for that is the young reporter's name.

And we fade out before the Great Decision.

My agents were ecstatic when they read the script. A love story by a neophyte writer. What "neophyte" meant in this context was that I had never written a script, which in turn meant that I could be sold for short money and no points, which in turn meant that as the story costs were not top-heavy, a package might be put together with a heavyweight actress/actor/director, which in turn meant that I would be shuffled right off to Buffalo. (I was not as wise in the summer of 1964 as I am in the summer of 1974, but that is what neophyte meant then and that is what neophyte means now.) All the script needed, my agents said, was a few changes and would I come to town to discuss them. Has anyone ever been so young that his heart skipped a beat at the prospect of a script conference with a roomful of William Morris agents? I was, that summer.

There were seven agents crowded in the office, all very short. The meeting was chaired by a henna-haired woman who, after making sure that I was comfortable, assured me that the purpose of the meeting was "constructive criticism."

"Constructive criticism," chorused the other six agents.

"Does anyone have any constructive criticism?" asked the chairperson.

Silence.

"I'm sure someone has some constructive criticism," said the chairperson.

One of the shorter agents raised his hand. "I hope

you don't take this amiss," he said to me, "because we all know what we're here for is constructive criticism."

Again the chorus: "Constructive criticism."

"Constructive criticism," I said. Was the heroine too unsympathetic? Was the young reporter too shallow? Or too young?

"Right," said the agent. "Now I'd just like to ask you one thing, uh, and I hope you won't take this personally, it's just constructive criticism, but when you retype the script, I'd like you to make the margins a little wider, if you know what I mean."

I was not sure I did.

"Leave a lot more white space on the page," he added.

There was general nodding around the room. "A good point," the chairperson said.

"White space," I said.

"White space," the agent said.

"That's constructive," the chairperson said.

The best time to do a picture, if you are a part-time screenwriter, is when you don't need the money. Then you are working because you like either the project or the people (or perhaps both), and your own vanity becomes fused with the vanity fair of the movie business. With luck, the picture might turn out to be pretty good; at worst, you've had a lot of laughs.

Technique is easily learned. I sat through three consecutive showings of *Seven Days in May* at a second-run drive-in in Long Beach to count the number of sequences that made up a well-crafted movie. (As I remember, there were forty.) But most instructive of all is seeing the bad movies of good directors. Truffaut's *Fahrenheit 451*, Antonioni's *Red Desert*, Peckinpah's *Major Dundee*, Penn's *The Chase*—in each there is a moment or sequence that stands out in such bold relief from the surrounding debris as to make the reasons for its effectiveness clear.

Surveying the architecture of even the most mendacious film can be exhilarating. Norman Mailer caught this feeling exactly in *The Deer Park* when the director, Charles Eitel, finds himself absorbed in a meretricious screen story retailed by the producer, Carlyle Munshin: "The professional in Eitel lusted for the new story . . . it was so beautifully false. Professional blood thrived on what was excellently dishonest."

Keep scenes short. A brothel is a good place for exposition, as is an assembly line or a baton-twirling contest for drum majorettes. In a quieter genre, when two people are talking, have one of them shaving or going to the bathroom or having his ears pierced. A radio dropped in a bathtub is a good way to kill someone and a waffle iron in the face makes a nice visual pattern. Don't forget props: studios call it characterization when an actor is plugged into a menthol inhalator or picks his teeth with a .38 or swabs his ear with a Q-tip.

"He used to be a writer," the agent said of his client, the producer. "Now he's a creator."

It took my wife and me three years and $2,000 to get our first picture made. It was based on a book called *The Panic in Needle Park* by James Mills and was about two heroin addicts on the streets of New York. We got involved in *Needle Park* because no one was asking us to do any film work. Both my wife and I liked the book and we brought it to my brother, who is a film producer. Between the three of us, we scraped up $1,000 for a year's option against a final purchase price of $17,500 and 5 percent of net profits. It was a year before we finally found time to write a treatment, or dramatic breakdown. By that time, the initial option was up and we had to ante up another $1,000 to hold the book for a second year.

We now had $2,000 of our own money invested in the project and no prospects for laying it off on a studio. Our agents were not sanguine; the story was "too downbeat." They suggested packaging it with Henry Fonda; we suggested that Fonda was perhaps forty years too old for the lead, and countered with Peter Fonda. They said that Peter Fonda was not package-able. Then they suggested writing the whole experience off as a tax loss. Studio after studio turned us down. Then our agents showed the treatment to the Levine organization, and to everyone's surprise, Levine bought it. Months later, we learned why. "Joe never reads anything," one of his executives told us. "You've got to sell him with one line."

We asked what our one line was.

" 'Romeo and Juliet on junk.' "

It was from the Levine experience that we learned the importance of guile in writing screenplays. "Romeo and Juliet on junk" was heavy freight, heavier still after we flew to New York and checked into a junkie hotel on the West Side. The roaches in the hotel were the size of gunboats, and neither the sheets nor the towels were changed until we went to Bloomingdale's and bought some of our own. A friend put us in touch with a pusher who dealt marijuana and cocaine to the various movie companies filming in New York. He was a sixteen-year-old high school student with braces on his teeth; his brother was a dealer and his mother an addict and he was the compleat entrepreneur, also dealing heroin from a grocery bike he pedaled around the neighborhood; all his dope was taped to the bottom of the basket on the bicycle.

He introduced us to his customers and for the next

several weeks we spent day and night with junkies. We plied them with Hostess Twinkies and they shot up in our room and importuned us for money. Mills's heroine was a lesbian-call-girl-turned-junkie, but during these sessions we found an addict more in keeping with the studio's sensibilities: junkie and hooker Levine would go along with, but lesbian he wasn't into.

It was not exactly the Montagues and the Capulets, but we were stuck with making it seem so. Our solution was to write in a voice-over the action in which one protagonist or the other would talk about a-heroin-kind-of-love. We never had any intention of recording the voice-over, but it did give Levine's people something they could read to Joe. In one sentence.

Another trick. Studio executives are notoriously literal-minded, and the easiest way to soothe them when they complain about the mood of a scene is simply to add a stage direction. Thus, if they maintain that:

BOBBY
You dumb bitch

is too grim, you change the line to:

BOBBY
(Engagingly)
You dumb bitch

The man in charge of Levine's West Coast office was a former agent who had doffed his agent's black suit for executive suede. (This was during the buck-skin-and-fringe period of Hollywood executive life when every studio vice-president looked like Buffalo Bill in tinted glasses.) He had the corner office and the right barber, but he felt a little exposed, in large part because his counterparts in New York were three thousand miles closer than he was to Levine's ear. "Nice guy, smart as a whip," he would say of his Eastern alter ego, "don't trust him." In the middle of a meeting he would often interrupt to ask the names of the more important captains in the better restaurants, and he was an inveterate Gucci-checker and lapel-measurer. Not that he was without self-confidence. "When I go on a set," he liked to say, "things happen."

A screenwriter I know was doing a racing picture. "I didn't know you were interested in auto racing," I said.

"I'm not," he said. "Bores me stiff."

"Then how do you handle the racing scenes?"

"With the magic stage direction," he said. " 'SEQUENCE TO BE STAGED BY DIRECTOR.' "

Festival fortnight in Cannes. The atmosphere was less film festival than agricultural fair. There were stalls for Scandinavian pornography in the lobby of the Carlton and slide shows explaining the merits of international co-production. The exhibits were run by thick-waisted men who looked like the proprietors of Middle-European Harvester franchises. The conversation was of negative pickup and cross-collateralization, of renting the Yugoslavian army and bribing the Guardia Civil. The lobbies were rich with rumor: Joseph Losey was not speaking to Luchino Visconti. Erich Segal was feuding with Sergio Leone. Buck Henry had seen seven pictures in one day. Jacqueline Susann had met Picasso.

We were staying at the Carlton. It was easy to fall into the pattern. The hall porter brought endless bottles of Chateau d'Yquem, a studio publicity man handed out crisp, new hundred-franc notes as petty cash, every night there was dinner for six, eight, twelve at La Reserve: it all went on the budget of the picture. We reread *Tender Is the Night*. From the balcony of our suite, we could look down on the

Croisette and beyond, past the "bright tan prayer rug of a beach" to Sam Spiegel's yacht bobbing on the Mediterranean. Scott and Zelda, Dick and Nicole Diver, Gerald and Sara Murphy. Abe North. Tommy Barban. Rosemary Hoyt. It would make a great picture; living well *was* the best revenge.

Back in Los Angeles, our agent had already set the ball rolling. *Tender Is the Night* was available; Fox held the remake rights and no additional payments had to be made to the Fitzgerald estate. We would, as the agents say, "take a meeting."

The vice-president in charge of production met us in his office. He had not, he said, read the "basic material," but the story department had pulled out a synopsis made in 1945. He showed us the synopsis: five pages, single-spaced. A few lines caught my eye: "On their way to Paris, Dick and Nicole and Abe and Rosemary visit the trenches of a World War I battlefield. Later, waiting for a train, an orchestra breaks into 'Yes, We Have No Bananas.' "

I handed the synopsis back to the vice-president in charge of production.

"I would gather," he said carefully, "that what interests you about this property is the glamour and glitter of the Edwardian age."

We never wrote the picture.

Film festival wardrobe: faded Levi's, tie-dyed T-shirt, torn bush coat, paint-spattered tennis sneakers, and a velvet dinner jacket.

There are writers in Hollywood with the reputation of being a "good meeting," as in "Irving is a fantastic meeting." A good meeting thinks fast on his feet, can argue forcibly that the sun rises in the east, and even more forcibly that it rises in the west if that is the way the studio sees it. He is an interpreter of silences and a reader of eyebrow movement, a master of options, strategic withdrawals, and tactical advances. And he has a fund of good gossip to bridge that awkward moment when he deposits the blame for one of his bad ideas on someone else's doorstep.

I am a terrible meeting. During the conferences on *Tender Is the Night*, the vice-president in charge of production asked how we planned to deal with the ending. We would not take Dick Diver to upstate New York as Fitzgerald did, my wife said. Instead we would end the picture with the penultimate scene in the novel: Dick blessing the Riviera beach with the papal cross as he prepared to leave France.

This was not exactly what the vice-president in charge of production had in mind. Couldn't "the two young people"—he could never remember the Divers' name from the synopsis, so always referred to them as "the two young people"—get back together?

It would seem, I said, to defeat the point of the book.

"That might be so," he said. "But your audience today would like to see these two young people get back together. Your audience today likes your up ending."

I made an attempt to be a good meeting. "But Ali MacGraw," I found myself saying, "died at the end of *Love Story*."

Nicole Diver, meet Jenny Cavalleri.

The producer had a mechanical joint roller because he could never get the hang of building his own. He poured the grass evenly, fiddled with the roller, and presto! a joint that looked like a Camel. He took a man-sized hit. "The day I got busted for dope," he said, "was the day I left the Republican Party and the Catholic Church."

The story conference is to screenwriting what crab grass is to the lawn. It encourages the most spurious sense of collaboration: if it allows the producer to feel "creative," it makes the writer ever more aware that he is an employee. Everyone involved feels impelled to pump significance into the most banal bloodletter; rarely this side of academe does one hear more about "illusion versus reality" than one does in a story conference, usually in a story conference about a western. Every sentence tends to begin with "What if . . ." as in "What if the young doctor blows up the boat?"

"As an existential act?"

"Right."

"The illusion-versus-reality-type-thing?"

"Right on."

"But his wife's in the boat."

"What if he only thought she was?"

"There's your illusion versus reality again."

In an effort to cut the losses, we have generally tried to hold story conferences at home. We live fifty miles up the coast from town, and the very length of the ride along the Pacific can turn what began as a meeting into an adventure. And always there is lunch, the same story-conference lunch: a cold leek soup, antipasto, baguettes of French bread, fruit, Brie, and white wine. The lunch is programmed to reinforce the notion that the turf is ours, and that it would be bad form for a guest to push aberrant ideas; we are no longer employees, but host and hostess. Sometimes it works.

The producer was showing me around his lavishly appointed office. His shelves were stocked with pre-Columbian artifacts and there were two Picasso etchings on the walls. "Here's a Miro," he said, adding helpfully "M-I-R-O."

Once you accept the idea that says because you get paid $200,000 to write a script and the director gets $500,000 to direct it, he's $300,000 smarter than you are, then Hollywood becomes a very amusing place to work.

*   *   *

"You're a Mel," a producer told a screenwriter friend of mine. The statement perplexed my friend, whose name was not Mel. "Screenwriters are all named Mel," the producer explained. "Mel Frank. Mel Shavelson. Mel Panama . . ."

"*Norman* Panama," my friend interrupted.

"He's still a Mel," the producer said. "Producers are named Marty. In this town, the Martys hire the Mels."

The screenwriter was bearish on the box-office prospects of his new film. I mentioned the director's considerable following on college campuses, but the writer was unimpressed. "Straight to cult," he said of the new picture. "It'll be a hit at Bloomingdale's."

At least twice a year I am asked to prepare an obituary on the death of Hollywood. I am always a veritable Old Testament of parables that no one outside of Hollywood seems to understand, all of them attesting to the ealth of the industry. There is my Marty Erlichman parable. Marty Erlichman is Barbra Streisand's manager. At the opening of a blockbuster hit I had a hand in writing for his client, Erlichman kept staring at me, as if trying to place the face. Suddenly he snapped his fingers and said, "You must be someone's manager." The point being that when times are flush, the manager's ultimate accolade is to think that someone who looks interesting must also be a manager, like himself.

Then there is my Phil Feldman parable. Phil Feldman is the president of a film company from whom I tried to promote a free trip to New York. I had written a picture for his company, the picture was a hit and I figured why not, I'm entitled. Two, three, five weeks went by and he never answered my "Dear Mr. Feldman" letter. So I decided to write him another:

Dear Phil,

I was immensely warmed and cheered by your letter. It really made us both chuckle.

I mentioned the proposal to our agents and they said it was definitely an option worth considering.

Mazel.

John

Two days later I got a call from Feldman's office. The boss was on a rampage. He could not find the file copy of the letter he had never written me and now he had forgotten which proposal he had never made which I was allegedly discussing with my agents. If it were a new proposal, he did not want me to take it to Paramount. I explained that it was a joke, that he had never written a letter (that being the point of the exercise), but that I knew there were three words that would always make a movie executive's palms twitch: "proposal," "agents" and "option."

When I offered these parables to the last editor who had asked me to write of Hollywood's death rattle, he could not see the lesson, remaining convinced that the industry was in a terminal coma. Or perhaps he just had trouble imagining Old Testament prophets named Marty and Phil.

I have come to dread Academy Award time each spring. The Oscars are always good for an annual smirk in the press, from Andrew Sarris in the *Village Voice*, say, or Vincent Canby in the *New York Times*. The choices are "moribund," the ceremony "tacky." As a matter of fact, the smirkers have never understood either the Academy or its awards. (I have no ax to grind; although eligible, I have by choice not joined the Academy of Motion Picture Arts & Sciences, as I would by choice not join any critics' circle or society

195

or organized sucker list of whatever name.) The Academy is essentially a trade union of some 3,000 members, a mixture of below-the-line sound men and lighting men, special-effects men and PR people, film editors and set dressers, as well as above-the-line actors and directors, producers and writers. The awards are the awards of any union in any company town, a vote for jobs, and hits provide jobs, flops don't. If the New York film critics, most of whom work for union-organized publications, opened their membership to several thousand typesetters from the Typographical Union and projectionists from IATSE and secretaries from the Newspaper Guild, I suspect that the Academy's choices would seem a lot less moribund.

A studio executive came to a writer friend of mine and said he had an idea for a film. "We're all very excited about it," the executive said. "The sky's the limit on development money."

"What's the idea?" the writer said.

"Relationships," the executive said. He beamed and pulled on his pipe.

The writer stared at him for a long time, waiting for him to add something else. "You mean men and women?" he said finally.

"That'd be part of it."

My wife and I were once taken to lunch by a producer with a hot idea: "World War II."

"What do you want to do with it?"

"You're the writers."

For the record, we have also been asked to do "an extension of *The Graduate*" and *"Rebel Without a Cause"* in the west Valley, 1978, with a girl in the James Dean part."

It was a deal in search of a story: Paul Newman and Robert Redford as New York police officers David Durk and Frank Serpico. Durk and Serpico, the two cops who had blown the whistle on corruption in the New York Police Department and forced the creation of the Knapp Commission. David Durk, the button-down gray-flannel-suit cop, graduate of Amherst College, former student of Alfred Kazin's. Frank Serpico, the undercover cop, who swung with chicks, wore a beard and a ring in his ear. Paul Newman as Durk. Robert Redford as Serpico, Butch and Sundance in the Big Apple, over a million beans between them, plus a percentage of the gross. Only they did not have a script.

The writer and the director of *Butch Cassidy and the Sundance Kid* had jointly turned down the project before we were approached, and when we listened to the tapes and read the two magazine articles on which the screenplay would be based, we knew why: there was no story. Especially no story when both Newman and Redford had script approval, as did the director: the writer on a project in which two superstars plus a director have script approval stands a good chance of getting ground into little pieces. We declined.

But in Hollywood when you turn down a go-project with two superstars, it is generally assumed that you only want more money. The ante was sweetened; again we declined. And sweetened again: our agent intimated that he could get us $100,000 for a first draft, and that he would ". . . work out the down side later." (I might add here that it is a good rule of thumb to cut an agent's intimation by 50 percent.) The head of the studio called at 7:30 A.M. and said he was glad we were coming aboard. I waffled. Again the ante went up. There was so much money involved that my palms began to sweat. And still we did not want to do the script.

It was the appearance of Sam Peckinpah in the package that made us change from "no" to "maybe." We had first met him in the bad years when he could not get work because of a distinctly un-Hollywood penchant for telling people exactly what he thought of them, their ancestors, their wives and children. We had often talked of doing a picture together, but nothing ever came of it. Now there were stars, money, and a studio; the only thing there wasn't, in fact, was a story.

Peckinpah had never met Paul Newman, and so a dinner was arranged at Newman's house in Malibu. We had not seen Sam in over a year, and he was as unmellow as ever. He said that he did not much like Redford and that if he had directed *Butch Cassidy* it would have been a better picture. Newman, who had some distinct reservations about the violence in Peckinpah films, never lost his aplomb. He had just finished directing *Sometimes a Great Notion,* from which the original director had been fired, and he said that he had ". . . cut it from a disaster into a failure." It was the kind of remark that Peckinpah, the director, could appreciate. Newman and Peckinpah—they were two professionals feeling each other out, and they seemed to like each other.

We talked about red wine. We talked about studio accounting. In fact we talked about everything except Durk and Serpico, which was the point of the exercise. It was only after we left, standing with Sam out in front of Newman's house, that the subject even came up.

"Sam," I said, "what the hell is this picture all about?"

"Write me a Western," Peckinpah said.

"Jesus, Sam, it's about two cops in New York City."

A small smile. "Every story is a Western."

We must have looked bewildered. As if lecturing to two rather slow small children, Sam said, "You put the hare in front of the hound and let the hound chase the hare."

"Oh."

"Simple."

We never wrote the picture.

* * *

The woman in our script had a twelve-year-old child. "If you're not married to that kid," Ali MacGraw's agent whispered at a party, "I can get Ali to read the script."

We have, in the course of a dozen or so films, stayed in suites at the St. Francis Hotel in San Francisco, the Ambassador East in Chicago, the Regency in New York, the Connaught in London, the Carlton in Cannes, the Eden in Rome, L'Hotel in Paris, and the Tequendama in Bogotá. I say this only to suggest one attraction about working in films that goes largely unmentioned: the attraction of borrowed luxury. Contracts specify an expense allowance of $1,000 a week and there is always a chauffeured limousine to help the traveler nagivate a strange city. In every way, the minor fix is in. Hand an expired passport to a production manager and within hours he will return it, renewed. Land in a foreign capital and a public relations man will glide you through customs, dispensing francs or lire or pesos or pound notes. ("If you have any dope, best tell me now so I can clear things," a PR man advised me at Heathrow; I received the same counsel from his opposite number at Orly.) The ripoff is endemic; studio bookkeeping is so byzantine that none of the profit participants ever really expect to see their points and as a result are not inspired to economy up front. It is this tendency toward largesse that makes a movie company on location so easy to spot. They laugh a little too long in hotel restaurants and talk a little too loud and drink a little too much; they always stick together and are the object of an attention they pretend to ignore. They are like exiles spending the currency of a government which, unbeknownst to the locals, collapsed yesterday.

We were asked to write a picture for Barbra Streisand. Unfortunately we did not think much of the book we had been asked to adapt; we had, in fact, turned it down twice before Streisand was involved.

But such was the lure of Streisand that we were almost able to convince ourselves that she could make even this story work. The director encouraged this delusion; he had not liked the book either, but with the Streisand magic, he said, perhaps we could pull it off.

With some trepidation, we entered into negotiation. But so seductive is the mythology of deal making that our reservations for the moment evaporated. It is all an elaborate entertainment. There are no surprises in a deal; both sides are aware beforehand of the broad strokes in the final settlement, yet the charade of haggling goes on. The sums involved often resemble the national debt of an emerging nation, frequently causing the negotiators to absent themselves from reality. "I know janitors who make $75,000," our agent once said, as he advised us to turn down a deal.

We were kept abreast of the negotiation by telephone. After an initial thrust and parry, our screenplay fee was set at $100,000. On signing, we would receive $15,000 and, on delivery of the first draft, another $35,000. For two sets of revisions, we would get another $25,000, and on the first day of principal photography, if no other writers had been called in, the final $25,000. The delivery date on the first draft was twelve weeks after a negotiated start date. At any point after the first draft we could be fired, but even if we were replaced and our script dismissed as unusable, we would receive the minimum first-draft payment of $50,000.

The fee was easy; now the real bargaining began. Our agent asked for points, which in a Streisand picture could be considerable. But unless they are also partners in the production, writers of an adaptation rarely get points, mainly because producers are unwilling to give a piece up front to a writer they might ultimately want to fire. Thus our request for points was turned down flat. Our agent then informed the producers: no piece, no srript.

The game was now the deal, not the screenplay. Instead of points, the producers offered a deferment out of profits. The first offer was for $25,000, and, when that was turned down, they raised the deferment to $50,000. Our agent accepted and then began to work out when and how the deferment would be paid. After much haggling, it was agreed that the deferment would be in two equal payments, the first at 2.2 times the actual negative cost of the picture (at which point the film would be past break-even and into initial profits), the second at 3.5 times negative. Payment would be pari passu (or pro-rated) with others holding a deferment position. So finally, after three weeks of negotiation, what had been established was that if we wrote the picture and if there were no other writers and if the picture was made and if it went into profits, we would make $150,000.

We balked. Not over the deal, but over the book. Even the possibility of $150,000 did not make us like it any better. More meetings, more bargaining. So much time had been expended on the negotiations that the producers were reluctant to audition other writers, even in the face of our desire to bow out of the project. Finally we suggested a compromise: instead of taking a lump-sum first payment, which would tie us into the picture for months, we would give the producers three weeks during which we would try to work out a viable narrative from the book. At the end of the three weeks, we would either go ahead under the original terms or call it a day. As guarantee of our good faith, our agent stipulated that we would work for $2,500 a week, or half our weekly rate. (Actually we did not have a weekly rate, but now he could claim we did, and he had a deal memo to prove it.)

And so we went to work. On the fifth day, we told our agent to get us out of the deal.

"How badly do you want out?" he said.

"They don't have to pay us."

We never wrote the picture.

Scene 235 took place in a cafeteria. The time was night. KATE was having a cup of coffee with her lover,

HUGH, a kind of young Eric Hoffer with patch pockets. They run into Kate's former lover, WARREN, a black academic who describes himself as "less a Tom than a Thomist." Warren and Hugh, who have never met, immediately take to each other. Their rapport makes Kate so nervous that she leaves the restaurant.

The actress objected to the scene. "So she's balled both guys. What's there to be nervous about?"

"She just is," my wife said.

"Do you get nervous when you're in the same room with two guys you've slept with?" the actress asked.

"Yes," my wife said.

The director, the producer, and I assiduously began examining our fingernails.

"Well, I didn't know the picture was about *your* hangups," the actress said.

Shirley MacLaine came to lunch to discuss *January and February,* as did Julie Andrews; we flew to Tucson to discuss it with Joanne Woodward and to San Francisco for meetings with Natalie Wood. For each of these ladies we rewrote the picture, by the by, adding some filigreeing from Vanessa Redgrave and Faye Dunaway. Which is how a picture about a social worker in Detroit and Cleveland evolved effortlessly into a script about a college professor's wife in Pomona whose life comes to a crisis at the Ojai Music Festival.

Then we quit the picture.

This was the original end of the piece. It elicited the following response from Robert Manning, the editor of the Atlantic Monthly, *to which I replied. This exchange between Manning and me was included in the piece as printed in the* Atlantic *in July, 1974.*

MEMO TO JOHN GREGORY DUNNE

FROM: THE EDITOR

I like your sweet-and-sour dissertation on

screenwriting and will run it in the July issue, with proper credits and a reminder that Fatty Arbuckle Memorial Week is in the offing. It leaves me wondering, though, if Hollywood is the drag you make it seem. I'd like to read more. Perhaps some ruminations about some of the screenwriting aces of the past, and perhaps a case or two in which everybody, writer included, was happy at the end. And perhaps a bit more about the makeup of the contemporary screenwriting community, if there is one. Do most of you live in and around Hollywood? Earn a good living at the trade? Have any fun? Or is there no such thing as an homogeneous group of men and women who make their livings or get their kicks mainly out of writing for the movies?

MEMO TO THE EDITOR

FROM: JOHN GREGORY DUNNE

The problem about your memo is that in essence I disagree with just about everything implied in it and will try to explain why as briefly as I can. I conceived of the piece as about some experiences Joan and I have had. We are book writers who moonlight on film scripts, as are most of the screenwriters we know well (people like Brian Moore and Judith Rascoe and Gavin Lambert and Christopher Isherwood), and whatever perceptions I have are based on the salient fact that movie writing is not a primary occupation. The professional screenwriters we know are either directors or aspire to be, because only by directing your own script can you control your own material. I once wrote that "writing scripts and not wanting to direct them is like wanting to be a co-pilot." That still says it all.

The fact is, screenwriting *is* a drag, despite the doubt voiced in your memo. The analogy to working for *Time* was well considered. We have both worked in practically every level at *Time*, and I did not, nor I suspect did you, consider it writing; what appeared in print belonged to the magazine or the managing editor or the surrogate Luce of the moment, not to the writer. Finish a book and there is a sense of accomplishment; finish a script and the shit starts. An example: When we turned in the script we just finished, it was suggested we rewrite the girl as a spade, because Diana Ross was available. We managed to procrastinate, but if the studio finally decides on Diana Ross, our choices are either to rewrite the girl as a black or to forfeit $50,000 and ten points. This is the given of screenwriting. This also is before the producer, director, or actors have weighed in with their ideas. (And this, I might finally add, is an original screenplay.)

Joan once wrote that a deal memo, which spells out contractual control, is the most important piece of paper on a production. This is novelist Josh Greenfeld on his collaboration with director Paul Mazursky: "If I don't like something of Paul's, it stays in; if Paul doesn't like something of mine, it goes out." This is Jules Feiffer on his collaboration with Mike Nichols: "A script is something Mike revises, often with my help." Those were two successful collaborations between friends; Jules and Josh recognized and accepted their junior partnership because their own work was elsewhere.

Since the decline of the contract system, there is no great homogeneous screenwriter community. Writers work at home instead of at studio offices and thus are spread all over (we, for example, live fifty miles from the nearest studio). I don't know if writers are making a good living. The Guild claims only a tiny percentage supports itself exclusively on movies or television, but even in the palmy old days only a tiny percentage of the Guild was ever in demand. As for the old stars, they were mainly stars because they were good around the right dinner tables.

Why then write for films? Because the money is good. Because doing a screenplay is like doing a combination jigsaw-and-crossword puzzle; it's not writing, but it can be fun. And because the other night, after a screening, we went out to a party with Mike Nichols and Candice Bergen and Warren Beatty and Barbra Streisand. I never did that at *Time*.

1974

4.

CONTINENTAL DRIFT

THE NIGHTINGALE
OF JACKRABBIT FLATS

They had begun arriving for the trial the night before, the old people in their Scout campers. It was a long drive, a hard two hundred miles from Tecopa, California, but it was cooler on the floor of Death Valley at night, and so they had set out after sundown through the vast empty desert, and finally they had arrived in Independence, California. They camped for the night on the main street, across from the Winnedumah Hotel, and in the morning they gathered in anxious little knots outside the Inyo County Courthouse, by a large boulder on which had been chipped these words from Genesis: MY LAND IS BEFORE THEE; DWELL WHERE IT PLEASETH THEE.

By 9 A.M. they were crowded into the courtroom, standing five deep in the back. It was already stiflingly hot, and the heat made the old people even more restless, more disturbed, and some of them shuffled around the polished aggregate floor outside the courtroom, reciting litanies of small griefs. A miner passed among them with a brown paper bag, distributing homemade tags which said "We're from Tecopa" or "We Need Pat."

Pat was Patricia Gardelius, and she stood silently by the defense table, a slender, handsome woman, just forty, in a beige dress. She was not the kind of woman one would expect to find on trial in a criminal case. She was a practical nurse in Tecopa, a desert community so poor that some of its citizens lived in caves, so isolated that a doctor flew in only once a week, from Lone Pine, 125 miles west across Death Valley. Out there in the wilderness, Patricia Gardelius had delivered babies, cared for the sick and bound up accident wounds, and now, on this oppressively hot summer day, the state of California was putting her on trial for practicing medicine without a license.

The old people of Tecopa had come to Independence not only out of devotion to Pat Gardelius but also out of a bitterness that had begun festering long before her arrest. In part, it was bitterness at the lush new California across the Sierra Nevada. But beyond that, perhaps at the heart of Patricia Gardelius's troubles, lay in the growing bitterness between Tecopa and the town of Shoshone, a few miles deeper in the desert—an acrimony born of the slow erosion of inherited privilege before an influx of new people and new ideas, and leading up to a drama which is now playing itself out like a desert version of *The Cherry Orchard*.

To understand, it is helpful to take a drive out to Tecopa. The Joshua trees stop growing first, and then the mesquite, and after that on Route 127, north of Baker, there is nothing but sand and sere, sun-blasted hills and occasionally, etched against the sky, a weathered cross marking the grave of some unknown, unmourned tramp miner. It is hot, deliriously hot, the average July high hitting 136 degrees in Badwater. The places north of Baker and east of Lone Pine have names like Badwater, Furnace Creek, Stovepipe Wells, the Funeral Mountains—and the names tell what life is like out on the eastern rim of California, sealed off from the rest of the state by the alkali desert and the bony spine of the Sierra Nevada. It is the end of the world, the jumping-off place to oblivion, the land God gave Cain, a place where a river is called the Amargosa, which is Spanish for "bitter," because its water, when there is any water at all, is undrinkable.

Tecopa is out there next to the Amargosa, a few

miles east of Route 127, past an abandoned mine and the burnt-out shell of an automobile rusting away in a dry wash, on an unnumbered road. A few mangy dogs bay across from a Chevron station. There is a post office and the Faith Community Church and the Enterprise Motel and Trailer Park and a long, green cinder block building called The Trading Post. At one end of the building is a café with a few tables and a lunch counter, which is closed during the heat of day. At the other end is a general store where the meat in the trays has a slightly greenish tinge. Between the café and store is the Snake Room, which serves beer only and does not provide glasses, unless the customer asks, and then he gets a paper cup. And that is about all.

A mile or two farther out, in Jackrabbit Flats, there are low, one-story bungalows which look as if they have been built of driftwood. Up in Tecopa Hot Springs there is a trailer colony; the people use corrugated-iron outhouses, some of them marked HIS or HERS. The trailers are surrounded by propane tanks and have aluminum foil crimped in their windows to deflect the sun and the heat. Eight miles north, by the landing strip in Shoshone, there are a number of caves, dug by hand out of the scorched hills in years past, and these caves are home to a constantly changing band of winos and retired miners. Littered around outside are batteries, lanterns, tire frames, and old cannibalized cars up on blocks.

Beyond the caves is Shoshone. Aside from some grass and a few more trees, there is little to distinguish Shoshone from Tecopa. But the mood is less somnolent. For years Shoshone was not so much a town as the private fief of State Senator Charles Brown, a native of Georgia, who came to this wasteland to make his home and his fortune. Charles Brown was a power in the desert, a man who got things done, a man ultimately not to cross. He is three years dead now, but his spirit still pervades Shoshone, and though his legacy of power is slowly evaporating, that power is still regarded by his family as a birthright, a birthright which somehow isolates them from the way life is now lived on the desert, the way it is lived, for example, in a place like Tecopa.

The mines and the mineral hot springs are the reasons Tecopa exists. The miners gather in the Snake Room evenings and talk about distant mines and distant adventures—the drunk that started off in Barstow and ended up in Elko, the sheriff in Butte who decided whether a stranger was a miner or a pimp by the calluses on his hands. The arthritic pensioners who live in the trailers in Tecopa Hot Springs disapprove of the Snake Room. They are there to take the waters in the cinder block baths. Under the flag of the richest, most populous state in the union, they sit naked in the springs, shielded from the sun by a corrugated-iron roof, and talk about human disintegration, ailing liver functions and "Iva Hanks, whose kneecaps are deteriorating." Time does not exist for these people, only social security and a desperate fundamentalism. "The Lord needs our money," they say in disapproval of the Snake Room regulars, and in the afternoons they sit in their trailers and talk about Tecopa. "Blink your eyes and you miss it," they say, "but we love it."

Even in the West, where distance is made into a virtue, Tecopa's isolation beggars the imagination. It is a community where the Montgomery Ward catalogue gets more use than the telephone book. People talk of "going out to Vegas" to shop or see a movie, and Las Vegas is 106 miles away. A lone garage man in Lone Pine comes over on Mondays, through Death Valley and over three lethal mountain ranges. A Catholic priest comes in to say Mass once a week, on Monday evenings at 6:30. The undertaker is in Bishop, 275 miles away, and death is a constant companion in a community of the old and the halt. And except on Wednesdays, when the doctor flies in from the hospital in Lone Pine, life and death in Tecopa are in the hands of Patricia Gardelius.

In the Snake Room and in the Faith Community Church, down in Death Valley and across the Nevada Line in Lathrop Wells, Pat Gardelius is regarded with something approaching reverence. The word she brings to mind is "capable," like those women on the wagon trains who cooked and cared for their children and primed rifles and dug arrowheads out of wounded bodies. Her husband, Douglas, is a miner, and she has four children by an earlier marriage. There is nothing of the do-gooder about her; there was a need, she had experience, she pitched in. Indeed, if Charles Brown was the symbol of rugged individualism on the desert, Pat Gardelius is the symbol of the helping hand. It was perhaps inevitable that these two outspoken people would sooner or later clash.

In the only language they know, the language of old newspaper headlines, miners unblushingly call Pat Gardelius an "angel of mercy," and each seems to have his own story about her to tell. "It was squirting blood like a pump," says a miner whose chest was almost caved in by a beam. "I'd have bled to death without her." A hoist man tells of the time she went five hundred feet down into a shaft to save the life of a miner named Larry Lee, Jr. "A boulder broke loose, crushed Larry's leg, and pinned him in the mine," the hoist man recalls. "That was before we had telephones. It was five hours before the doctor came. Pat stayed with Larry all that time down in that dark hole. Larry lost his leg, but he owes his life to our nurse."

There are other stories: about Albert Beasler, who lost his heel in a mine accident; about Ben Robinson, who was gored by a bull; about Walter Sewell, who lost 70 percent of his blood when his ulcers hemorrhaged and was kept alive by Pat Gardelius with glucose injections until the doctor flew in. There are more mundane stories about snakebites and sniffles, colds and coronaries, burns and births. "Drove over to Lone Pine when the pains were only five minutes apart," says a young mother holding an infant in her arms. The hospital in Lone Pine is 186 miles away by road. "Worried? No I had Pat with me."

And there are stories about automobile accidents. To appreciate a desert accident, it is necessary to drive over those empty blacktop roads, where there is nothing against which to gauge speed and the needle on the speedometer creeps up insidiously toward 100 mph. Then there is a dip, a soft shoulder, and the car is splattered over the highway. The coyotes come then, if there is a body, and by the time the Highway Patrol arrives, there is often an arm missing or a leg, or sometimes even a head. Long ago an accident report brought Pat Gardelius out into the desert to spend a night alone with a body—a huge 350-pound corpse. According to its identification papers, the body was that of a scientist at the Atomic Test Site in Mercury, Nevada. During the night a car with siren wailing careened up to the wreck and a security agent got out. There were secret papers somewhere about, and when the agent could not immediately find them, he accused the nurse of moving the body. "Sure," she recalls telling him, "I drug it across the desert." He began berating her, and she exploded. "You silly little bastard, you think I drug *that?* He weighs three hundred and fifty pounds." The agent finally found the papers and left her then, alone with the body, and the coyotes came; and from before midnight until after dawn she sat in her car, blinking her lights, racing her engine, and honking her horn to drive them off.

Sometimes an accident victim does not die immediately, and the effort to save the flickering life becomes a race against time and nature. "We had just finished looking at the *Late Show* when the call came," Pat Gardelius says of one such case. A car coming over the Charles Brown Highway from Pahrump, Nevada, had crashed. The man was killed instantly; his companion, a girl of twenty-two, was crushed and unconscious. An ambulance had been summoned from Lone Pine, nearly two hundred miles distant, but the girl was in such bad condition that if she was to be saved, the ambulance would have to be met somewhere on the road, somewhere in Death Valley. With her husband, Pat Gardelius drove to the scene of the crash and treated the girl for shock. "I didn't treat the injuries," she says. "It's shock that kills people." She gave her a pain killer and plasma and helped lay her on a stretcher in the back of a station wagon which belonged to the Inyo County deputy sheriff stationed in Shoshone. Then the nurse and the sheriff started across Death Valley. "There's no seat in the back of that station wagon," Pat Gardelius says. "I was sitting with my fanny on the floor and my legs out in front of me and no support for my back, trying to give the poor girl some plasma. Going around curves at night as fast as we were going, it's not easy to keep an IV going." Five miles past Stovepipe Wells, they met the ambulance from Lone Pine and passed the patient over, then drove the ninety miles back to the spot on the road where Douglas Gardelius was guarding the body of the dead man. "You can't leave a body by itself out on the highway," Pat Gardelius says. "It's morally wrong."

Morality takes on meaning in the desert world of Pat Gardelius. It is not something abstract, to be exercised only by groups and countries; it is something fundamental in your attitude toward your fellow man, living or dead. "It's not always easy helping the people of Tecopa," she says. "In fact, I wish there was a doctor here. Sometimes I just hope, pray and improvise."

Pat Gardelius's moral qualms about her own fallibility do not trouble Tecopa. Desert people prefer to think in reverential terms. Except for one unknown person out there on the desert, one person who perhaps resented the reverence, resented the improvisation, resented the mantle of morality that had fallen by default on Pat Gardelius. And one day last spring that one unknown person wrote a letter.

* * *

The letter brought Ira D. Sims to Tecopa. He is a short, anonymous-looking young man with glasses, thinning hair, and a slight weight problem. He drove over from Fresno, spent the night in Barstow, then in the morning drove the remaining 122 miles to Tecopa. He asked for the doctor's office and was told that it was on the dirt road behind the Rioh Garage.

Pat Gardelius was making a house call that morning and was late getting to the office. Ira D. Sims was waiting outside when she arrived. He complained of a headache, upset stomach, sore throat, earache, and general flu symptoms. He seemed in pain, Pat Gardelius recalled later, "though he wasn't screaming. I took him at his word." She spent ten minutes examining him, then gave him a shot of penicillin and streptomycin, two boxes of pills and a bottle of medicine for the earache. Ira D. Sims paid her $10 for the medicine and was told to check back the next day, when the doctor was scheduled to fly over from Lone Pine.

Ira D. Sims did not show up the next day, but he did return to Tecopa a week later. He brought with him a deputy sheriff and a warrant for Patricia Gardelius's arrest. He said that he was an investigator for the California Department of Professional and Vocational Standards and that he was charging her with practicing medicine without a license in violation of Section 2142 of the California Business and Professional Code.

The arrest of Patricia Gardelius enraged Tecopa. The Tecopa Progressive Association fired off an angry letter to California Attorney General Thomas Lynch protesting the state's "shabby treatment" of the town. In the Snake Room there was talk of seceding from California and joining Nevada. Miners described in detail what they would do if they ever learned the identity of the anonymous complainant to the Department of Professional and Vocational Standards. "That son of a bitch is liable to wind up with a powder stick and a short fuse in his hip pocket," said one leather-faced desert rat who had mined from Canada to Mexico and back.

Later it turned out that Ira D. Sims had also had a warrant served on the town's only barber for operating a shop without a license, his shop being a chair in the back of the Snake Room. Nor had Ira D. Sims stopped there. He had driven to Furnace Creek, down on the floor of Death Valley, where he had a sheriff arrest May Dorval, a doughty, eighty-three-year-old registered nurse, also on a charge of practicing medicine without a license. All in all, it was quite an expedition to the desert for Ira D. Sims.

The question that nagged at desert people as Patricia Gardelius awaited trial was who had written the anonymous letter. It was not only a breach of trust but—worse in the eyes of many—it was a breach which brought in the outside world, in the person of Ira D. Sims. "Anybody thinks I want to prosecute a nurse from Death Valley—big, glamour-deal Death Valley—must think I'm a big bird," growled Inyo County District Attorney Robert Loundagin. He is a paunchy, slow-moving man with a blotchy red face, a gravelly voice and eminent common sense. "These bureaucratic investigators, they got to justify their own existence, so they justify it by heckling someone. I just wish they'd let us alone."

Distrust of outsiders is endemic to Inyo County, and not without reason. At the turn of the century, western Inyo, in the shadow of the Sierra, was lush farmland, nourished by the waters of the Owens River. Then, in a giant water swindle engineered by Los Angeles land speculators, the river waters were siphoned off and diverted south to the parched San Fernando Valley, where land prices soared and the speculators made a $100-million killing by selling off tracts· they had previously bought at rock-bottom prices. Their acres withering, Inyo farmers banded together in vigilante groups and nine times blew up the aqueduct south into Los Angeles County. Beaten but still proud, they fired their last salvo in the spring of 1927 with a full-page advertisement in the Los Angeles newspapers which began, "We, the farming communities of Owens Valley, being about to die, salute you."

Now, isolated from the rest of California, Inyo spreads out from the Sierra like antimatter, a desolate, embattled land slightly smaller than Belgium, inhabited by only 12,000 people. There is a wagon-train ethic out there on the desert, a pride that the beleaguered desert existence is in itself an assurance of mutual trust. No one seemed more deserving of that trust than Patricia Gardelius, no one less likely to be betrayed by an anonymous letter.

She is a woman of the frontier, born in remote Jarbidge, Nevada, a hundred miles north of Elko and a hundred miles west of Twin Falls, Idaho; her mother was a nurse there and also the town mortician and justice of the peace, and so the idea of "helping out" was implanted early. Pat Gardelius took two years of nurse's training at Sacred Heart Hospital in Spokane, Washington, leaving to get married before she got her certificate.

She had four children, three boys and a girl, but the marriage ended in divorce, and in 1953 she married Douglas Gardelius, a quiet, infinitely patient miner who legally adopted her four offspring. She had spent all her married life in a succession of mining towns, and finally in 1954 she moved to the Tecopa area, where Douglas Gardelius had come to work in the mines.

Tecopa did not seem to offer much more than the towns she had left behind. There had once been a railroad, the Tonopah & Tidewater, running up to the mines, but it closed down after the war and the tracks were torn up several years later. There were no private telephones and only three pay stations, one in Tecopa, one at the Springs and one in Shoshone. "And half the time they were out of order," says Pat

Gardelius. Nor was there any public electricity; what power there was came from small, private diesel plants. Telephone service was finally installed three years ago, electricity two years ago.

The Gardelius family settled first in Shoshone, later moving to Jackrabbit Flats. There is an airfield in Shoshone—a wind sock, a dilapidated hangar and a gravel strip with a dip in the middle—and it is here that the doctor from Lone Pine lands on his weekly visit. The doctor's name is Walter Wilson, and he has been flying in from Lone Pine once a week for twenty years. He is a slender, smiling man of sixty with a highly developed set of Inyo County grievances against the outside world. A devout Seventh-Day Adventist, he regards his weekly visits to Tecopa as "missionary work." It was only a matter of time before the doctor discovered that Pat Gardelius had some nurse's training. Her children were growing up, she had time on her hands, and so she began working, at first more or less as a receptionist, a couple of hours a week. "I didn't look for this job," Pat Gardelius says. "It just sort of found me. And then it grew and grew, to seven days a week, and sometimes all day and all night too."

There were standing instructions from Walter Wilson for every situation she was likely to encounter. Every day she called Lone Pine to report new patients and to receive more specific orders. In emergencies she was on her own until the doctor could fly in. "You just do what needs to be done," says Pat Gardelius. "And most anything out here could be an emergency." Almost imperceptibly her authority increased, and an arrangement was worked out under which she received as pay one-third of the income taken in by Walter Wilson's Tecopa office. To the retired pensioners in Tecopa Hot Springs, old, arthritic and alone in their trailers, she helped make up for the sons who lived in Chicago, the daughters who did not write. They needed to feel wanted, needed someone to fuss over their ailments, real and fancied. "Everybody who passes out out here," says Pat Gardelius, "you get a call that so-and-so has had a heart attack."

Old couples traveling out to the mineral springs in the desert dropped off their medical records at her office before finding a permanent mooring in the trailer park by the healing waters. There were pills and capsules and medicines in the office, some of them prescription-only drugs, but Pat Gardelius had instructions from Dr. Wilson to distribute them as she saw fit. "It wouldn't do the doctor any good to write out a prescription and say, 'Take it down to the corner drugstore,' " she says, "cause the nearest corner drugstore is in Vegas."

Wednesday, when the doctor came, patients would begin filing into the office early in the morning, signing a roster to show their place in line—a nursing mother, a miner with his arm in a sling, an old woman with her upper plate missing. The office is a one-story, corrugated-iron building with a large waiting room, several treatment rooms, and an alcove for the dentist who occasionally flies in with Dr. Wilson. Shoved up against one wall is an unpainted, homemade cradle. It is usually lunchtime before Dr. Wilson arrives, often with a large box full of Queen Anne cherries picked from his own trees in Lone Pine for the assembled patients, and from then until nearly midnight every week, he and Patricia Gardelius would administer to a seemingly endless procession of the sick.

Sometimes there would be house calls. One day shortly after his blue Cessna touched down, Dr. Wilson went directly to the cave colony on the edge of Shoshone. Metal stovepipes poked up through the sand, and wedged in the entrances of the caves was a motley collection of doors liberated from outhouses, trucks and railroad cabooses. The day before, Patricia Gardelius had treated an old miner and cave-dweller named Jack Norman for a heart attack; he had been fixing a flat tire, the temperature was 106 degrees, and he was eighty years old. When Wilson arrived, Norman, wearing a battered gray pith helmet, a dirty sport shirt and a hearing aid, was waiting outside his cave. There were three water barrels lashed together in front of the cave, and a hand-lettered sign that said FALL-IN-SHELTER. "I thought I was going to go under," he said, greeting Dr. Wilson. "Would have, too, hadn't been for that Pat."

Inside the cave the earth walls were lined with aluminum foil. There was an unmade bed, and by it, a system of pulleys which led outside to a handmade wooden frame, on which was a mirror. Dr. Wilson began manipulating the pulleys until the mirror outside caught the midday sun, reflecting it off the aluminum foil. "Only solar lighting system in the country," Walter Wilson said. In the new light, pictures pinned to the aluminum foil became visible, pencil and pastel drawings sketched by Jack Norman from old magazine photographs—Connie Mack, Knute Rockne, Gracie Allen, State Senator Charles Brown, and John, Robert and Jacqueline Kennedy. On a shelf above the bed was a hand-carved twenty-mule team and a wooden Saint Bernard with a tot of brandy hanging from its neck; on the dog Jack Norman had lettered, MAN'S BEST FRIEND AND DOG. The old miner sat on his bed, amid all his worldly possessions, as Dr. Wilson examined him. He was very deaf and Walter Wilson had to shout. "You're too old to exercise like that, Jack. The old heart won't take it. You don't want to go under now, do you?" Jack Norman nodded vigorously. "Would have checked out yesterday, hadn't been for that Pat."

It was this kind of dependence that aroused in Patricia Gardelius a sense of responsibility toward Tecopa. With her children in school, she became interested in school problems, joined the PTA, and when that was not active enough, ran for the Board of Education of the Death Valley Unified School District. "The first time you run, you don't know what you're getting into," Pat Gardelius says. "The second time you're just plain gullible."

Her election to the school board was perhaps the

start of the trouble. The Death Valley Unified School District is immense, 9,000 square miles of desert with only two primary schools, one in Tecopa, the other in Death Valley Junction—and one high school, in Shoshone. High school students bus to Shoshone from as far south as Baker, forty-eight miles away, as far north as Stovepipe Wells, eighty-five miles; as the result of an interstate agreement, the high school even takes students from across the Nevada line in Pahrump. There are eighty-eight students in the high school today; a few years ago there was a graduating class of only one, and the undermanned baseball team lost a game by a score of 34-0. It is a poor school district, and because salaries are generally lower than in the rest of California, teachers must be recruited in such badly paying states as Montana and North Dakota. "We only hope that they're good enough so we can't keep them here," says District School Superintendent Claude Ellison. "Good ones are snapped up by richer districts. Bad ones you're stuck with."

In addition, the district's intrinsic problems were exacerbated by a growing bitterness between Shoshone and Tecopa. Everything in Shoshone belonged to Charles Brown: the land, the few houses, the gas station, the general store, the lunchroom and the saloon, which is called the Crowbar, and which, unlike the Snake Room, is licensed to sell hard liquor. For twenty-four years Charles Brown sat in the California legislature as Senator from Inyo, Mono and Alpine counties, the largest and most sparsely populated district of the state. Most urban dwellers do not even know the name of their duly elected State Senator, but in Inyo, Mono and Alpine counties, Charles Brown was known as a man with a paternal regard for his constituents. He was better known, and in many cases better thought of, than the Governor of the state.

Solidly entrenched though they were, Shoshone and the family of Charles Brown still watched the migration of social security pensioners to the trailer colony in Tecopa Hot Springs with growing unease. Even had they wanted, the pensioners could not buy land in the Springs, and in any case, they were happy in their trailers, free of upkeep and property taxes. But to the family of Charles Brown, voters who are not taxpayers are something less than a desirable element, people with no stake in the county, people who might upset the status quo. Nor was it reassuring to Shoshone that the pensioners bound themselves to Pat Gardelius, for hers was a voice in local affairs that Shoshone did not particularly like to hear. As a member of the school board, she figured prominently in an acrimonious dispute over the renewal of the contract of a teacher at the high school in Shoshone. The teacher—a friend of the Brown family—had been accused of making fun of the parents of her students, and had been judged incompetent by the school superintendent. Over the protests of the Browns, Patricia Gardelius voted to uphold the superintendent, and the contract was not renewed. "Ignorance prevailed," says Bernice Brown Sorrells.

A short time later, in 1960, Charles Brown was voted out of office after twenty-four years. The Tecopa vote was not the difference in the election, but it was a first defeat, a shadow of things to come, and Shoshone grew increasingly resentful of voters who were not taxpayers. Two years later, in 1962, these voters proposed a new bond issue for a new elementary school in Tecopa and a new gymnasium and two new classrooms for the high school in Shoshone. "We have a terrible time trying to get teachers," Pat Gardelius says. "What they had to live in was bad enough. What they had to teach in was even worse."

The school-bond fight was bitter. "Pat doesn't back away from a fight," says Claude Ellison, the school superintendent. "Fact is, sometimes I think she enjoys one. The bond fight was a dilly. Charley Brown said to me, 'Just let me get out of the hole.' Get out of the *hole?* My God, he was a millionaire." The voters in Tecopa passed the bond issue over the strong objections of the electorate in Shoshone. Shortly after the election, former State Senator Charles Brown died. "Charley was a good man," Pat Gardelius says. "We disagreed on a lot of things, but he always played it straight."

The bond fight severed any semblance of good feelings between Shoshone and Patricia Gardelius. Today Bernice Brown Sorrells can scarcely disguise her contempt. "A poverty pocket," she calls the trailer colony in Tecopa Hot Springs. She is a handsome, gray-haired woman in her late forties, and she was once a close friend of Pat Gardelius, "Pat was a mouse of a girl when she came here," Bernice Brown Sorrells says, "bright but uneducated." And now? "An unskilled person breaking the law."

The isolation of the desert holds no fears for Bernice Brown Sorrells. "We're not so isolated as those people in that poverty pocket would have you believe," she says. "You can get to Vegas in an hour and a half, and it's only an hour to Lone Pine by plane. You can get to a doctor. But those people don't want to get to a doctor. They just want somebody to cater to them, a place to go where they can talk about their ailments." The Sorrellses are breaking ground for a new development of low-cost houses. "We're going to have restrictions," Bernice Brown Sorrells says. "This isn't going to be any poverty pocket."

These bitter feelings were not assuaged by the fact that Patricia Gardelius met them with tolerance. "I feel kind of sorry for Bernice," Pat Gardelius says. "She never knew what defeat was until Charley got beat." Even worse, Pat Gardelius's sympathy did not keep her from adding other defeats. Last spring Maury Sorrells, Bernice Brown Sorrells's husband, decided to run for the school board as a member from Shoshone. Though not running herself, Patricia Gardelius declared herself against him. On election day Maury Sorrells was overwhelmingly defeated. That same day Patricia Gardelius was arrested.

Most of Tecopa came to the trial of Patricia Gardelius, two hundred miles across the floor of Death

Valley and over the Funeral, the Panamint, and the Inyo-White Mountains. These travelers were old, most of them, and they wore Panama hats and faded sundresses, and a woman with a Magic Marker pencil moved among them, offering to write on the back of any plain dress: "Tecopa Needs Pat." They had brought box lunches with them, and as they waited for the trial to begin, they examined the jury panel, wondering if any among them would possibly vote Patricia Gardelius guilty, wondering if they had brought enough food to last through a long trial.

Up until fifteen minutes before court opened, the district attorney's office was trying to get the Department of Professional and Vocational Standards to dismiss the case. "This whole thing could have been handled better on an administrative level," says Robert Loundagin, the Inyo County District Attorney. "There's no doubt that there was a prima facie violation of the law. Over the years, I suppose it's only natural to usurp more authority than you're entitled to. But this woman saves lives out there. This should have been handled by the State Board of Medical Examiners. They could have cautioned the doctor that the nurse was exceeding her authority and that would have been the end of it. But no, these damn-fool bureaucrats insist we go ahead with a trial."

Though Melvin Belli, the San Francisco attorney who was for a time the defense attorney for Jack Ruby, volunteered to take Patricia Gardelius's case, she elected to stick with an Inyo County lawyer before an Inyo County jury. His name is Willis Smith, and he is a short, cocky attorney from the cattle town of Bishop. The case was prosecuted by Assistant District Attorney Kenneth Murphy, like Loundagin a friend of Patricia Gardelius. "In a sense," he said in his opening statement, "I'd rather cut off my arm than try this case." But the issue, he continued, was not whether Patricia Gardelius did good for the people of Tecopa; it was whether she had broken the law. Willis Smith quickly challenged the contention that Patricia

Gardelius had acted in violation of the laws of California. The fact that there was no doctor within 106 miles, he argued, created an emergency in Tecopa, and if there was an emergency, the law was not broken. Furthermore, he said, Patricia Gardelius had been entrapped by Ira D. Sims, and such entrapment was illegal.

The main witness was Ira D. Sims. Under cross-examination, he admitted that he had received the anonymous complaint one month and three days before he had first gone to Tecopa. His voice heavy with scorn, Willis Smith hammered on the point that the Department of Professional and Vocational Standards could not have considered the alleged violation too serious if it had taken one month and three days to investigate it. Willis Smith also lingered lovingly on the fact that a grown man like Ira D. Sims made his living going around the state claiming he had a headache. He further elicited from Ira D. Sims the information that he had allowed Patricia Gardelius to treat one last patient before having her arrested.

"You didn't think it was *dangerous* for her to treat one more patient?"

"Apparently not," said Ira D. Sims.

Ira D. Sims did not return to the courtroom to hear Willis Smith's summation. In a bravura performance, the little lawyer from Bishop strutted before the jury box calling the heavens to witness the perfidy of the absent bureaucrat who had acted on an anonymous complaint. Stabbing his finger at Sims's empty chair, Willis Smith said, "The good Lord saw a creature in the Garden of Eden tempting Adam and Eve, and the good Lord said that the tempter should walk on his stomach for the rest of eternity, and that is what should happen to Ira D. Sims." His voice lowered as he called on Inyo County's ancient distrust of outsiders. "We don't need people like Ira D. Sims in Inyo County," Willis Smith said. "We don't need people like Ira D. Sims in the state of California."

The jury was out two hours. "I wonder who the

troublemaker is," Assistant District Attorney Murphy muttered as he waited with Willis Smith for the verdict. Shortly before 7 P.M., the jury returned and the foreman announced, "Not guilty." The courtroom erupted in cheers, and scores of weeping Tecopans engulfed the defense table, kissing, hugging and congratulating Patricia Gardelius.

Things will never be quite the same again on Route 127, north of Baker. The talk is of the heat and ailments and Patricia Gardelius. She still comes down from Jackrabbit Flats every morning for a cup of coffee in the café before going to the office in the corrugated-iron building behind the Rioh Garage, and she is still on call day and night, seven days a week. But things have changed, in Shoshone as well as in Tecopa, and the changes have not been for the better. Night lights were finally put in at the airstrip, and late in July, trying them out for the first time, Maury Sorrells crashed and was killed instantly.

Friendships are ended and there is bad feeling on the surface, where before it only simmered beneath. In Independence the district attorney's office wonders why its recommendation that the Gardelius case be dismissed was not heeded. In the Inyo County sheriff's office, there is a tendency to reflect Shoshone's view of Patricia Gardelius. "A lot of those people up there aren't sick," says under-sheriff Mike Elerick, a slender, impassive man with clear, pastel-blue eyes. "They just talk themselves into getting sick if they're not getting enough attention. They need qualified medical attention, not an unskilled nurse. If she makes a mistake and someone dies, those people who love her so much now will be the first ones to want to hang her from the highest yardarm." Despite these views, he does not think that the sheriff's office is compromised by calling on Patricia Gardelius in the event of an emergency. "She's a public utility," he says. "We call on her just like we would a tow truck."

In Tecopa there is talk, idle talk mostly, of having

Pat Gardelius run for the state legislature, and though she ridicules the rumor, it is enough to send paroxysms of rage through Shoshone. There is also talk in the Snake Room that miners have purchased two five-gallon cans of tar and some old feathers in case they ever discover who sent the anonymous letter. "If I found out, I'd never tell," Patricia Gardelius said over a cup of coffee in the café. "I wouldn't want that on my conscience." The sun was vanishing in the desert and the temperature was sliding under 100 degrees. "And besides," she said, "I'd probably have to clean him up."

1965

GOLDEN BOYS

Frankie Duarte had the flu. Seco Luna was available. A good Mexican boy. From Mexico. A left-hander. One hunded twenty-two pounds. Raul Tirado's manager said no. Twenty-two was too heavy. The contract with Duarte stipulated twenty. He didn't want his boy in with a southpaw. The matchmaker said Seco Luna would make one twenty. Raul Tirado's manager persisted. He didn't want his boy in with a left-hander. Even a left-hander Frankie Duarte had beaten. The matchmaker said it was Tuesday. The main event was Thursday. There weren't that many boys available on such short notice. It was a $1,500 pay night out the window. Raul Tirado's manager said all right. Reluctantly. At one twenty. The other boy couldn't come in an ounce over twenty.

So went the Tuesday before the weekly Thursday-night fights at the Olympic Auditorium in downtown Los Angeles. The Olympic is a relic from another age, the last fight club in America with a weekly card, fifty-two weeks a year. When I was growing up, the weekly fights were a part of the fabric of urban life. I used to watch Willie Pep (has any fighter ever had a better name?) dazzle and bewilder opponents at the ramshackle Hartford Auditorium. We had no Yankees or Packers to root for in Hartford, no team to consume the local imagination, but we did have featherweight champions. Louis "Kid" Kaplan. Bat Battalino. Willie Pep. I think back on it now and it embarrasses me to remember that certain words heard on the radio could bring tears to my eyes: " . . . from Hartford, Connecticut, the featherweight champion of the world, Willie Pep." I thrilled when Willie beat Chalky Wright for the title, I cried when he was slaughtered by Sandy Saddler the night he lost it, I envied him the girls he displayed at the Hartford Auditorium. In the mists of memory, these girls are always blond and had what in my youth we called big knockers. The champion's girl friend with a pair of charlies that would knock your eyes out was, in fact, as much a part of my childhood as World War II. Since those were the days when the St. Louis Browns had a one-armed centerfielder, my athletic heroes, my "boyhood idols" in the language of the sports pages, were naturally intact prizefighters. I wanted to be Phil Terranova or Lulu Constantino or Al "Bummy" Davis. Sunday mornings I went to Mass early just to see Genaro Rojo, a good local boy, a welterweight always referred to in the *Hartford Courant* as a "crowd pleaser," which meant he got hit a lot, bobbing and weaving behind his left shoulder on the way to the communion rail, squeezing rubber balls to strengthen his hands. I used to think it was the only way to receive communion until I learned that the rap on his hands was that he had knuckles like potato chips.

And then the weekly fight game collapsed. Television killed it, and prosperity and the opening up of professional team sports to black athletes, who no longer had to get their brains scrambled in order to escape the ghetto. There were no fighters and no audience and the weekly fight clubs where a good boy could learn his trade disappeared. Today Muhammad Ali is the most famous athlete in the universe, but I bet there is not one person in ten thousand who knows that Irish Art Hafey is the number three ranked featherweight in the world or that Vicente Saldivar is 19 and 0 with 11 KO's. Nor did I, until I started to go to the fights again at the Olympic.

I suppose it was a matter of reintroducing myself to my youth. The Olympic is an anachronism, a fifty-year-old, ten-thousand-seat tenement that stinks of piss and liniment, leased to the roller games Saturdays and to the wrestlers Wednesdays and Fridays. But it is the weekly fight card that gives the Olympic its special character. Historically, poverty has been the breeding ground of prizefighters, and in the Chicano barrios of east Los Angeles is a ghetto peculiarly adapted to the perpetuation of the Olympic. It is a ghetto that seems comprised solely of flyweights, bantamweights, superbantams, featherweights and lightweights. For a Chicano athlete, the road out of the barrio is limited. There are no 122-pound tight ends, no five-foot rebounding forwards, no featherweight home-run hitters. Without the Mexican small men, the weekly fights at the Olympic simply would not exist. Over the years, the fighters who have filled the Olympic have had names like Art Aragon and Jesus Pimentel and Cisco Andrade and Raul Rojas and Bobby Chacon and Mando Ramos and Baby Sal Sorio and Enrique Bolanos and Danny Lopez. In any given week, Mexican Americans make up at least 60 percent of the paid attendance. It is not the Gucci crowd that one sees at the Rams or Lakers games; none of the top agents are there as they are in their season-ticket boxes at Dodger Stadium. It is an audience of gold teeth and polyester pants and T-shirts and AmVet badges. The big draw is a Mexican against an Anglo white hope and the crowd can grow ugly if a decision goes the wrong way. In 1964, the Olympic was quite literally wrecked when a riot erupted after a Mexican favorite lost a close decision to a Japanese rival; flooring, billboards, steel chairs—anything that could be ripped and thrown—were tossed into the ring. Today every customer who enters the Olympic is patted down police-style at the door in a check for hidden bottles of booze.

What makes the Olympic ultimately interesting, however, is neither the sociology of poverty nor the anthropological patterns that produce featherweights. It is the fight game itself. It is a game that by any natural logic or order of selection should be extinct, but which motion pictures have caused to survive in the national image bank. *Golden Boy. Body and Soul. Champion. The Set-Up. Fat City. Somebody Up There Likes Me.* Because of them, we all know the bleak concrete of the dressing room, the cold blaze of the ring lights, the ash-blonde at ringside with the red fox fur, the old manager with the pinkie ring and the orange cigar holder and the red plastic feather in his plaid fedora. And the legendary jeers: "Hit him, you bum, you got the wind with you." To visit the Olympic is to wonder if the movies took their clichés from the fight game or the fight game took its clichés from the movies. The Olympic's promoter is a casting director's dream. Her name is Aileen Eaton and she is always called the First Lady of Boxing. It would perhaps be more accurate to call Aileen Eaton the Only Lady of Boxing. She is sixty-six years old, she went to work for the Olympic thirty-five years ago after her first husband died and she took it over after her second husband, the club's promoter, also died. She is frail, she has faded red hair and of course she is as tough as a stevedore. "She is," says a manager who works with her so often he does not wish to be identified, "a stainless-steel tulip." Barbara Stanwyck played the part in *Golden Boy.*

Fight night at the Olympic begins at twelve noon with the weigh-in. Abandoned cats roam the aisles and corridors, pigeons bomb from the rafters. The walls of the ancient auditorium are covered with faded tinted photographs of old-time strong men and wrestlers and fighters and announcers. "Bud Taylor, the Terre Haute Terror." "The Popular Sport Harvey." "Bert 'Geev Eet to Heem' Colima." At ringside the scales are set up and the fighters climb on. The preliminary boys make from $125 to $200 each for the privilege of getting their noses flattened and their ears cauliflowered. Yet this is a better option than some. "I could be a jockey," said a bantamweight standing at ringside, flicking a piece of pigeon shit from his synthetic sweater, "and a horse could fall on me and he weigh fifteen hundred pounds and he would hurt me, I think."

It seemed an irrefutable point.

The managers and trainers and cut men and hangers-on watched the weigh-in out of the corners of their eyes and talked about old fights and new boys.

"Your boy's in with a runner."

"If it weren't for the ropes, he'd back into Mexicali. But my boy will catch him before he hits Tijuana. Who's your new boy?"

"A Mexican heavyweight."

"I see a Mexican heavyweight, I bet everything I can steal on the other guy."

"Your boy got hit by a lot of right hands last week."

"He's only had ten fights."

"If he's fighting in a school yard, he shouldn't've been taking the right hands he was taking last week."

A featherweight got on the scale, peeling off a T-shirt lettered LET'S HAVE AN AFFAIR. The scales were adjusted. One twenty-four and a half. The featherweight got off the scales and ripped open a bag of cheese popcorn.

"That shit will give you cancer," his manager said, taking it from him. To an onlooker, well within earshot of his boy, the manager said, "Sticking up gas stations is what he's good at."

"And bar fights," the second man said. "He's six-and-oh at the Casa Mazatlán, I hear."

"I saw your brother fight a long time ago," the manager said. "At St. Nick's. Eight-round semifinal. He was in with a colored boy."

"He lost."

"Split decision. A dirty fight it was, too. Lots of rabbit punches."

"They're good at the rabbit punches, the colored."

It was not communication; it was ritual.

Seco Luna did not make the weight. He skipped rope, he shadow-boxed, but he was still a pound over his contracted weight of twenty. An official from the State Athletic Commission gave him until four o'clock to make one twenty; if he didn't, he would be fined 10 percent of his purse and his manager would lose his fee. He boiled himself down to one nineteen and three-quarters.

When I arrived back at the Olympic that night, there was a crap game going on in the parking lot. I searched for the Olympic's legendary scalper, a Mexican Barnum who peddles $5 seats for $2—except they are tickets to last week's fight. He didn't seem to be working that evening. Seco Luna and five of his friends and handlers arrived in an overcrowded Pinto. As he walked across the lot carrying his equipment bag, Seco Luna suddenly stopped and peered into the match-maker's Cadillac. The car had a lettered license plate that read ROUND 1. Seco Luna went from the passenger's side of the driver's side, examining every detail of the Cadillac. I think I have never seen an envy and a yearning so naked.

It was a dull night at the Olympic. Ignacio Orosino decisioned Alejandro Lopez in the four-round opener. Ramon Contreras TKO'd Eladio Leal, the Cuban Kid. Rico Dineros decisioned Cole St. John and Alberto "Superfly" Sandoval KO'd Juan Rodriguez. In

233

the main event, Raul Tirado was slapping Seco Luna around pretty good until he accidentally butted Luna over the eye, causing the referee to stop the fight. It went into the books as a technical draw. What I remember most about the fight was not Seco Luna's left hand or his counterpunching. I remember that he did not wear a bathrobe but a serape.

As I left the Olympic, the ring announcer was tub-thumping for the upcoming weeks. "The undefeated boy from Mexico . . . the uncrowned featherweight champion . . . the hard-hitting Filipino boy . . . the sensational Mexican boy."

Good boys all. Each one of whom wanted a Cadillac with a license plate that read CHAMP. I suppose the golden boys of my childhood wanted that, too. Bummy Davis was shot and killed trying to stop a stickup in a saloon in Brooklyn. And the last I heard, Willie Pep was tending bar.

1976

REALTOR TO THE STARS

Mike Silverman likes animals. Mike Silverman goes on safari. Mike Silverman has a pet ape. The name of Mike Silverman's pet ape is Charlie. Charlie wears Gucci trousers. Mike Silverman is the realtor to the stars.

I was sitting in Mike Silverman's Beverly Hills real-estate office beneath a permanently affixed movie screen on which, to relax prospective buyers, he projects slides of the animals he photographs on safari.

Frankly, if I were in someone's office to buy a house and this creation behind the desk turned off the lights and flicked on a picture of an ape in Gucci trousers, I would make smoke for the county line, but then I am not the ordinary buyer of your basic "BACHELOR PAD—3 br, mds, den, $1.75 mil."

Mike and Charlie are living proof that the reality principle does not operate in much of the real estate sold between Beverly Hills and the Pacific Ocean. It is an area where the potential buyer with only $100,000 to spend will be told churlishly to try "south of Wilshire, east of Doheny." Houses lease for $7,500 a month, 2 br condominiums go for $300,000. Each block north of Santa Monica Boulevard in Beverly Hills adds $100,000 to the purchase price of a house and there are entire neighborhoods where prices begin at half a million—and escalate quickly to two million. In the Malibu colony, beachfront is up to $2,500 a foot and "shacks" on forty-foot lots start at $250,000. There is as much imperative to these prices as there is to spending $3,000 for a Galanos dress or $300,000 for a Léger. What you are buying is fantasy and asking about the copper plumbing or the light in the basement is like kicking the tires of a Rolls-Royce.

Part of the reason is the glamour quotient. Directions are given by personal rather than geographical coordinates, as in, "Turn left at the Jimmy Stewarts" or "It's on Mulholland between Jack and Warren" (and if you have to ask who Jack and Warren are, you belong in that social Siberia south of Wilshire and east of Doheny). At the beach, "Ryan" lives at La Costa and "Billy and Audrey" in Trancas and you plot your destination between O'Neal and Wilder. Houses have pedigrees and if the bloodlines can be traced from James Caan to Kim Novak to Ingrid Bergman, so much the better.

This studbook tradition was best satirized by my friend, producer Collier Young, owner through four marriages of a house on Mulholland he calls The Mouse House. One Christmas, having been married

235

to both ladies, he sent out a card reading, "Christmas Greetings from The Mouse House, former home of Ida Lupino and Joan Fontaine."

Oddly enough, it is often easier to sell a house for $500,000 than for $50,000. The purchaser of the half-million-dollar house is insulated from the vagaries of the economy and need not scratch for the last dollar. The man who sells him that house is like the Starkeeper in *Carousel*, watching stars rise and fall, predicting when that perfect piece of star property will come back onto the market. Nearly three-quarters of Mike Silverman's business used to be with show people; now it is considerably less than half. Today his perfect buyer is a person of "mature years with two marriages and a couple of heart attacks who wants to enjoy the time he has left." Silverman is a compendium of *Time* magazine adjectives—tall, silver-haired, impeccably dressed. He came west from New York nearly twenty-five years ago as a freelance commercial artist. Times were tough, he got into real estate. What he learned selling $30,000 houses off the Sunset Strip was that it did not take that much more work to sell them for ten times as much a few miles farther west in Beverly Hills.

Silverman's background in commercial art gave him a feel for what he calls the art direction in selling a house. In other words, a fire in the fireplace, a Rigaud candle burning on the coffee table, music on the stereo, two dozen white tulips, calligraphed invitations on the mantel, a chilled bottle of Pinot Chardonnay. "A glass of wine in a two-million-dollar house is awfully nice, don't you agree?" Mike Silverman said, sounding for all the world like Paul Henreid talking to Bette Davis in *Now, Voyager;* at any moment I expected him to light two cigarettes at once.

Mike Silverman has twenty people working for him. He will not handle a house under $150,000 (and only rarely one in that range); his average sale is $300,000, his commission 6 percent. The first eight residential prices listed on the board outside his office the day I visited him were 320, 450, 1.5, 450, 1 mil, 270, 350, 495. Houses fit for Peggy Lee. Or Tony Curtis, Cher, Sonny, Rex Harrison, Debbie Reynolds, Alice Cooper, Frank Sinatra, Dino De Laurentiis—to give you some of Silverman's better credits.

As the realtor to the stars, Mike Silverman is not the easiest person to get to see personally. Credentials are checked, access protected. "Does Mr. Silverman know you?" his secretary asked when I called for an appointment. (The last time a secretary asked me that, I told her that her film-director boss owed me $2,500 for an ounce of cocaine and I wanted it soonest or his car would blow up. He got on the phone quick.) Silverman not only has a PR man, he seems to have been invented by a PR man. Listening to him talk is like reading an anthology of old Leonard Lyons columns. My friend. My good friend. My very good friend. Charo. Frank. Zsa Zsa. "Number two client," Mike Silverman said, pointing to a picture of Zsa Zsa Gabor in a Swedish tit magazine where Silverman's PR man had placed a story about his client. Mike Silverman handles a new house for Zsa Zsa Gabor before and after her marriages. "Number one client," Mike Silverman said, pointing to a picture of Frank Sinatra in the same magazine. Mike Silverman is selling Frank Sinatra's house in Palm Springs. The house ("STAR'S HOME—HELIPORT") is on the market for $1,400,000 and Silverman has advertised it in a newspaper in Egypt that also features an advertisement for the Aladdin Hotel in Las Vegas. "I figure some sheikh might pick it up," Silverman says.

To date, Silverman's biggest residential sale has been for $2 million. "A steal," he says. Often he uses a helicopter to let a prospect case a house from above, check out the neighborhood, compare the size of the swimming pool next door. "We're in a wild market," he says. "There doesn't seem to be any ceiling." Recently Dino De Laurentiis went into escrow on a house for $1,100,000, then pulled out when the estate was used as a movie location and bought a $2 million

237

house instead. "I have a lot of anecdotes like that," Mike Silverman said.

Indeed, Mike Silverman seemed to speak only in anecdotes. He flipped through some animal pictures. "I was once chased by a rhino going forty miles an hour," he said. Pause. Beat. "I was in a Jeep going fifty."

"I have a full telephone involvement in my john," Mike Silverman said. "I once missed a deal because I was in the john and couldn't get to the phone."

Mike Silverman was running out of anecdotes. There is, after all, not that much to selling a house. You list it, you wait for someone to call. You chill the Pinot Chardonnay and make sure the firewood is not green and the tulips aren't wilted and the Rigaud has the proper fragrance.

"How old are you?" I asked.

He stared, hands tented under his nose. I had the feeling he was going to give me the asking on his age. I was right. "Forty-seven would be about right," Mike Silverman said.

His hand moved over his desk as if in search of one last anecdote. He picked up a press photograph. "Here's me and Elke Sommer at an art opening. Being a bachelor I get invited to all the art openings."

"You must have an active social life then?"

He examined the question for hidden explosive devices. "Not at all," he said finally. "I devote three nights a week to heavy reading."

"What?"

"Books." It seemed to strike him as not quite sufficient. "I also watch documentaries on television."

I got up to go.

"My press agent has a lot of anecdotes about me," Mike Silverman said.

Oh, yes. I live in Trancas. Three miles past Billy and Audrey.

1976

MAD MILO

There are 214 private detectives listed in the Los Angeles Yellow Pages. No Archer. No Marlowe. No Spade. No Continental Op. I needed a shamus for a writing caper I had planned. Local color, MO, that sort of thing. I picked Nick Harris. I liked his ad: DISCREET SHADOWING FOR PEACE OF MIND.

"Nick Harris passed on," the secretary said when I telephoned.

"When?"

"1943."

"Oh."

"I'll connect you to Milo."

Milo. The perfect name for a shamus. Evoking one of the greats. Miles Archer. Deceased partner in the partnership of Spade & Archer. (" 'Miles,' Spade said hoarsely, 'was a son of a bitch.' ") Milo. The boss. Working in the great tradition.

Milo picked up the phone. "Milo Speriglio," he said. "Press liaison."

Samuel Spade's jaw was long and bony, his chin a jutting V under the more flexible V of his mouth. His nostrils curved back to make another, smaller, V. . . . He looked rather pleasantly like a blond satan.

—DASHIELL HAMMETT, *The Maltese Falcon*

Milo Speriglio looks like a capital "I." He is slight and reed thin, perhaps five eight and 140 pounds, a thirty-second-degree Mason who chain-smokes Kool cigarettes and wears a diamond ring on his right pinkie with the Masonic emblem on the right side and tiny diamond stones worked into the initials M.S. on top. His eyes are cool and heavy-lidded, his suit caramel-colored, his shirt a discreet orange print, his office, both walls and carpeting, baby blue. He is forty years old, he has run for mayor of Los Angeles on a law-and-order and antibusing platform (finishing fifth among the twelve candidates in the primary), and he shares the terrace beyond the glass doors of his office with the League of Women Voters. There is a large oil painting of a striking long-haired blonde on the baby-blue wall opposite his desk, a self-portrait, it turns out, by his wife; two of her other paintings also hang on the baby-blue wall—one of a tiger, the other of a sun-dappled seascape. I think of Philip Marlowe's office: "A reasonably shabby door at the end of a reasonably shabby corridor in the sort of building that was new about the year the all-tile bathroom became the basis of civilization."

Milo is talking. His voice is soft, barely audible, and he seems to disappear in the black Naugahyde chair behind the U-shaped desk, his face all but hidden by the smoke screen from the Kools. He has, he says, one hundred seventy full-time operatives, and their rates, depending on the complexity of the case and the qualifications of the personnel on it, run from twenty-three to fifty-five dollars an hour. His own rates, when he works on a case, are much, much more. The client must sign a contract and pay a retainer up front, and as with BankAmericard, there is a monthly charge for late payment of the balance. I glanced at the four-page rate card, stopping at a box headed SEMEN TEST. It reminded me of Scobie in *The Heart of the Matter*: "You never knew in a search what you would find. A man's bedroom was his private life: prying in drawers you came on humiliations; little petty vices were tucked out of sight like a soiled handkerchief; under a pile of linen you might come on a grief he was trying

to forget." CHILD-CUSTODY INVESTIGATIONS. PHONE
TAPS & ROOM BUGS PROFESSIONALLY DETECTED. SKIP
TRACES. DETERMINING SPOUSE'S FAITHFULNESS. DIS-
CREETLY DETERMINING WHAT WAS DONE—WHERE
& WITH WHOM. The rate card seemed to italicize Milo
Speriglio's own personal evaluation of himself in the
Yellow Pages: A LEGEND IN HIS OWN TIME.

We began with a case that was instrumental in making Milo Speriglio a living legend. The Tabby case.

J.G.D.: Tell me about the Tabby case.
MILO: Tabby was the name of a cat and this was probably the biggest cat case ever held in this country.
J.G.D.: How did it come about?
MILO: Two clients, male and female, came into the
office and told my secretary they wanted to see me,
and me only, to investigate a missing cat. They had
seen me on a press conference on television and
they had noticed the crossed swords I have hanging
on the wall in my office. They had recently gone to
a very famous psychic who had told them a man
with crossed swords was going to find Tabby. It
turned out they were quite wealthy clients from
London.
J.G.D.: How long had Tabby been missing?
MILO: About six months prior to our being brought
into the case. We handled it like it was an FBI case.
We had about thirty agents working on it.
J.G.D.: a purebred cat?
MILO: No, actually it was just an inexpensive cat, but
it was very important to them. We are very good at
animals. We get an average of ten or twelve dog
cases a year. Dogs are much easier to find than cats.
Right now we are running an 85 percent success
record in finding dogs.
J.G.D.: Why are dogs easier to find?
MILO: I don't know. They just seem to be. Cats we
run less than 50 percent successful. The weirdest
case we ever had in the animal field was a canary.
J.G.D.: You had to hunt a canary?

MILO: Which we did not find, yes.

J.G.D.: How do you go about hunting lost pets?

MILO: Well, there are no guide rules. We treat it like it was an actual person—when was it last seen, et cetera, et cetera. There is a lot of field work; unless we have photographs, it's hard to tell if you have the right animal if there are no tags on it.

J.G.D.: Where did you find Tabby?

MILO: In the hills, about eighteen miles from where the clients lived.

J.G.D.: Was it stolen?

MILO: No. It had several animal bites on it, so it was only roughing it.

J.G.D.: What was your fee on the Tabby case?

MILO: That particular cat case ran twenty-five thousand dollars. But that was unusual. The average dog case runs about three hundred to four hundred dollars.

J.G.D.: We've talked about missing animals. What about missing persons?

MILO: Females are harder to find than males. Because of the name change with marriage. But in the past ten years, this agency is working on a 92 percent find rate. That means we find 92 percent of the people we're asked to find. And that includes people missing thirty or forty years. We have found them in just about half the states in the United States.

J.G.D.: Any particular case stick in your mind?

MILO: The sex-survey case.

J.G.D.: The sex-survey case?

MILO: Right. One of the major universities in California took a sex survey of a bunch of girls. They wanted to determine the sex life of these particular girls. And then two years later, they wanted to do a follow-up survey. They couldn't locate five hundred fifty of the females in the survey and they hired us to find them. The girls were sixteen years of age at the time of the survey and now they were eighteen, and these five hundred fifty had moved away from home and they couldn't find them.

J.G.D.: It must've been expensive.

MILO: We were working on a volume rate.

J.G.D.: Because you were looking for five hundred fifty missing female persons?

MILO: Right.

J.G.D.: How many did you find?

MILO: Ninety-seven percent. Which surprised the hell out of us. Because we're working on a 92 percent average, which is the highest in the country.

J.G.D.: How did you get into this?

MILO: Well, I have a pretty interesting background. Prior to being a private investigator, I was a disc jockey and recording artist. I used to go under the name of Mad Milo.

J.G.D.: Mad Milo?

MILO: Right. That was my professional name. I don't sing, so I invented a new type of record. I would take a hit record—you can legally steal a few bars off any record—and I would lay in a voice-over. You ever heard of *"Elvis on Trial"*?

J.G.D.: No.

MILO: We actually put Elvis on trial on that record. I was sort of a judge. I would say, "Elvis, what do you have to say about such and such?" And he would sing a few bars of one of his hits. "Don't be cruel," he would sing, and so forth.

J.G.D.: It must have been lucrative.

MILO: I made zero pennies.

J.G.D.: It seems a big jump from Mad Milo to being a private eye.

MILO: This might go along with the theme of your story because this is what really happened. Television was kind of fascinating in those days. *Peter Gunn* was the number-one show and I thought I would like to be a private detective like that.

J.G.D.: Why?

MILO: Because I was used to leading an exciting kind of life, like being in the disc-jockey field and what have you.

J.G.D.: I see.

MILO: But you have to have experience. I went to the Yellow Pages and called Nick Harris, but you had to have four thousand hours of previous experience before they even considered you. The next place I called, the same thing. Experience. The third place, I said I had four and a half years' experience. And the woman in charge said her husband just died and she needed somebody.

J.G.D.: You said you had four and a half years' experience, but you didn't?

MILO: Yeah. About two and a half months passed, and I became general manager of the company and stayed another four years. Then I opened my own agency.

J.G.D.: How many cases have you had?

MILO: Way over a hundred fifty thousand.

J.G.D.: *A hundred fifty thousand?*

MILO: Right. That I have handled or directed.

J.G.D.: Can you carry heat?

MILO: No, not legally. Not in Los Angeles County. They won't issue gun permits to private investigators.

J.G.D.: What do you carry then?

MILO: We carry an item we also distribute.

J.G.D.: What's it called?

MILO: Stinger dog repellent.

J.G.D.: I see.

MILO: It's red pepper with an oil base.

J.G.D.: In an aerosol can. Like mace.

MILO: This is legal. Seventy one-second shots. Or you can shoot it continuously.

J.G.D.: It takes the place of a heater?

MILO: Right.

J.G.D.: What are you best known for?

MILO: Being the North Pole.

J.G.D.: What?

MILO: Being the North Pole. Where Santa lives.

J.G.D.: Oh.

MILO: It was an accident. Several years ago, we started getting calls from little kids asking if they could talk to Santa Claus and we said, "You must have the wrong number." But it got to the point where we were getting too many calls, so we started to investigate to find out what the heck was going on.

J.G.D.: Being a private detective, you were uniquely equipped to make this sort of investigation.

MILO: Right. And we found out they were misdialing a Dial-a-Santa number, which was one digit off ours. So we decided, well, rather than disappoint the kids, we would go along with it. So we instructed our girls to start answering the phone, "North Pole." And as time permitted, the various investigators would become Santa and later the girls on the switchboard became Mrs. Claus.

J.G.D.: And you continued it.

MILO: Right. When the Dial-a-Santa went out of business. Last year, we got more calls than we ever had in the past. It made all the wire services. All the local newspapers did stories and it made radio and television. In fact, we're still getting calls on a daily basis from parents wanting to know what are these phone bills they are getting.

J.G.D.: What are you up to now?

MILO: I've started a publishing company. Seville Publishing.

J.G.D.: That's an interesting name.

MILO: I named it after my car.

J.G.D.: Then you don't see yourself being a private eye for the rest of your life?

MILO: No. No way. No way possible.

J.G.D.: What do you want to do?

MILO: I'm going to have to find something exciting somewhere along the line, even if it's just on a part-time basis. I would be bored to death just being a publisher. I'm kind of old to get into things I used to do years ago. Skating with the roller derby, things like that.

1977

WINTER CRUISE

The rain sluices down through the canyons of Los Angeles and seeps into the bones. Christmas crèches hang askew from the drenched palm trees along Wilshire Boulevard, etched against the cold gunmetal sky like some presentiment of the Second Coming. I finger travel folders. Cartagena. Acapulco. Puerto Vallarta. Mazatlán. La Paz. A trade wind whispering through the frangipani blossoms. The music of a thousand guitars.

I pick up the cruise ship in Acapulco. It is her maiden voyage, and she sits at her berth trim and so white she might have been carved from a mountain of soap. Only at the anchor chain is there a hint of rust. I tour the ship. There is a nightclub, four cocktail bars, three dance floors, a theater, a swimming pool, shuffleboard, Ping-Pong. Every room is first class. From the purser I get a list of future cruises. There is the Family Plan Cruise, the Art and Photography Cruise, the Flower and Archaeology Cruise, the Life Begins at 40 Cruise. Each, I was told, was unique, each two weeks of fun and frolic in the tropics, away from the cares of home and family.

I am assigned a place at the second sitting in the dining salon. My table companions are a retired farmer and his wife from the Imperial Valley and a lady realtor from Burbank named Bette. Her hair is a young and hopeful Sunshine Gold, and she calls herself "the Merry Widow." She smiles and winks, her tongue licking her upper lip. "A grass widow actually," she says. Bette seems to know everyone on board. There are Bob and Ralph and Harry. I ask their last names. "No last names," she says. "No lasting entanglements." The farmer's wife peruses the breakfast menu. She orders prune juice, some Kadota figs and a dish of stewed prunes. "The water," her husband says. His wife stares him into silence. "I told Claude that Merle Oberon lives in Acapulco," she says. "He says to me, 'Does Merle Oberon drink the water?'"

That night, before we sail, there is a charity gala on board celebrating the world premiere of a new Hollywood film. There is a cluster of movie people on the Lido deck and some international whores. They seem a race apart from the passengers, from those wives with their hair newly blued, those husbands uncomfortable in brocade dinner jackets. A former president of Mexico is supposed to attend the gala, and before he arrives I watch one of Acapulco's first citizens, an American, rearranging the place cards to get a better seat at the head table. "Which one is the president?" an elderly woman in harlequin glasses asks her husband. "He's one of those Mexicans," her husband answers. Bette asks her escort of the evening to take a picture of her with the movie stars, and when he refuses, she stands by herself, swaying to the music of the mariachis. "My God, look at that creature in the mauve," a man behind me giggles. It is someone I had once known in New York. He looks like the picture of Dorian Gray, so drunk he can hardly stand. "She looks like Carmen Miranda." I laugh and feel disloyal.

In the morning we are underway. The west coast of Mexico looms dimly off to the starboard. The passengers lie toasting in the sun. Noses begin to peel, and varicose knobs turn brown. The daily schedule for the three-day run to Los Angeles is inexorable. In my cabin I read the daily riddle in the shipboard newspaper: "Why is a ship a she?" Answer: "Because when coming into port, she always heads for the buoys." After breakfast I go to Count Calories with Kirk on the Lido deck, and following that I walk up to the Grand Saloon for a Complimentary Dance Lesson with Chiquita and Montalvo. The pace never quickens, the conversation is always the same. "She has angina, you see. . . . And so after the operation. . . . My first trip since Clem passed on. . . . You'd think they'd have a size sixteen. . . ."

The cruise directress has a relentless smile. "That dear Mr. Hannon, do you know what he said when we passed through the Panama Canal locks? 'Do we get bagels?' " I nod. She explains. *"Locks. Bagels."* I smile. We are waiting to get costumes for the masquerade party that will be held that night. On the ship's bulletin board is the notice: CAPTAIN'S FARE-WELL PARTY TONITE—FIRST SITTING CAPTAIN'S COCKTAILS 6:30—SECOND SITTING CAPTAIN'S COCK-TAILS 8:00. I hear the cruise directress talking to another group of revelers. "Locks," she says. "And bagels." A spurt of laughter. "And Mr. Carter a semi-finalist in the Ping-Pong tournament. Sixty-nine years young."

The grand march of the masqueraders begins promptly at 10:30 in the Grand Saloon. Most of the contestants are wearing bedsheets and are variously identified as either Arabs or Roman senators. Bette is a semifinalist. She is dressed as a pumpkin. She is wearing black tights and is swaddled in orange cloth with four balloons placed strategically front and rear. The winners in the "Original" category are a husband and wife decked out as hippies, the winner in the "Artistic" category a woman swathed in green velvet with a picture frame around her head—the *Mona Lisa*. After the final balloting, Bette comes into the bar with a hatpin in her hand. She invites the single men sitting on the barstools to prick her balloons. The balloons pop, one by one. The bar empties. A last round of margaritas. Bette is kissing cheeks. Suddenly she begins to cry. "I'm a respectable woman," she says. "I'm forty-nine years old. I've beaten cancer. Why can't I have a good time?"

The last day out the weather is rough. Many of the passengers remain in their cabins. The dining saloon is almost empty. Stewards tie Red Cross sick bags to the railings. In the lounges there is a subtle change in the conversations. The passengers no longer talk of Cartagena and Acapulco, but of Glendale and Santa Ana. Photographs of children and grandchildren appear. There is a general discussion of tipping procedures. The cruise directress settles the argument—a dollar a day per person for the dining-room waiter and the same for the room steward. Friendships made for life a week ago on the Acapulco nightclub tour now seem less possible, less relevant. "You ever get up to the Bay Area now, Ava, you look us up."

"Don't get up that way much anymore, but we'll see," Ava says. "Don't have your address, but don't suppose you folks will be hard to find. The telephone book. We'll see. Nice meeting you, I'm sure."

They straggle off the boat the next morning, laden with duty-free liquor, rum mostly, and Kahlua. The band waiting on the pier is playing "California, Here I Come." I see Bette after clearing customs. She waves and blows a kiss. "Aloha," she says.

1967

BOTTLED POETRY

At the top and again at the bottom of the Napa Valley, an hour or two northeast of San Francisco, there is a redwood sign alongside Highway 29 that reads WEL-COME TO THE WINE COUNTRY, followed by a quote from Robert Louis Stevenson, ". . . and the wine is bottled poetry." The Napa Valley is indeed wine country. Along the forty-nine-mile stretch of Highway 29 in Napa County, there are over fifty wineries, so many offering tasting tours that it is quite possible in a journey from Oakville, say, to Calistoga to get a cheap and quite pleasant buzz. But until May 24, 1976, the bottled poetry of the Napa Valley was generally regarded by wine connoisseurs as bottled Sara Teasdale.

On that day in Paris, an English wine merchant held a blind wine tasting in honor of the American Bicentennial. The white wines in the tasting consisted of four classic French Burgundies (a Bâtard Montrachet, a Puligny Montrachet, a Clos des Mouches and a Merseault-Charmes) and six California Chardonnays; the reds pitted such *grands crus* Bordeaux as Château Mouton-Rothschild (1970), Château Haut-Brion (1970) and Château Montrose (1970) against such upstart California Cabernets as a Freemark Abbey (1969), a Heitz Cellar "Martha's Vineyard" (1970) and a Stag's Leap Wine Cellars (1973). The nine judges were all French and there wasn't a stiff or a ringer in the bunch: the head sommelier at Tour d'Argent, the owner of Le Grand Véfour, the co-manager of the

Romanée-Conti vineyards and a half-dozen other wine writers and wine bureaucrats. The tasting was held on the patio of the Hôtel Intercontinental, which was festively draped with the tricolor and the Stars and Stripes. Each judge was given a scorecard (the wines were to be rated on a scale of one to twenty), a hard roll to clear the palate and an ice bucket to serve as a spittoon. After a glass of Chablis *pour un rince-bouche,* the judges began to taste.

Now the French were not at all sentimental about the Bicentennial (HOW FRANCE WON THE AMERICAN REVOLUTION was a headline for the occasion in *Paris-Match*), nor were they about to be sentimental about any bottled iambic pentameter from the Napa Valley. Condescension was the rule of the day. "Definitely California, no nose," said one judge. "The best of the Americans," offered another. The problem was that the noseless Californian and best of the Americans were both French, and when a third judge twirled and sniffed and said, "La belle France," he was holding a Napa white. When the scorecards were tallied, the results mortified the French judges. The winner among the reds was the Stag's Leap Wine Cellars (which draws its name from a large jutting rock in the Napa Valley); the clear victor among the whites (six of the nine judges placed it first) was Napa's 1973 Château Montelena.

A few months after the Paris testing, I decided to visit Château Montelena. I was prompted not by chauvinism (the only wine I buy is a Spanish Rioja) but by a survey in *Fortune* on the change in American drinking habits, specifically from hard spirits to wines, whose sales rose 37 percent over the last five years. Actually I was aware of the change long before *Fortune*, largely because I am still a member in good standing of that diminishing constituency of "older drinkers" with what *Fortune* calls ". . . the special taste that is satisfied by whiskey." From the late sixties on, it has been virtually impossible to get a drink in the trendier households of Hollywood, where vodka is regarded as booze and a drink is generally something blue with a gardenia in it that's made in a blender and named after an island, or a volcano; on the kitchen blackboards in these houses, there is usually chalked some message like, "2 cases vino—ein blanc, ein rouge—Zig-Zag papers." What particularly fascinated me in the *Fortune* survey was the information that 74 percent of the hundreds of millions of gallons of wine consumed in America was produced in California. And so I headed north into the Napa Valley.

It is an eerie place, a narrow valley between two mountain ranges, a sliver of land that seems lost in time. Town and valley seem to belong to an era before the combustion engine. The mind takes a long time to adjust to the reason: there are no shopping malls along Highway 29, no developments of ticky-tacky tract houses. Local ordinances, one is told; an agricultural preserve of arable acres. The landscape is carpeted with vineyards and occasionally, every mile or so, a vast Victorian stone pile rises out of the vines, the home of some nineteenth-century wine baron, all turrets and cupolas and verandas and stained-glass windows. The effect is Edgar Allan Poe. One thinks of mass murders on the polished hardwood floors, dead bodies occupying overstuffed chairs shrouded with linen antimacassars.

Château Montelena sits at the top of the valley, near Calistoga, a tiny town floating on an underground hot spring, which makes it a mecca for old people with bodies battered by arthritis and the other customary complaints of senior citizenship; the name of the motel where I stayed was Dr. Wilkinson's and it offered, like the others in town, mud baths and high colonics. The Montelena winery was built in 1882 in the style of a French château. Its walls are three to twelve feet thick and much of it is hollowed into a hillside to allow the aging wine the proper amount of cool and damp. The history of the château mirrors the wine-making history of the valley. Although wine has been produced commercially in the valley since 1861, the Napa wine industry in its current incarnation is only forty years old. The reason, of course, is Prohibition, which forced most of the old wineries to plow under their vineyards or go into receivership or sacramental wine or minor bootlegging.

For decades after the passage of the Volstead Act, Château Montelena's vineyards were neglected, its winery dormant. Then in 1958, the château was purchased by a Chinese couple who had fled Mao's China with their bankbook intact. There in the Napa Valley they sought to re-create their estate in north China. They built a lake and surrounded it with willow trees; in the lake they put a number of islands and on several of the islands they actually built pagodas. Coupled with the mock French of the château, the mock chinoiserie is startling. A Chinese junk painted with dragons lies beached on the lakeshore and ducks and geese paddle and honk in the water. Because the lake has no source, however, it needs an aerator to keep the water clear and unstagnant. The aerator sticks out of the water like a periscope and I had the definite illusion, while sitting in one of the pagodas, that the shade of Mao Tse-tung was under the lake in a submarine checking to see where the people's money had gone. I was on my third bottle of Château Montelena at the time.

In fact, a belt of the grape is advisable after a day touring Napa wineries, Château Montelena not excepted. There is something to remember here about wineries in general and California wineries in particular: not outside of a roomful of William Morris agents will you hear more talk about art. The art of the grape. The art of wine making. The art of fermentation. The art of bottling. Basically, however, visiting a winery is about as interesting as watching a haircut. The smell is nice, but a steel-jacketed fermentation tank has none of the intrinsic magnetism of a Bessemer converter, say, or a five-color press. In a weekend spent at half a dozen wineries, I learned only three things I didn't already know—first, that a cooper is a barrel maker;

second, that white wine can be made from red grapes; and third, that Napa vintners do not think that French wine is better. On reflection, I believe these to be three things I should have known in the first place.

What we are dealing with is not an art but an illusion, the illusion of pastoral manufacture, of a preindustrial yeomanry. This is the illusion that lends the Napa Valley its peculiar nineteenth-century crafts aspect. Paradoxically, it is also an illusion that attracts conglomerates and absentee owners and tax shelters. In 1972, Château Montelena was purchased by a southern California supermarket developer and his lawyer, and as their head illusionist, or wine maker, they selected a Yugoslavian refugee named Miljenko Grgich. After eighteen years in the Napa Valley, Grgich's only concession to New World custom has been to anglicize his name to "Mike" ("because easier to spell"). In his dogged devotion to an almost fundamentalist concept of the American dream, Grgich reminded me of another group of Yugoslavs I met in the California vineyards, the grape growers in Delano first struck by Cesar Chavez in the mid-sixties. I admit a fondness for the clannish and stubborn Slavs in California's wine and grape country. They still speak in the accents of their ancestors and not in the featureless inflections of affluent California and cling more tightly to the frontier mentality than do the men whose great-grandfathers helped to create it. The complexities of the twentieth-century industrial society already lapping at the edge of their vineyards completely elude them. Now fifty-two, Grgich is part of this single-minded tradition. When I asked him why he had left Yugoslavia, he replied, "Because I am strictly believing in free enterprise."

The only thing that sends Grgich into greater raptures than the free-enterprise system is the making of wine. Clad in a black beret and a purple pullover, he walked me over every inch of Château Montelena's winery and vineyards, giving me a crash course in viticulture and enology. I learned approximate fermentation times and how stems, skins and seeds are recycled as fertilizer and that Chardonnay is aged in imported Limousin oak barrels and Cabernet in imported Nevers barrels, information as useful to me as an explanation of the pathetic fallacy would be to him. Grgich actually talks to the wine (a claim made by every head illusionist), sensing when it is ready for the barrel. "Is living thing," he said. "Book no good, science no good. I smell. I taste. I know." How? "I am artist." I gave the obligatory nod.

Now it was time to taste. No more art, no more illusion, just the reality. Grgich picked a '72 Chardonnay, a '73 Zinfandel and a '73 Cabernet and led me out to one of the pagodas. I noticed the bridge appeared crooked. "Chinese believe evil spirits travel in straight line," he said. "So bridges zigzag." I generally have a low tolerance for wine chat, but as this was the first time I had ever been where the evil spirits could not get at me, I decided to give it a shot. The tasting was conducted by Château Montelena's sales manager. We uncorked the first bottle. We swirled and breathed and then I found myself talking about the precocity and the good forward nose and the softening of the tannins and bottle age and complexity and the young Cabernet taste.

"An exceptional finish."

"Goes along with the rich nose."

"I'd say a spicy nose."

"Rich and spicy."

"Long on the palate."

"A hint of complexity."

"More of an innuendo."

"Comes from the oak."

"Limousin?"

"No. Nevers for the Cabernet."

"Of course. Nervous."

"But agreeable."

"Absolutely."

"A long wine."

"Vraiment," I said.

No evil spirits traveled the zigzag bridge, but the complexities of the grape reached me, perhaps because I did not realize that in a tasting you are supposed to swirl, taste and then spit out instead of swallowing. I drank everything. My brain was so addled with drink that it was sometime after I arrived home that I thought to call Château Montelena to find out where I could get some of the prize '73 Chardonnay.

It is just the thing after three Scotches.

1976

TEXAS POOR

To drill an oil well costs in the neighborhood of $100,000. The chances of finding oil, if the well is the first in a new field, are roughly one in eight, the chances of the well being profitable, if oil is discovered, one in forty-three. It is a game played on credit, and if the credit is not forthcoming, a man is broke. Indeed it is possible for a man to have drilled 115 million barrels of oil in his lifetime, to live in a $700,000 house, to wear on his finger a diamond as big as the Ritz, to have personal assets estimated at a million dollars and still, in the terms of the oil game, be considered broke. One way to get into this predicament is to default on a $29 million loan. Of such anomalies is the story of Glenn McCarthy.

There is a whole generation now to whom the name Glenn McCarthy is meaningless. Their eyes only unglaze when told he was the model for Jett Rink in Edna Ferber's *Giant*. "The James Dean part," they say, and it is a response that saddens me. Nearly twenty years ago, when I was a boy in prep school, Glenn McCarthy was, for good or ill, the symbol of everything Texas stood for, the prototype wildcatter. He came out of Houston's Fifth Ward, a section so tough, he liked to recall, that ". . . the cops were afraid of the people, and there was almost always a dead man somewhere in the street in the morning." He pressed pants, drove rivets, ran filling stations, a brooding, vaguely menacing man with the looks of a Mississippi gambler who did not like to have anyone else tell him what to do. It was the ideal disposition for a wildcatter, and in places with names like Chocolate Bayou and Bailey's Prairie and Coleto Creek, he began to drill, operating on a shoestring, often unable to pay his crew, announcing instead, "Anybody wants to walk off the job, I'll whip hell out of him." And then the improbable happened. McCarthy struck oil, parlaying the well into an empire of natural gas, radio stations, a steel plant, a chemical firm, a private air force.

Other poor Texans have struck it rich, but theirs have remained merely Horatio Alger stories. With McCarthy there was something more, a kind of vulgar élan. He brawled his way through the Houston night, shooting craps at $1,000 a throw, driving his Cadillac at a hundred miles an hour with a bottle of whiskey at his side. His concept of civic betterment was to build the Shamrock Hotel, a vast, ugly pyramid that Frank Lloyd Wright described as "tragic." Its opening was memorialized in Texas annals as "the night Houston ate peas with a knife." It was St. Patrick's Day, 1949. The invitations to the opening were gold on white doeskin. There were sixty-three different shades of green in the hotel and, as a St. Patrick's Day touch, McCarthy had 2,500 shamrocks flown over from Ireland. Thousands of friends, guests and freeloaders jammed the hotel, some flown in on planes McCarthy had chartered, others trained in on the *Super Chief,* which he had rented for the occasion.

The opening was the peak of McCarthy's career. Already the seams of his empire were beginning to split, and in the Petroleum Club oilmen were laying odds that Jesse Jones would pick up the Shamrock at ten cents on the dollar. Jesse Jones didn't but the high-rolling was over. McCarthy was fearfully overextended; he had more than $30 million on loans he could not meet, and with his sources of credit drying up, he could no longer play the wildcatter's gambling game. The Shamrock went, and then, one by one, the other enterprises. Plans gathered dust, plans, for example, to build a domed sports stadium in Houston fifteen years before ground was broken for the Astrodome. "He could have saved just about everything if he had been willing to incorporate," a friend has said. "Or he could have made a deal with Sinclair. They offered him a hundred million for his holdings and another fifty million to pay off all his debts. He could have paid his taxes and put seventy-five million cash in the bank. But that's not the way independents operate. No matter what the risk, they prefer to go it alone."

Today McCarthy is still going it alone. He describes himself as "slightly active" in oil, he runs the Cork Club, a private night spot in downtown Houston, and there is Glenn McCarthy's Wildcatter Whiskey, every bottle of which carries a picture of him taken in his younger, wilder days. There are those who would not regard this as living in penury, but in the oil game money is relative. What counts is the ability to deal now, not yesterday's successes. There are no points for crapping out.

Not long ago I flew over to Houston to see how the vicissitudes of time and fortune had affected McCarthy's life-style. We met over lunch in the men's bar at the Cork Club. There was a sense of overwhelming maleness in this masculine preserve. The chili was so hot it felt like an acetylene torch in my stomach, deer heads were mounted on the wall, and there were three nude paintings, the kind in which the artist lavishes attention on nipples pink as rose petals and large as acorns. McCarthy is fifty-nine now, his jowls are looser and there is more silver in his hair than I expected. His voice is a deep, low, almost nasal rumble. The talk at the table was of hunting and rattlesnakes. One of the men told about seeing someone bitten in the hand by a diamondback "big around as that catsup bottle there," and as he described how the victim's arm slowly began to turn black, he laughed until the tears came.

"You ever get hit by one of them sumbitches, Glenn?" another man asked.

Slowly McCarthy raised his leg over his knee and pulled up his cuff. Just above his right ankle was a triangular scar. "Got me in the gristle," he said. "Didn't hurt me none. I was drunk. Just rolled over and went to sleep. Alcohol must have saved me. Must have killed that sumbitch."

It was the authentic voice, the voice of a man who has lived the kind of life that allowed no second takes. Later we went down to McCarthy's office, two floors below the Cork Club. The room is dominated by two pictures of himself, one an oil portrait, the other an almost life-sized photograph of him standing on a ridge glowering at the camera, a hunting rifle nestled in his arm. He excused himself to put some medicine in his eyes, which were burned some time ago in an oil-well fire. I examined the office. There was a cigarette lighter shaped like an oil derrick on his desk, a shotgun cartridge in an out box, a bottle of Wildcatter Whiskey, a clutter of maps, blueprints and geological surveys, and a drawing of a building that had never come to be. When McCarthy returned, one of the men who had been at lunch spread a map on his desk.

"This old boy owns this land got more money than he got sense, Glenn," he said. "There's oil here and here and here. He just wants a well drilled in six months. He said he'd lease it to me, and I said, 'Hell, no, I'm not in the oil business,' and I thought of you. I don't want to make a jillion, I want you to make a big strike, Glenn."

McCarthy studied the map noncommittally. I wondered if he was thinking, as I was, who was promoting what, or whom. It did not seem to be a proposition that would have been offered him twenty years ago. "I'll have to make a survey," he said finally. "I'll let you know."

A few minutes later there was a telephone call from a Hollywood theatrical agent booking a singer into the Cork Club. In question was the singer's contract, and as McCarthy argued over the phone, his voice began to rise. "Now, goddammit, you're trying to pull a fast one on me," he said. He listened and then his face began to get red, and he started to shout. "I don't want any fancy talk, you hear? You play that way, and I'm going to call this whole thing off. You want it that way? Then all right, goddammit, it's off." He slammed the phone down.

The style had not changed. It occurred to me how tough it must have been to do business with McCarthy in the past when he had millions at his disposal. I left him poring over the maps of the proposed oil lease, giving orders, asking questions: How deep were the other wells in the area, what rock formation were they in? He was dubious about the area's possibilities, but in the days when he was king of the wildcatters, he had made a fortune when lesser men called him a fool. As we shook hands, I asked him if there was anything special he remembered about the flush years. He thought for a long time. "I remember the Shamrock opening," he said. "There was a lot of talk about Communism at the time. I wanted something that would personify the American way of life."

1967

EUREKA!

1.

I moved to California on the fifth day of June 1964. I can be very specific about the date: I had to swear to it in a legal deposition, signed and witnessed and admitted into evidence in Civil Court, City of New York, in and for the County of New York, as an addendum in the case of *New York Telephone Company, Plaintiff*, vs. *John Gregory Dunne, Index No. 103886/1964*. The charge against me was nonpayment of a bill from New York Telephone in the amount of $54.09. The record of the proceeding, Index No. 103886/1964, noted that a subpoena had been issued ordering me to court to answer the charge, and a process server, fully cognizant, as the record shows, that his "statements are true under the penalties of perjury," swore under oath that he had served me with said subpoena on July 7, 1964, in person at my residence, 41 East 75th Street, City of New York, County of New York. The case of *New York Telephone Company, Plaintiff*, vs. *John Gregory Dunne* was heard on July 24, 1964, and in due course I was found guilty as charged, fined $5 plus $9 in court costs and $1.16 in interest on the unpaid bill, making the total default $69.25. A warrant was also issued for my arrest for failure to answer a court order, namely the subpoena allegedly served on July 7, 1964.

Sometime later that summer, the papers pertaining to Index No. 103886/1964, Civil Court, City of New

York, in and for the County of New York, were forwarded to me at my new home in Portuguese Bend, California, a peninsula protruding into the Pacific Ocean on the southwestern tip of Los Angeles County. The equilibrium of my first western summer was upset. The sealed crates containing the records of my past were drawn from storage and opened. A check of my bank statements confirmed that the bill from New York Telephone had been paid on time, the evidence being a canceled check, No. 61, dated March 23, 1964, drawn in the amount of $54.09 on the Chase Manhattan Bank, Rockefeller Center Branch, and paid to the order of the plaintiff, the New York Telephone Company. Witnesses attested that I had not been out of Los Angeles County since my arrival on the fifth of June, making it difficult for the process server, whatever his affirmations that his statements were "true under the penalties of perjury," to have served me with a subpoena on the upper East Side of Manhattan on July 7. I engaged Carmine DeSapio's attorney and on his instructions sent this information to the president of the New York Telephone Comapny, copy as well to Mr. John McInerney, Clerk of the Civil Court, City of New York, in and for the County of New York. By return mail I received a letter from the president of New York Telephone apologizing for the unfortunate error, saying that the judgment had been vacated and that copies of the vacating order as well as his letter of apology had been put in my file. I was so warmed by this prompt recognition of corporate error that I immediately wrote back the president of New York Telephone, copies to Mr. Frederick Kappel, chairman of the board at AT&T, and to Mr. David Rockefeller at the Chase Bank, and told him to do something carnally improper to himself.

And so I was in California, on the lam, as it were, from the slam. Manifest Destiny, 1964. What was western expansion, after all, but a migration of malcontents and ne'er-do-wells, have-nots with no commitment on the stable society left behind, adventurers committed only to circumventing any society in their path. For eight years on the upper East Side of Manhattan, I had been a have-not and a malcontent. I dreamed of being an adventurer. When I was twenty-five, I had put up $100 to buy a piece of an antimony mine in Thailand. I was not sure what antimony was, but I saw myself in riding boots and a wide-brimmed hat in the jungles of Siam. There was a whisper of opium and there were women always called sloe-eyed, wearing *ao dais* and practiced in the Oriental permutations of fellatio. The daydream, of course, was compensation for the reality I was then living. I was a traffic clerk in an industrial advertising agency, little more than a messenger in a Brooks Brothers suit and a white buttoned-down shirt and a striped tie, taking copy and layouts for industrial toilet fixtures to the client in the Bronx. At night I tried to write a novel titled *Not the Macedonian*. The first line of the novel—the only line I ever wrote— was "They called him Alexander the Great." Not, of course, the Macedonian. My Alexander was a movie director. In Hollywood. I had never met a movie director, I had never been in Hollywood. For that matter, I had never been west of Fort Carson, Colorado, where I had spent the last three months of a two-year stint as a peacetime Army draftee. Nor had I ever told anyone, least of all the girl I was then supposed to marry, that my fashionable address in New York's silk-stocking district was a rooming house, populated by men who had been beaten by the city. One roommate was a lawyer from South Carolina who had failed the New York Bar exam three times and was afraid to go home. Another was a drunk who had been out of work for eleven months. The owner-landlord of this townhouse between Madison and Park packed four people to a room, each at $56 a month, and day and night he prowled the corridors and stairwells looking for transgressions of his house rules. Once he threatened to evict me for tossing Q-Tips in the toilet, another time for violating the food protocols. His kitchen was run on a nonprofit honor system; a price list was posted (2¢ for a saltine, 5¢ for a saltine with a dab of peanut butter, 7¢ for a saltine with peanut butter and jelly, etc.) and the tenant was expected to tot up his expenses on a file card. Snitches reported to the owner-landlord that I had been negligent in the accounting of my nightly inhalation of Hydrox and milk. My only defense was rapture of the snack. I threw myself on his mercy and was sentenced to permanent loss of kitchen privileges.

Each day I scoured the "Apartments to Share" column in the *Times* real-estate section, but it was not until a man in a green-flocked apartment on East Fifteenth Street told me there was only one bed in his flat that I realized the meaning of the phrase in the ads, "Must be compatible." I haunted the sleazy one-room employment agencies along Forty-second Street and up Broadway, looking for a better job. I felt that if I only broke through to $75 a week it would be the first step to the cover of *Time*. In the evenings I concocted resumés, listing jobs I had never held with references from people I had never met. The most elaborate fiction was the invention of a job on a daily newspaper in Colorado Springs. During my service at Fort Carson, I had noted that this paper did not give its reporters bylines and so I bought up enough back issues at the out-of-town newsstand on Times Square to create for myself an unbylined city room background. The employment agents were impressed. Except one, a man with rheumy eyes and dandruff flaking down on his shiny blue suit. Even now I sometimes awake with a start remembering that awful day when he told me he had checked out one of my *soi-disant* Colorado references, who reported that he had never heard of me.

I can say now what I dared not say then: I was a jerk.

In time, however, my nonexistent job on the city desk of the Colorado Springs newspaper helped me find employment with a trusting trade magazine, an opportunity that I later parlayed into a five-year sojourn on *Time*. There I learned discipline, met deadlines and became adept at dealing with the more evasive transitions, the elusive "but," the slippery "nevertheless," the chimerical "on the other hand." I also learned that the writer on a news magazine is essentially a carpenter, chipping, whittling, planing a field correspondent's ten- or twelve-page file down into a seventy-line story, in effect cutting a sofa into a bar stool; in the eyes of his editors, both are places to sit.

Since days in *Time*'s New York office are counted as enhancing one's world vision, I became, after three years, the magazine's Saigon watcher, even though I had never been there. In 1962, I persuaded my editors to pay my way to Indochina, my alleged sphere of expertise, where I fornicated for five weeks and in what now seems a constant postcoital daze floated to the nascent realization that the war beginning to metastasize in Vietnam was a malignant operation. It was a difficult induction to explain to my editors back in New York. A whore in Cholon did not seem much of a source, notwithstanding the brother she claimed was in Hanoi, from whom, in her text, she received periodic messages over an RFD route I suspected was not sanctioned by President Diem or Archbishop Thuc. It was just a feeling. I had the feeling when I monitored a conversation about Swiss bank accounts over drinks at the Cercle Sportif in Saigon, an abstract discussion punctuated by long silences, the simple question, "Do you favor Lausanne?" seeming to carry an absurd consignment of symbolic freight. I had the same feeling when I flew around the countryside for a few days with a four-star U.S. Army general from MACV. The bases he dropped in on reminded me of Fort Bliss or Fort Chaffee from my own Army days. The latrines were spotless, whitewashed stones lined the pathways between tents and the young volunteer American officers wore starched fatigues and spit-shined boots and their hair was clipped to the skull two inches over the ears. There were graphs and maps and overlays with grease pencil notations, and after every briefing there was coffee and optimism, but no American officer in whatever section we happened to be visiting could explain why the roads were not secure at night. Losing control of the roads at night was the nature of the war, the general said. He seemed to think this a reasonable explanation and stressed that the plans and procedures of his command were "viable"; I learned new and ambiguous meanings for the word "viable" during my short stay in Vietnam. A Turk nicknamed Cowboy had a less ambiguous expression. Cowboy was a former colonel in the Turkish air force who, after being declared redundant and forced into premature retirement, had signed on with the CIA for the Bay of Pigs. At $2,000 a month he was working off that contract in Vietnam, hedgehopping over the hills to avoid ground fire, summing up what was happening in the jungles below in two words: "All shit."

Cowboy carried no weight in the Time-Life Building. Briefed at the Pentagon, lunched at the White House, my editors saw the light at the end of the tunnel; they thought my sibylline meanderings the pornography of a malcontent. In the ensuing religious wars about Vietnam that rent *Time*, I sided with the doubters in the Saigon bureau and asked to be relieved of the Vietnam desk. My penance was reassignment to the Benelux portfolio, along with responsibility for the less doctrinaire capitals of Western Europe—a beat that encompassed by-elections in Liechtenstein, Scandinavian sexual mores and Common Market agricultural policy. "How small," I wrote, "is a small tomato?'' I became sullen, a whisperer in the corridors. I did not get an expected raise, a short time later I married, a short time after that, still a malcontent, not yet a have, I quit my job. Ignorant of the impending posse from the New York Telephone Company, the adventurer routed himself to California.

Eureka, as the state motto has it: ''I have found it.''

I had found it.

2.

What I found first was culture shock. Imagine: an Irish Catholic out of Hartford, Connecticut, two generations removed from steerage, with the political outlook of an alderman and social graces polished to a semigloss at the Hartford Golf Club. Imagine a traveler with this passport confronting that capitol south of the Tehachapis called El Pueblo de Nuestra Senora La Reina de Los Angeles. My wife was a fifth-generation Californian and was in a sense returning home (although her real home was the equally impenetrable flatland of the Central Valley), but to me it was a new world: *the* new world. I watched Los Angeles television, listened to Los Angeles radio, devoured Los Angeles newspapers trying to find the visa that would provide entry. ''Go gargle razor blades,'' advised a local talk show host pleasantly; it was a benediction that seemed to set the tone of the place. Dawn televised live on the Sunset Strip: a minister of the Lord inquired of a stringy-haired nubile what she liked doing best in the world. An unequivocal answer: ''Balling.'' Another channel, another preacher. This one ascribed the evils of the contemporary liberal ethic—my own contemporary liberal ethic, as modified in generations of smoke-filled rooms—to one ''J. J. Russo.'' It was some time before I apprehended that the Italianate ''J. J.'' was in fact Jean-Jacques Rousseau. In a newspaper I read of a man living on the rim of Death Valley who walked alone out into the desert, leaving behind a note that he wanted to "talk to God." God apparently talked back: the man was bitten by a rattlesnake and died.

Fundamentalism, the Deity, the elements—those familiar *aides-mémoire* that titillate the casual visitor to the western shore. I did not need a pony to find the immediate subtext of banality and vulgarity. It took a long time, however, to learn that the real lesson in each of those parables was to quite another point. Los Angeles is the least accessible and therefore the worst reported of American cities. It is not available to the walker in the city. There is no place where the natives gather. Distance obliterates unity and community. This inaccessibility means that the contemporary de Tocqueville on a layover between planes can define Los Angeles only in terms of his own culture shock. A negative moral value is attached to the taco stand, to the unnatural presence of palm trees at Christmas (although the climate of Los Angeles at Christmas exactly duplicates that of Bethlehem), even to the San Andreas fault. Whenever she thought of California, an editor at the *New York Times* once told me, she thought of Capri plants and plastic flowers. She is an intelligent woman and I do not think she meant to embrace the cliché with such absolute credulity; she would have been sincerely pained had I replied that whenever I thought of New York I thought of Halston and Bobby Zarem. (My most endearing memory of this woman is seeing her at a party in New York, as always meticulously pulled together, except that the side seam on her Pucci dress had parted. The parted seam was the sort of social detail that marked her own reportage, which had a feel for texture absent in her *a priori* invention of a California overrun with plastic greenery.) "I would love to see you play with the idea of California as the only true source of American culture " she wrote my wife and me, fellow conspirators, or so she thought, in her fantasy of the western experience. "I mean, what other state would have pearlized rainbow-colored plastic shells around its public telephones?''

Notice "plastic," that perfect trigger word, the one word that invariably identifies its user as culturally superior. When I arrived in California in 1964, the catch words and phrases meant to define the place were "smog" and "freeways" and "kook religions," which then spun off alliteratively into "kooky California cults." Still the emigré, I referred to my new country as "Lotusland"; it was a while before I realized that anyone who calls Los Angeles "Lotusland" is a functioning booby. In the years since 1964, only the words have changed. California is a land of "rapacious philodendron" and "squash yellow Datsuns," Marion Knox noted on the Op Ed page of the *New York Times;* seven months in the Los Angeles bureau of *Time* seemed to Ms. Knox an adventure in Oz. "Angel dust." "The 'in' dry cleaner." "Men in black bathing suits, glossy with Bain de Soleil." (Perhaps a tad of homophobia there, a residual nightmare of Harry's Bar in Bloomingdale's.) "The place of honor at . . . dinner parties," Ms. Knox reported, "is next to the hotshot realtor." I wonder idly whose dinner parties, wonder at what press party do you find the chic hairdresser and the hotshot realtor. I also think I have never read a more poignant illustration of Cecelia Brady's line in *The Last Tycoon:* "We don't go for strangers in Hollywood."

In *Esquire,* Richard Reeves spoke of "ideas with a California twist, or twisted California ideas—drinking vodka, est, credit cards, student revolts, political consultants, skateboards . . ." An absurd catalogue, venial sins, if sins they be at all, some not even Californian in origin. Ivy Lee had the Rockefeller ear before the term "political consultant" was invented, not to mention Edward Bernays and Benjamin Sonnenberg, who were plugged into the sockets of power when normalcy was still an idea to be cultivated. And what is est after all but a virus of psychiatry, a mutation of the search to find one's self, passed west from Vienna via Park Avenue, then carried back again, mutated, on the prevailing winds. (Stone-throwing in glass houses, this kind of exchange, a Ping-Pong game between midgets, est on one coast, Arica on the other, vodka drinking in California, Plato's Retreat in Manhattan, lacquered swimmers on the Malibu, their equally glossy brothers three time zones east in Cherry Grove.) The trigger words meant to define California become a litany, the litany a religion. The chief priests and pharisees attending the Los Angeles bureaus of Eastern publications keep the faith free from heresy. A year ago a reporter from *Time* telephoned my wife and said that the magazine was preparing a new cover story on California; he wondered if she had noticed any significant changes in the state since *Time*'s last California cover.

Still they come, these amateur anthropologists, the planes disgorging them at LAX, their date books available for dinner with the hotshot realtor. They are bent under the cargo of their preconceived notions. "The only people who live in L.A. are those who can't make it in New York," I once heard a young woman remark at dinner. She was the associate producer of a rock-and-roll television special and she was scarfing down chicken mole, chiles Jalapenos, guacamole, sour cream, cilantro and tortillas. "You cook New York," she complimented her hostess. "Mexico, actually," her hostess replied evenly, passing her a tortilla and watching her lather sour cream on it as if it were jam. Another dinner party, this for an eastern publisher in town to visit a local author. There were ten at dinner, it was late, we had all drunk too much. "Don't you miss New York?" the publisher asked. "Books. Publishing. Politics. Talk." His tone was sadly expansive. "Evenings like this."

The visitors have opinions, they cherish opinions, their opinions ricochet around the room like tracer fire. The very expression of an opinion seems to certify its worth. Socially acceptable opinion, edged with the most sentimental kind of humanism, condescension in drag. "Why can't you find the little guy doing a good job and give him a pat on the back?" the managing editor of *Life* once asked my wife. Little people, that population west of the Hudson, this butcher, that baker, the candlestick maker, each with a heart as big as all outdoors. Usually there is a scheme to enrich the life of this little person, this cultural dwarf, some effort to bring him closer to the theater or the good new galleries. Mass transit, say. I remember one evening when a writer whose expertise was in menopausal sexual conduct insisted that mass transit was the only means of giving southern California that sense of community she thought it so sadly lacked. I did not say that I thought "community" was just another ersatz humanistic cryptogram. Nor did I say that I considered mass transit a punitive concept, an idea that runs counter to the fluidity that is, for better or worse, the bedrock precept of southern California, a fluidity that is the antithesis of community. She would not have heard me if I had said it, for one purpose of such promiscuous opinionizing is to filter out the disagreeable, to confirm the humanistic consensus.

He who rejects the dictatorship of this consensus is said to lack "input." Actors out from New York tell me they miss the input, novelists with a step deal at Paramount, journalists trying to escape the eastern winter. I inquire often after input, because I am so often told that California (except for San Francisco) is deficient in it, as if it were a vitamin. Input is people, I am told. Ideas. Street life. I question more closely. Input is the pot-au-feu of urban community. I wonder how much input Faulkner had in Oxford, Mississippi, and it occurs to me that scarcity of input might be a benign deficiency. Not everyone agrees. After two weeks in California, the publisher of *New York* magazine told Dick Cavett at a party in New York, he felt "brain-damaged." Delphina Ratazzi was at that party, and Geraldo Rivera. And Truman Capote, Calvin Klein, Charlotte Ford, George Plimpton, Barbara Allen with Philip Niarchos, Kurt Vonnegut, Carrie

Fisher with Desi Arnaz, Jr., Joan Hackett and Arnold Schwarzenegger. I do not have much faith in any input I might have picked up at that party.

3.

California is not so much a state of the Union as it is an imagi-nation that seceded from our reality a long time ago. In leading the world in the transition from industrial to post-industrial society, California's culture became the first to shift from coal to oil, from steel to plastic, from hardware to software, from materialism to mysticism, from reality to fantasy. California became the first to discover that it was fantasy that led reality, not the other way around.

—WILLIAM IRWIN THOMPSON

Perhaps, it is easiest to define Los Angeles by what it is not. Most emphatically it is not eastern. San Francisco is eastern, a creation of the gold rush, colonized by sea, Yankee architecture and Yankee attitudes boated around the Horn and grafted onto the bay. Any residual ribaldry in San Francisco is the legacy of that lust for yellow riches that attracted those early settlers in the first place. Small wonder Easterners feel comfortable there. They perceive an Atlantic clone; it does not threaten as does that space-age Fort Apache five hundred miles to the south.

Consider then the settling of southern California. It was—and in a real sense continues to be—the last western migration. It was a migration, however, divorced from the history not only of the West but of the rest of California as well, a migration that seemed to parody Frederick Jackson Turner and his theory on the significance of the frontier. In Turner's version, the way west was not for the judicious—overland, across a continent and its hard-scrabble history. Those who would amputate a past and hit the trail were not given to the idea of community. Dreamers or neurotics, they were individualists who shared an aversion to established values, to cohesion and stability. A hard man, Turner's western wayfarer, for a hard land.

The settlers of southern California traveled the same route across the Big Empty—but on an excursion ticket. By the mid-1880's, the frontier, as Turner noted, was for all intents and purposes closed, the continental span traced by a hatchwork of railroad lines. Where there were railroads, there was murderous competition, and when in 1886 the Santa Fe laid its track into southern California, it joined in battle with the Southern Pacific for the ultimate prize, the last terminal on the Pacific shore, a frontier of perpetual sunshine where the possibilities seemed as fertile as the land. The rate wars between the Santa Fe and the Southern Pacific denied sense. From the jumping-off points in the Missouri Valley, fares to southern California dropped from $125 to $100, and then in a maniacal frenzy of price-cutting to twelve, eight, six, four dollars. Finally on March 6, 1887, the price bottomed out at one dollar per passenger, one hundred copper pennies to racket down those trails blazed by the cattle drives and the Conestoga wagons, to cross that blank land darkened by the blood of the Indian wars.

What the railroads had essentially created in southern California was a frontier resort, a tumor on the western ethic. Bargain basement pioneers, every one a rebuke to Turner's hard man, flooded into southern California, 120,000 of them trained into Los Angeles alone by the Southern Pacific in 1887, the Santa Fe keeping pace with three and four trainloads a day. In such a melee, where personal histories were erased, the southland was an adventurer's nirvana. Land speculators preyed on the gullible, enticing them with oranges stuck into the branches of Joshua trees. But even when the land bubble burst, the newcomers stayed on, held captive by the sun, the prejudices and resentments of their abandoned life, the dreams and aspirations of their new one, cross-fertilizing in the luxuriant warmth.

And still they came, a generation on every trainload. If New York was the melting pot of Europe, Los Angeles was the melting pot of the United States. It was a bouillabaisse not to everyone's taste. "It is as if you tipped the United States up so all the commonplace people slid down there into southern California," was the way Frank Lloyd Wright put it. In *Southern California Country,* Carey McWilliams replied gently to Wright: "One of the reasons for this persistent impression of commonplaceness is, of course, that the newcomers have been stripped of their natural settings— their Vermont hills, their Kansas plains, their Iowa cornfields. Here their essential commonplaceness stands out garishly in the harsh illumination of the sun. Here every wart is revealed, every wrinkle underscored, every eccentricity emphasized."

Expansion, McWilliams noted, was the major business of southern California, the very reason for its existence. The volume and velocity of this migration set the tone of the place. From 1900 to 1940, the population of Los Angeles increased by nearly 1600 percent. Everyone was an alien, the newcomer was never an exile. In an immigrant place where the majority was nonindigenous, the idea of community could not flourish, since community by definition is built on the deposits of shared experience. The fact that the spectacular growth of Los Angeles exactly coincided with the automotive age further weakened the idea of community. Where older cities, radiating out from a core, were defined and limited both by transportation and geography, Los Angeles was the first city on wheels, its landscape in three directions unbroken by natural barriers that could give it coherence and definition, its mobility limited only by a tank of gas.

The newness of Los Angeles—it is, after all, scarcely older than the cenury—and the idea of mobility as a cultural determinant lent the place a bumptiousness that was as appealing to some as it was aggravating to others. In a word, southern California was different, and in the history of the land, what is different is seldom treasured. Exempt from the history of the West, the cut-rate carpetbaggers who settled in the southland could adopt the western ethic and reinterpret it for their own uses. The result is a refinement of that ad hoc populism that has characterized California politics in this century, an ingrained suspicion of order, the bureaucracy of order and the predators of order. It is a straight line from Hiram Johnson to Howard Jarvis, and when Jerry Brown intones, "Issues are the last refuge of scoundrels," he is speaking in the authentic voice of a state where skepticism about government is endemic.

This attitude toward politics, as well as southern California's particular and aggressive set toward the world, could be dismissed as a sunstroked curiosity as long as the region remained a provincial and distant colony, and so it did remain until World War II. Even with the steady infusion of people and ideas and capital, southern California had almost no industrial base until the war. There was plenty of technological know-how—Ls Angeles was the first city in the country to be entirely lit by electricity—and even before the turn of the century there was a sense that the city's destiny did not lie in divine guidance from the Atlantic. "The Pacific is the ocean of the future," Henry Huntington said then. "Europe can supply her own wants. We shall supply the needs of Asia."

Cowboy talk: there was no industry to supply the needs of Asia. Agriculture dominated southern California (Los Angeles until 1920 was the nation's richest agricultural county) and the population boom had spawned an improvised ancillary economy of the most demeaning sort. It seemed a region of maids and clerks, of animal hospitals and car dealerships and roadside stands, of pool services and curbstone mediums. "Piddling occupations," James M. Cain wrote in 1933. "What electric importance can be felt in a peddler of orange peelers? Or a confector of Bar-B-Q? Or the proprietor of a goldfish farm? Or a breeder of rabbit fryers?" In this service economy, Hollywood was the ultimate service industry—it required no raw materials except celluloid, which cost little to ship either as raw stock or finished film—but its payroll was enormous and from 1920 to 1940 it gave southern California a simulated industrial base. In 1938 the movie industry ranked fourteenth among all American businesses in gross volume, eleventh in total assets.

And then came the war. The figures tell the story. In an eight-year period, 1940 to 1948, the federal government invested $1 billion in the construction of new industrial plants in California, and private industry kicked in $400 million more; industrial employment rose 75 percent; Los Angeles alone juggled $10 billion in war production contracts. These were just numbers, however, as ephemeral as any wartime figures. What was important was the technological scaffolding propping up the numbers. As Carey McWilliams points out in *The Great Exception*,* California "unlike other areas . . . did not *convert* to war production, for there was nothing much to 'convert'; what happened was that *new* industries and *new* plants were built overnight." "New" is a word that often takes on a suspect connotation when applied to California, but here were new plants untainted with the technological obsolescence afflicting so many older industries in the East. New processes using the new metals and new chemicals indigenous to California. New industries, such as aerospace and computers, which were mutually dependent, and in the case of aerospace particularly suited to the geography and climate of southern Cal-

---

* It should be noted here that McWilliams's two books, *Southern California Country* and *The Great Exception*, are essential to any study of California. I think they are great books, not only because I am now and often have been in McWilliams's debt, but more importantly because they are cool and informative, history as literature in every sense.

ifornia, a place where hardware could be tested on the limitless wastes of the Mojave 365 days a year.

In effect the war allowed southern California to find a sense of itself. The self discovered was not particularly endearing. Think of Frederick Jackson Turner's hard man, glaze him with prosperity, put him in sunglasses and there you have it—a freeway Billy the Kid. There was an extravagance about the place, a lust for the new, and it was this lust that allowed southern California to capitalize on the technologies of the future, to turn its attention away from the rest of the nation, from the bedrock of history itself. The boom years made Los Angeles an independent money mart, no longer an economic supplicant, its vision west across the Pacific to Japan and Australia, toward those frontiers envisioned by Henry Huntington; look if you need proof at the Yellow Pages and those branch offices in Tokyo and Sydney. To some the lusts of southern California seemed to lead only to venereal disease. "Reality . . . was whatever people said it was," J. D. Lorenz wrote in *Jerry Brown: The Man on the White Horse*. "It was the fresh start, the self-fulfilling prophecy, the victory of mind over matter. In a land without roots, reality was image, image replaced roots, and if the image could be constructed quickly, like a fabricated house, it could also be torn down quickly." It is part of the fascination of southern California that it would enthusiastically agree with Lorenz's creed. Better the fresh start than roots choking with moral crab grass, better the fabricated house than the dry rot of cities, better mind over matter than a paralysis of will.

Prosperity stoked the natural bombast of the southern California frontier. Los Angeles, that upstart on the Pacific, looked back on the eastern littoral with a cool indifference that bordered on contempt. See what community got you, it seemed to say; what good are stability and cohesion if their legacy is the South Bronx? Economic independence, coupled with that western urge to be left alone, made southern California in some metaphoric sense a sovereign nation, Pacifica, as it were, with Los Angeles as its capital. And here is the other negative that defines Los Angeles: it no longer regards itself as a second city.

The history of nationhood is also largely the history of a nation's single city—that London, that Paris, that New York (with Washington as its outermost exurb) where politics, money and culture coalesce to shape a national idea. Every place else is Manchester or Marseilles. The claim of Los Angeles to be the co-equal of New York could be dismissed as the braggadocio of a provincial metropolis except for one thing. Los Angeles had Hollywood, the dream factory that is both a manufacturer of a national idea and an interpreter of it. Hollywood—the most ridiculed and the most envied cultural outpost of the century. Think of it: technology as an art form, an art form, moreover, bankrolled and nurtured by men who, in Louis Sherwin's surpassing remark, "knew only one word of two syllables and that word was 'fillum.' " At times I admit a certain impatience with Hollywood and all its orthodoxies. I hear that film is "truth at twenty-four frames a second" and wonder if any art has ever had a credo of such transcendental crap. Try it this way: "truth at sixty words a minute." But that is a factor of age and taste. When I was an undergraduate, the trek of the ambitious and allegedly literate bachelor of arts was to the East; to be heard, one was published, and the headquarters of print was New York. Now that trek is a trickle. The status of image has usurped the status of type. The young graduates head west, their book bags laden with manuals on lenses and cutting, more conversant with Jewison than with Joyce, almost blissfully persuaded that a knowledge of *Dallas* and *San Francisco, Casablanca* and *Maracaibo* is a knowledge of the world at large.

It is this aspect of the Hollywood scene that eastern interpreters fasten upon. Zapping the vulgarity is less demanding than learning the grammar, the grammar of film, and by extension the grammar of Los Angeles, and of California itself. In the beginning, there was the vulgarity of the movie pioneers, many of whom were from Eastern Europe. No recounting of that era is complete without referring to those early movie moguls as former "furriers" or "rag merchants." It was an ethnic code, cryptological anti-Semitism. For furrier read Jew. No, not Jew: the Sulzbergers were Jews, and the Meyers; these unlettered rag-traders were nothing but ostentatious, parvenu sheenies, and there was always a good giggle in the Goldfish who changed his name to Goldwyn. I think of the Marxist critic who in the space of a few thousand words spoke about Josef von Sternberg, who "spurns as canard the rumor that he was born Joe Stern of Brooklyn"; about Mervyn Leroy, of whom "it is rumored that his real name is Lasky"; and about Lewis Milestone, "whose actual name is said to be Milstein."

It was easier to laugh than it was to examine the movie earthquake and its recurring aftershocks, easier to maintain that Los Angeles's indifference to the cultural heritage of the East was evidence of an indigenous lack of culture. But the lines had been drawn, the opinion media of the East versus the Western image media of movies and television, and the spoils were the hearts and minds of America. This country had always been defined by the East. Everything was good or bad to the extent that it did or did not coincide with the eastern norm; the making of cultural rules, the fact of being the nation's social and cultural arbiter, imbued confidence. The movies were a severe shock to that confidence, all the more so because those images up there on screen did not seem to have an apparent editorial bias. "The movies did not describe or explore America," Michael Wood wrote in *America in the Movies*. "They invented it, dreamed up an America all their own, and persuaded us to share the dream. We shared it happily, because the dream was true in its fashion—true to a variety of American desires—and because there weren't all that many other dreams around."

The opinion media and the image media—each has an investment in its version of the American myth, each a stake in getting it wrong about the other. To the opinion media, southern California is the enemy camp, and their guerrilla tactic is one of deflation. In their version, the quintessential native was born in Whittier and carries the middle name Milhous. Apostates and quislings are spokesmen: the refugee from Long Beach, now a practicing Manhattan intellectual, who reports that life in Los Angeles is the life of a turnip; the film director who curtsies to his critical constituency and says that if Solzhenitsyn lived in L.A., he would have a hot tub and be doing TM. Hatred of New York is seen as an epidemic. "What do you hate (or dislike) about New York City?" begins a letter from *New York* magazine. "We are asking a number of persons . . ." *Esquire* finds this hatred, and Woody Allen in *Annie Hall*. It is a kind of negative boosterism that I find infinitely depressing. "As a well-known New York hater, you . . ." It was a correspondent from *Time* on the telephone. (*Time* again: its Los Angeles bureau is a Sun City for corporate remittance men.) I told the *Time* man that while I was gratified at being described as "well-known," I did not know how I had achieved the reputation of "New York hater." He admitted it was not from anything I had ever written. Nor anything I had said; we had never met. Nor anything he had heard secondhand. I persisted: how had I achieved that dubious repuation. "You live here," he said finally.

The call troubled me for a long time. If I had not thought much about New York's financial crisis (the actual reason for the call), I certainly took no pleasure in its plight (the assumption of my caller). It just never crossed my mind. And there it was, the canker, the painful sore of reciprocity: Los Angeles was indifferent to New York. It was the same indifference that for decades New York had shown, and was no longer showing, to the rest of the country.

4.

The splendors and miseries of Los Angeles, the graces and grotesqueries, appear to me as unrepeatable as they are unprecedented. I share neither the optimism of those who see Los Angeles as the prototype of all future cities, nor the gloom of those who see it as the harbinger of universal urban doom. . . . It is immediately apparent that no city has ever been produced by such an extraordinary mixture of geography, climate, economics, demography, mechanics and culture; nor is it likely that an even remotely similar mixture will ever occur again.

> —REYNER BANHAM, *Los Angeles:*
> *The Architecture of Four Ecologies*

"The freeway is forever" was the slogan of a local radio station the summer I arrived in California. Here was the perfect metaphor for that state of mind called Los Angeles, but its meaning eluded me for years. Singular not plural, *freeway* not *freeways,* the definite article implying that what was in question was more an idea than a roadway. Seen from the air at night, the freeway is like a river, alive, sinuous, a reticulated glow of headlights tracing the huge contours of a city seventy miles square. Surface streets mark off grids of economy and class, but the freeway is totally egalitarian, a populist notion that makes Los Angeles comprehensible and complete. Alhambra and Silver Lake, Beverly Hills and Bell Gardens, such an exit, each available. "The point about this huge city," observed Reyner Banham, "is that all its parts are equal and equally accessible from all other parts at once."

Driving the freeway induces a kind of narcosis. Speed is a virtue, and the speed of the place makes one obsessive, a gambler. The spirit is that of a city on the move, of people who have already moved here from somewhere else. Mobility is their common language; without it, or an appreciation of it, the visitor is an illiterate. The rear-view mirror reflects an instant city, its population trebled and retrebled in living memory. Its monuments are the artifacts of civil engineering, off-ramps and interchanges that sweep into concrete parabolas. There is no past, the city's hierarchy is jerry-built, there are few mistakes to repeat. The absence of past and structure is basic to the allure of Los Angeles. It deepens the sense of self-reliance, it fosters the idea of freedom, or at least the illusion of it. Freedom of movement most of all, freedom that liberates the dweller in this city from community chauvinism and neighborhood narcissism, allowing him to absorb the most lavish endowments his environment has to offer—sun and space.

The colonization of Los Angeles has reduced the concept of space to the level of jargon, to "my space" and "your space." Space is an idea. I do not think that anyone in the East truly understands the importance of this idea of space in the West. Fly west from the Atlantic seaboard, see the country open up below, there some lights, over there a town, on the horizon perhaps a city, in between massive, implacable emptiness. The importance of that emptiness is psychic. We have a sense out here, however specious, of being alone, of wanting, more importantly, to be left alone, of having our own space, a kingdom of self with a two-word motto: "Fuck Off." Fly east from the Pacific, conversely, and see the country as the Westerner sees it, urban sprawl mounting urban sprawl, a vast geographical gang-bang of incestuous blight, incestuous problems, incestuous ideas. People who vote Frank Rizzo and Abe Beame or Ed Koch into office have nothing to tell us. It is, of course, simple to say that both these views from the air are mirages, but even a mirage proceeds from some basic consciousness, some wish that seeks fulfillment. What, after all, is community? Space in the West, community in the East—these are the myths that sustain us.

When I think of Los Angeles now, after almost a decade and a half of living not only in it but with it, I sometimes feel an astonishment, an attachment that approaches joy. I am attached to the way palm trees float and recede down empty avenues, attached to the deceptive perspectives of the pale subtropical light. I am attached to the drydocks of San Pedro, near where I used to live, and to the refineries of Torrance, which at night resemble an extraterrestrial space station. I am attached to the particular curve of coastline as one leaves the tunnel at the end of the Santa Monica Freeway to drive north on the Pacific Coast Highway. I am attached equally to the glories of the place and to its flaws, its faults, its occasional revelations of psychic and physical slippage, its beauties and its betrayals. It is the end of the line.
It is the last stop.
Eureka!
I love it.

1978

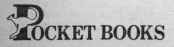